W9-CKL-213

PERNAMBUCO
in the Brazilian Federation
1889-1937

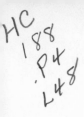

PERNAMBUCO
in the Brazilian Federation
1889-1937

ROBERT M. LEVINE

STANFORD UNIVERSITY PRESS

Stanford, California   1978

Sources of photographs on pp. 101–6: 1, 5, 6, and 12. *Diário de Pernambuco*, Recife. 2, 9, and 11. Editôra Abril, Recife, publishers of the magazine *Veja*. 3. Gilberto Freyre, *Olinda: 2° Guia Prático, Histórico e Sentimental de Cidade Brasileira*, 4th ed. (Livraria José Olympio Editôra; Rio de Janeiro, 1968). 4. Associacão Commercial, Recife. 7. Dr. Caio Cavalcanti. 8, 10, and 13. Author.

Stanford University Press
Stanford, California
© 1978 by the Board of Trustees of the
Leland Stanford Junior University
Printed in the United States of America
ISBN 0-8047-0944-0
LC 76-47968

Published with the assistance of
the Andrew W. Mellon Foundation

To Marjorie H. Levine
and to the memory of
Mollie Fried and Irma Chakrin

Preface

THIS BOOK FORMS part of a collaborative project that has produced independent but parallel studies of three Brazilian states under federalism: Pernambuco, Minas Gerais, and São Paulo. The basic rationale for this project is set forth in the Introduction, pp. xv–xxii, which appears in all three books.

I am thankful to my colleagues, Joseph L. Love and John D. Wirth, for the opportunity to have worked so long and intimately with them on this collaborative research effort. We remained in frequent contact with one another from the early conversations about a joint project to the last stages of editing. The volume outlines are similar, not only from chapter to chapter but, as far as feasible, within each chapter itself. Though we attempted to keep repetition at a minimum, each book necessarily draws on a common stock of information that was freely shared throughout the research and writing. Many tasks were shared, while others were assigned individually. Love and Wirth compiled the code book for the collective biographies of the three state political elites; Love and I designed the SPSS program for the comparative biographical study. We spent twelve months in 1969–70 in Brazil, and met three times. Later, Love and Wirth spent a summer in Rio and Brasília, and I worked in the Public Record Office in London. We arranged to meet at least once a year since 1967.

With a few exceptions, I have used modern spelling for Portuguese words, proper names, and places in the text. In the Notes and Bibliography, however, I have followed the convention of citing authors and titles as they appear on the title page. The currency of Brazil for the period

under study was the milreis (written 1$000), and the largest monetary
unit was the conto (or 1,000 milreis and written 1:000$000 or simply
1:000$). In 1942 the milreis was replaced by the cruzeiro, one milreis
being equal to one cruzeiro. Dollar equivalents are given in Appendix C.

Many archivists, scholars, and other interested persons generously
lent their aid in the research for this work. I would particularly like to
thank the following persons for their assistance: in Recife, Lúcia Nery da
Fonseca of the Arquivo Público Estadual; Olímpio Costa Júnior of the
Biblioteca Pública; Gavin D. Black, formerly of the Great Western Railway Company; Vamireh Chacon and Gadiel Perruci of the Federal University of Pernambuco; the redoubtable Gilberto Freyre of Apipucos; and
Henriqueta Castello Branco.

My thanks also go to José Antônio Gonsalves de Mello Neto, Pernambuco's leading historian, and to "Sr. Nestor" of the Instituto Arqueológico, who repeatedly reminded me that "time is money."

I am also appreciative of the advice and cooperation given by former
governor Alexandre José Barbosa Lima Sobrinho, who received me in
Botafogo; the late Carlos de Lima Cavalcanti and his brother, Caio; the
late Marshal Juarez Távora; José Américo de Almeida; Amaury Pedrosa;
Luis Costa Pôrto; Nelson Coutinho; Gileno Dé Carli; and Geraldo Rosa e
Silva.

Among the many associates who offered aid during the course of my
research and writing are Jaime Reis, David Denslow, Linda Lewin,
Nathaniel Leff, Herbert S. Klein, Peter Eisenberg, João Alfredo dos An-
jos, Marc Hoffnagel, Antônio Paixão, Frank D. McCann, Ralph della
Cava, and Richard T. Rapp. Howard Craig Hendricks's dissertation research on the Recife Law School treats in depth a historical issue touched
on by this study; Craig and Carol Hendricks both aided my research in
numerous ways.

Research funds were provided by the U.S. Office of Education, the
American Philosophical Society, the New York State Research Foundation, and the Foreign Area Fellowship Program of the Social Science Research Council. A Senior Fulbright-Hays Lectureship, under the spon-
sorship of Dr. Manuel Diegues Júnior, enabled me to test some of my
hypotheses and interpretations in Brazil during the summer of 1973.

Above all, I am grateful to Joe Love and John Wirth. Beyond the professional aspects of the study, probably the most valuable aspect of all was

the lengthy exercise in collaboration. Its rewards supplement whatever contribution this individual volume may make. And finally, my thanks to Barbara E. Mnookin, my editor at Stanford University Press, for her patience, fortitude, and common sense.

ROBERT M. LEVINE

State University of New York,
Stony Brook

Contents

Six pages of photographs follow p. 100

Figures and Tables

FIGURES

TABLES

Introduction

THIS IS ONE of three independent but coordinated studies on the regional dynamics of Brazilian federalism from the beginning of the Republic in 1889 to the establishment of the Estado Novo in 1937. The objective is to write comparative history from the regional perspective, that is, to pinpoint similarities and differences among three leading states, while identifying modes of interaction at the national level. The role of São Paulo, which is located in the Center-South, and which received the greatest benefits from export-led growth, is examined by Joseph L. Love. Politically powerful Minas Gerais, situated between the prosperous southern states and the impoverished Northeast, is analyzed by John D. Wirth. Pernambuco, the Northeast's most important state, is treated by Robert M. Levine as a case study in political and economic decline.

The period under study begins with the devolution of power from the centralized Empire to the states, and follows the course of the Union's gradual assumption of authority and responsibility over the ensuing half-century. Recentralization began well before the "Old Republic" (1889–1930) was abolished by coup d'état in 1930; it was formally and stridently proclaimed by the Estado Novo dictatorship, Getúlio Vargas's unitary regime from 1937 to 1945.

Our purpose is to bring together insights into the complex dynamics of state-level social and political structures, which have always been crucial in Brazil, but particularly during the nation's most decentralized phase, the years under study. Political events define the chronological limits of these studies, yet the coups of 1889 and 1937 and the very different constitutions that attended them are partly arbitrary benchmarks. Important political events in the states did not always mirror national events, nor did they bear the same meaning. Moreover, the neatness of this periodization is blurred by socioeconomic continuities that dilute the impact of what historians used to call "turning points." We refer both to the historic North-South shift in power and resources, which started around 1850 and rendered the Northeast an internal colony of the dynamic South, and also to the modernizing forces—social differentiation, urbanization, the growing internal market—which the political events overlay.

Though the issues of federalism are ostensibly a set of political problems, the economic, social, and cultural contexts receive extensive treatment in these books. This fact is evident from the format of the studies, which are organized on thematic rather than chronological lines. To calibrate change over time, however, each author used a chronology appropriate to his own state while relating regional events to those at the national level and those in the other states.

We also use the concept of political generations to order the several themes. Leaders born before 1869 were socialized under the Empire, with its centralized bureaucracy. Those born in the 20 years before 1889 knew the Republic as young men in the period of its greatest decentralization. Leaders in the third political generation came of age after 1910, when the impetus for a more integrated polity affected the military, fiscal, and economic policies of the nation and the states. The origins, career expectations, and experiences of these three political generations are discussed in Chapter 5. Generational analysis also informs the chapter on integration which follows it.

These volumes explore the regional dimensions of change, adaptation, and rigidities of the Old Republic and the initial phase of the Vargas government. Structural changes were extensive: in the economy, coffee and rubber exports reached their apogee and went into sharp decline; manufacturing underwent its initial surge in a complicated set of rhythms. For much of this period economic growth was largely dependent on exports and foreign capital, including investments in government bonds for infrastructural development. By the 1930's, Brazil had shifted its dependence in financial and economic affairs from Great Britain to the United States. This coincided with the acceleration of industrialization by import substitution.

Brazilian society likewise was transformed: the nation received a net inflow of between two and one-half and three million immigrants in the years 1889–1937, more than any other comparable period in its history. By the 1930's, internal migration was also greater than in any previous decade. Rapid urbanization and improvements in public health accompanied these population shifts. By 1940 the nation had two cities, Rio de Janeiro and São Paulo, with populations over one million, and 21 other cities with populations in excess of 100,000. In the cities the early labor movement was the crucible for anarchist and communist activity, only to be channeled and controlled from the top down by a government apparatus in the 1930's. In the complex interplay between federal and state units, government assumed new tasks not only in social control but also in social welfare, education at all levels (grossly neglected before 1889), and commodity marketing inside and outside the country. The period under study was also the classic age of banditry and messianism, principally but not exclusively in the Northeast, though both phenomena were vestigial by the time of the Estado Novo.

The political system established by the constitution of 1891 seemed anomalous in Latin America, even anachronistic in light of the centralizing tendencies in Mexico, Colombia, and Argentina. Yet a decentralized Republic suited the interests of powerful export-oriented groups, and the ancient patron-client system found its political expression in the *política dos governadores* by 1900. This system, directed by the president of the Republic and the governors of São Paulo and Minas Gerais, was an arrangement for the mutual support of incumbent elites at all levels of government. With a preponderantly rural population and low levels of political participation (only 1–3 percent of the population voted in federal elections before 1930), *coronelismo*—boss rule—prevailed in the countryside and made urban political groupings irrelevant until the 1920's. Without the moderating power of the Empire to remove incumbents from office, the Republic had no constitutional solution to the problem of entrenched establishments. Violence at local, state, and federal levels remained an indispensable tool in politics, sometimes involving the army, sometimes not.

In the 1930's Vargas consciously pursued a policy of deinstitutionalization of the most important state machines of the Old Republic—the Republican Parties of Minas Gerais, São Paulo, and Rio Grande do Sul. Meanwhile new antiliberal parties on right and left threatened the hybrid liberal-corporatist constitution of 1934. The Estado Novo dictatorship, outlawing all parties, was the culmination of the effort to depoliticize Brazil, as well as to centralize its government; yet success was limited, as our examination of the states reveals.

States are the units of analysis because they were the foci of political loyalty and political organization: there were no enduring national or multistate parties in the era in question. Even Pernambuco usually behaved as a politically self-centered region, despite its being the "natural" leader of the Northeast. In fact, Pernambuco's failure to marshal the Northeast as a bloc in Congress is an important theme in that state's history. Aspects of regionalism that did not follow state boundaries—markets, for example—are examined, but for the most part these books focus on the states.

We believe the three states covered were the logical choice for study, especially since Love had previously written *Rio Grande do Sul and Brazilian Regionalism*. In the era under examination, São Paulo and Minas Gerais were the economic, demographic, and political leaders, and only Rio Grande could hope to challenge their control of federal policies and institutions. Pernambuco was the most important state in Brazil's leading "problem" area—the poverty-stricken Northeast—and it provides a dramatic and, in many ways, representative case study of Brazilian regionalism from the "underside." Nonetheless, we realize that regionalism and its socioeconomic context cannot be fully understood without studies of other units, especially Bahia, Rio de Janeiro, and the old Federal District. Much remains to be done.

Region and regionalism are defined with reference to the problem at hand, which is to study politics and its social and economic bases over several decades. Thus, a region is defined as having the following characteristics:

1. It is part of a larger unit and interdependent with other regions that, together with the first, constitute the larger unit.

2. It has a definite geographic size and location, being politically bounded.

3. Each region has a set of component subregions, which are contiguous.

4. The region generates a set of loyalties on the part of its inhabitants, which vary in importance and intensity over time.

5. Loyalty to the region, however, is subordinated (nominally at

least) to loyalty to the larger unit—the nation-state—among the politically effective sectors of the region's population; this loyalty may also vary in importance and intensity.

Regionalism is here defined as political behavior characterized, on the one hand, by acceptance of the existence of a larger political unit, but, on the other hand, by the quest for favoritism and decisional autonomy from the larger unit on economic and social policies, even at the risk of jeopardizing the legitimacy of the prevailing political system. Thus the emphasis is not on regional peculiarities per se (e.g. folklore, patterns of dress and speech), but on those factors that can be demonstrated to affect the region's political, economic, and social relations with the other regions and the larger unit of government, in this case a nation-state.

Attitudes toward regionalism changed during the period under review. The hopeful modernizers of 1889 saw decentralization as a device to obtain a more efficient allocation of resources than could be achieved through the central government. By contrast, the authoritarian centralizers of 1937 blamed "selfish regionalism" for a host of social, economic, and political dislocations they vowed to set right by action at the center. Both groups thought of regionalism in policy terms, but reached radically different conclusions on its validity. Grounded in Brazilian historical experience, this prescriptive aspect of regionalism becomes part of the definition.

Regional elites believed their states were socioeconomic as well as political units which demanded allegiance. But when state was pitted against nation, their allegiances were ambivalent, as shown in the experience of São Paulo in the 1930's. Furthermore, their success in establishing the significance of the region was in doubt, or at least ambiguous. Outright failures occurred, notably in the case of Pernambuco, which could not establish political coherence. Exogenous market forces and the terrain channeled economic growth in ways the leaders of Minas did not want. Opportunities to live and work in Rio de Janeiro, the center of patronage and stylish city-state, eroded the regional ideal among Pernambucanos and Mineiros, in striking contrast to their Paulista counterparts. Above all, the interpenetration of manifold and complex structures across regional boundaries sapped regional coherence.

In holding to the regional ideal, however, the elites soon realized that regionalism was not necessarily incompatible with a strong federal government. State and nation were not necessarily antagonistic; they were part of a continuum along which the balance of forces shifted. Compartmentalized state economic policies were abandoned as early as the severe depression of the late 1890's. The elites soon came to measure and define regionalism in relation to other units and the central government. Shaping the terms of these relationships was in fact the essence of regional policymaking. Viewed this way, regionalism becomes more complex and significant than it would be if the problem were only that of nonviable states struggling against the centralizing tide.

Relationships changed as the nation became more integrated. By the time of World War I, elites were even less inclined to counterpose region to nation, although the aim of state policy was still to extract favorable terms. Thus the state elites welcomed integration when they could influence or control it, and on the whole accepted it when they had to. We devote considerable attention to the integration process, which began well before the 1930 Revolution.

In the Brazilian case, integration was the product of two congruent forces, namely, the interpenetration of social, economic, and political life across regional boundaries *and* the partial transfer of decisions and resources to a national level of political organization. We believe that the former reinforced, but did not directly cause, the latter. Thus we give attention to the interaction of congresses and meetings at state and national levels. Yet the ambiguities of the centralizing impetus are revealed in detailed case studies of state budgets and fiscal policies, and in our discussion of military forces.

Two concurrent kinds of relationships marked the integration process. One, on the horizontal dimension, occurred within and among groups based on common bonds, affinities, and shared interests. The other, structured vertically, was the process of interaction among unequals: clientelism is a prime instance. Having examined both types of social interaction, we found striking the weakness of group and interest associations and the persistence of vertical structures, though this varied by state. Furthermore, it is clear that the elites modernized selectively, minimizing social mobilization. By this yardstick Brazil was far from being a fully integrated society by 1937.

In probing the complex processes whereby the parts fit together, we also focus explicitly on the role of state policymakers—what they wanted, tried to get, and settled for. Though political integration was far from uniform or complete by 1937, we think our analysis of regional decision-makers is a way to understand what was achieved. By looking at the terms of interaction we hope to carry analysis beyond the vague proposition that the elites, in learning to cooperate, willed national integration.

Our initial hypothesis was that the states functioned as "halfway houses," pioneering in areas of social and economic legislation, and slowly ceding responsibilities to the federal government after World War I. It later became clear, however, that government responsibility at *both* state and federal levels was increasing down to 1930, and that some state responsibilities were still vigorous until 1937 and beyond. This is another way of saying that regionalism was not the antithesis of interpenetration and integration, which took place on all levels of government.

One of the most instructive aspects of the regional approach is the opportunity for comparison, and there are several topics for which comparative regional analysis is especially appropriate.

1. The political consequences of different patterns of economic growth are seen more clearly: Pernambuco in decline, Minas with a relatively weak economy, and São Paulo in rapid expansion developed different political strategies at the state and national levels.

2. The alleged causal links between the level of socioeconomic development and types of political organization are brought under triangulation, allowing for a better view of other factors affecting leadership and organizations.

3. Different center-periphery relationships are highlighted in these studies. Pernambuco tended to predominate among the Northeastern states, but was itself a satellite of the central government; Minas was on the margins of the Center-South; São Paulo enjoyed a rapidly expanding domestic market; all had their export links and contrasting patterns of international financial obligations.

4. Similarities and differences in identically defined political elites are thrown into relief by the comparative analysis of computerized biographical data.

5. The role of the states in fostering or impeding political and economic integration emerges from the comparative study of state militias, budgets, specialized congresses, and associational activity.

As histories of Pernambuco, Minas, and São Paulo, these studies are schematic, not exhaustive. The stress is on structures, parallels, and linkages, rather than on detailed narrative exposition, for which there is still need. We hope that some of the richness of a unique regional society emerges in each volume. Inevitably, each study reflects the type, amount, and quality of source materials and previous studies available to the individual authors, who are responsible for their own volumes. In sum, each study stands alone; but all three follow the same design, which is the product of collaborative effort.

It was our intention not only to illuminate the Brazilian past but also to make a contribution to the literature on social and political change. The three works are case studies of major subnational units during the early phases of modernization. In charting the strategies of the elites to promote or retard change and the political consequences of shifts in the economic base, we hope these volumes will be read by students of the processes of capitalist modernization as well as by those interested in the unique features of Brazilian history.

We also hope to contribute to the comparative literature on regionalism and federalism. The problems and perspectives of regionalism are far from dead in the United States, where such issues as revenue sharing and state vs. federal control of energy resources are widely debated. Furthermore, it seems clear that many of the world's underdeveloped countries are experiencing profound currents of regionalism (often reinforcing ethnic cleavages), as social mobilization brings new groups into the political process. One form this can take is separatism and civil war, as the recent tragedies of Bangladesh and Nigeria illustrate. There is also a possibility that regionalism will lead to a more creative definition of the nation, as may be occurring in parts of Western Europe. Finally, in Brazil itself the issues of federalism are by no means dead, and it has yet to be demonstrated that the allegiance of the masses to the nation-state of Brazil parallels those of political and economic elites.

R.M.L.

J.L.L.

J.D.W.

PERNAMBUCO
in the Brazilian Federation
1889-1937

CHAPTER ONE

Man and the Land

PERNAMBUCANOS attribute their state's "strangely oblong" shape and reduced size to the political misfortunes that befell the region with the imposition of centralized monarchy after Independence. Punished for regionalist insurrection, Pernambuco was shorn of two-thirds of its former territory, including its access to the opulent pastoral and mining tracts ranging south to Minas Gerais.[1] An awkward demographic legacy followed: its nearly three million inhabitants during the 1930's ranked it fourth among the members of the federation while its Portugal-sized land area—2 percent of Brazil's—ranked it thirteenth.

Yet from the earliest colonial days Pernambuco dominated the vast Brazilian Northeast, both economically and politically; and specifically, in the period under concern, the neighboring states of Alagoas, Paraíba, Rio Grande do Norte, and Ceará, which I call its satellite bloc.[2] Geographically, the Northeast encompasses three distinct ecological zones that cut across and subsume political boundaries: the Zona da Mata, the humid coastal strip; the transitional Agreste; and the Sertão, the stark and irreducible backlands. Economic development and social organization, both in the state and throughout the region, have largely followed the lines of these zones, with the result that Pernambuco, like Minas Gerais, is not a coherent economic unit. This fact, a key to the dynamics of Brazilian federalism, is a central theme of this study.

The Land

The Mata. Much of the population of the Northeast is crowded into the Zona da Mata, a narrow belt that runs south along a plain from the

Ceará-Mirim valley in Rio Grande do Norte to the latitude of Salvador in Bahia. Within Pernambuco the Mata forms three distinct regions: the tablelands north of the capital, Recife, parallel to the shore; the dry Mata, west from São Lourenço da Mata; and the humid Mata, south and west of Recife to Quipapá. Always the most densely populated area in Pernambuco, this zone could continue to claim the bulk of the state's inhabitants at the end of our period.

The land of the Mata is typically hilly, the ample coastal rainfall is generally well distributed, and the soil, where it has not been worked out or washed away, is fertile and deep, reaching depths of 10 to 20 meters or more in places.[3]

The Mata's economy is based almost exclusively on one crop: sugar. The classical pattern of plantation agriculture was established here in the first century of Portuguese settlement, and by 1600 Pernambuco led the world in sugar production. Hundreds of *engenhos*—sugar plantations with rudimentary mills for processing cane—spread out from the first capital, Olinda, pushing cane cultivation into the Mata's river valleys. The sugar aristocracy that emerged in this process showed little interest in the region beyond, and settlement clung to the coast well into the nineteenth century. Through this period slash-and-burn agriculture stripped the zone of its forest cover, exposing the soil to erosion and gradually leaching out its fertility. Roads and railroads, when they came, added to the destruction: civil engineers in the region constructed most grades at relatively sharp angles, leading to further erosion, mudslides, and other kinds of damage. Most of the terrain is now covered with second growth.[4]

Sugar and, to a lesser degree, cotton made the Northeast the first major exporting region of Brazil and increased the influence of Recife, the region's principal port. Built in the mid-seventeenth century, Recife with its natural harbor and favored location at the confluence of the Capiberibe and Beberibe rivers soon displaced the original capital, Olinda, as Pernambuco's most important city. Indeed, until the mid-eighteenth century it was the second-largest city in Brazil (after Salvador) in terms of population and exports.

Hot and humid, with an average of 185 days of rainfall a year, Recife for some unaccountable reason enjoyed a reputation for salubrity among foreign travelers in the nineteenth century. Possibly this was because of the cooling sea breezes that prevail during most of the year; but even so, temperatures drop little at night, and the average daily highs range from

Fig. 1. Pernambuco and its satellite bloc. The Agreste zone as shown includes the transitional *caatinga*, or scrubland, bordering the Sertão. Data for the zonal borders was taken from Kempton E. Webb, *The Changing Face of Northeast Brazil* (New York, 1974), pp. 11, 52.

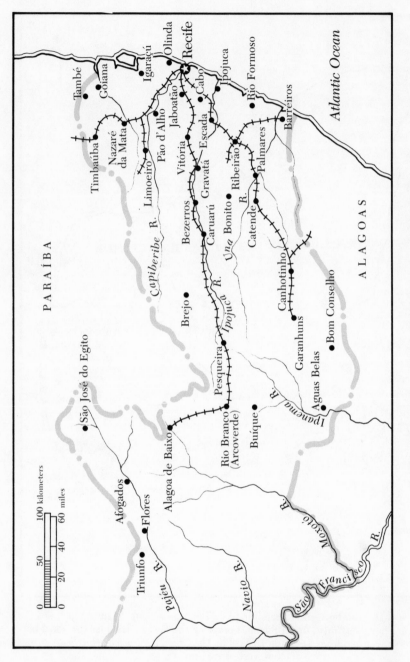

Fig. 2. The major rivers and the rail system (in 1933) of Pernambuco.

30° C (86° F) in December to 26° C (79° F) in July. Relative humidity averages from 79 percent in January to 89 percent in March; the air is especially heavy and damp in the swampy marshlands inhabited by the poor.[5] In the surrounding Zona da Mata, particularly to the south of the city, moisture seems literally to hover in the air; droplets of condensation coat the lush green undergrowth of the regenerated forest. Violent flash rainstorms often hit the coast, flooding the lowlands and washing away hillside soil; and floods periodically devastate the metropolitan area, transforming unpaved streets into rivers of mud. In the worst years the rising Capiberibe has covered nearly two-thirds of the city, with whole districts turned navigable and untold lives lost.[6]

Virtually all navigation along the state's several rivers is limited to the Mata. The Portuguese colonists invariably positioned their first settlements—Goiana, Igaraçú, Serinhaém, São Lourenço da Mata—near the mouths of river estuaries, giving them reasonably easy access to the capital, Olinda. But even to this day few of Pernambuco's rivers can be navigated beyond their estuaries. Boats ply the Goiana River merely to the end of the town of Goiana's canal; the Capiberibe can be navigated only to Dois Irmãos, formerly rural but by the twentieth century a suburb of Recife. Navigation on the Formoso, Ipojuca, and Serinhaém rivers extends only to the towns bearing their names, and on the Una River only to the outskirts of the town of Barreiros; all these towns are within 11 or 12 kilometers of the coast. The São Francisco River, gateway to the heart of the interior of Pernambuco, Bahia, and Minas Gerais, is not navigable along 465 kilometers of its 3,165-kilometer length because of rapids, waterfalls, and seasonal parching. In any case, in 1824, as punishment for Pernambuco's role in the regionalist uprisings of the period, the Crown stripped the entire Comarca de São Francisco from the province, removing from its jurisdiction both the mouth of the river and hundreds of miles alongside it southwest of Petrolina. Had Pernambuco retained control of the vast river system, it is possible that later efforts to improve navigation would have been pressed with greater energy.[7]

For many, perhaps most, of the residents of the Mata, conditions are hard. As the geographer Mário Lacerda de Melo observes, a plentiful supply of cheap labor, from colonial times to the present, has been responsible for the survival of the zone's sugar economy—and for its extremely low standard of living.[8]

The Agreste. The Mata ends at the base of the Borborema escarpment, only 56 kilometers from the coast in the north and 130 kilometers in the south, giving way to the drier Agreste.[9] In contrast to the rich soil of the Mata, the Agreste's grayish surface layer is shallow—one to three meters or less—and of silicate origin, rich in mineral content but sandy and easily drained. On the windward side of the Borborema, the Agreste is humid and densely inhabited; on the leeward side it is dry and sparsely settled, opening the way to the vast Sertão beyond. The northern Agreste, delimited by the Pernambuco-Paraíba border, has less rainfall than the southern part. Here cotton and livestock predominate. Cattle roam free and croplands are enclosed against wandering goats and pigs. In the southern Agreste, higher altitudes and more precipitation allow a greater variety of livestock and crops, including bananas, cassava, coffee, cotton, beans, corn, sisal, and manioc. The inhabitants of the Agreste are relatively better off than their neighbors in the coastal areas. Whereas the impoverished rural workers in the sugar-growing Mata subsist on manioc flour, black beans, and occasional jerked beef or salt cod, the Agreste farmers often eat cheese and milk as well. But most Agreste farmers are—and have always been—poor. Farms are smaller in this zone than in the Mata or the Sertão; there is little mechanization; and farming methods in general are primitive.[10]

The Agreste, a visiting writer observed in 1937, is but a "milder version of the Sertão. The air stirs, invaded by the intense light of the sun. There is no shade. The beauty of the land remains, but the sun punishes it in all but the winter months. The people are sullen; life is harsh. . . . The horizon is endless; nothing limits movement."[11] Here (the observer continues), in this zone of nondescript trading cities, with neither cathedrals nor secular traditions, "the land has been abandoned by the large landowners; it is divided between the marginal small farmer and the claim staker."[12]

It was the arrival of the railroad in the 1850's that confirmed the Agreste's commercial role. The dusty markets became important centers for distribution and trade: Garanhuns, linking southern Pernambuco and northern Alagoas with Recife; Caruarú and Pesqueira, at the gateway to the Sertão in the central part of the state; and Campina Grande in the State of Paraíba, the major interior Brazilian city north of Belo Horizonte.

Pernambuco's Agreste zone is divided by some geographers into three subregions: the northeast, central-west, and meridional. Though larger than the Mata, the zone comprises only 19 percent of the land area of the state (98,281 square kilometers); the two zones together are thus dwarfed by the Sertão, which with barely one-nineteenth the population of the Mata accounts for a full 70 percent. Along the coast there is a zone of rainfall averaging between 1,000 and 2,000 millimeters, but precipitation drops off sharply in the meridional zone to the southwest; the interior Sertão receives as little as 500 millimeters, and the town of Cabaceiras averages only 250.

Cotton was introduced to the Agreste in the early eighteenth century and quickly became a mainstay of the region's agriculture, especially after the 1840's. Some large plantations thrived briefly, mostly during the cotton boom caused by the American Civil War, when small property owners and even *moradores* (sharecroppers) took up cotton production. When world prices fell after the war, however, some Agreste growers abandoned cotton for coffee. Agricultural diversity coupled with a steady trend to minifundia (holdings of no more than ten hectares, or 25 acres) have contrived to make the Agreste very different, in economic structure and social organization, from both the Mata and the Sertão.[13]

The Sertão. The Sertão, the awesome region of Euclides da Cunha's epic *Rebellion in the Backlands*, emerges from the *caatinga* (scrub, or "white" forest, in the Tupi language) zone in the western Agreste and runs for hundreds of kilometers until it reaches the tropical rain forests of Maranhão, nearer to the Amazon basin than to the Atlantic coast. The Sertão spreads across seven states: Piauí, Ceará, Paraíba, Bahia, Pernambuco, Rio Grande do Norte, and Minas Gerais. This is the region of the drought. The countryside is healthfully semiarid under normal conditions, but sere and desolate when the rains fail to come. Ninety percent of the year's rainfall—ranging from 150 millimeters in parts of Ceará to 500 millimeters, according to location and altitude—occurs from January through May, the months of greatest evaporation.*

---

* Rainfall that comes before Christmas, called the *chuva de cajú*, is considered a godsend. Da Cunha describes the backlander's traditional and pathetic experiment on Santa Luzia's Day: "On December 12, at nightfall, he sets out six lumps of salt in a row, where they will be exposed to the action of the dew; they represent, respectively, from left to right, the six coming months, from January to June. At daybreak the next morning, he observes them. If they are intact, it presages drought; if the first has dissolved somewhat, has been transformed into a soggy mass, he is certain of rain in January; if this happens to the second, it will rain in February." If no rain falls by March, the sertanejo knows that there will be none for at least one more year. (*Rebellion in the Backlands*, pp. 105–6).

The region receives 3,200 hours of sunlight annually. On occasion no rain has fallen in parts of the Sertão for as long as 36 months. Low humidity and the thinnest of soil cover over the crystalline rocks induce rapid evaporation and low water retention; rivers in the dry season become ribbons of sand.[14] Occasionally, a season's rainfall comes in the form of brief torrential downpours over a few days' time; the soil washes away, and the water is lost.

The Sertão is not afflicted by the endemic hunger of the Mata; rather, it is subject to violent "epidemics of starvation" when the droughts come. We have a record of a devastating drought in the Northeast as early as 1583, when thousands of starving Indians fled to the coast in search of food. Other major droughts occurred in 1723–27, 1736–37, 1744–45, 1777–78, 1809, 1834–35, 1835–37, 1844–45, 1877–79, 1889–90, 1915, and 1931–32.

When drought strikes, evil seems to seize hold of the earth. An eighteenth-century traveler observed that children who had been walking returned to the crawling stage. Others have noted that during drought dogs and cattle become crazed and choke on cactus spines; bats and rattlesnakes swarm; edible roots turn poisonous. The sertanejo is frequently stricken by day blindness, unable to see until the torrid sun sinks beneath the earth. Not even the vultures, it is said, can tear the leathery hides of the withered carcasses of fallen horses.[15]

In normal years the land is dotted with cacti and other spiny xerophytes capable of storing water and thus useful for livestock forage. In the rainy season hydrous plants grow; the landscape suddenly flushes a pale yellow-green. The Sertão is generally flat and monochromatic, traversed by temporary streams that disappear when the rains cease and the land reverts to a tracery of thorns and branches. But exceptions exist. Humid oases (brejos) are found at higher elevations, where rainfall is more evenly distributed, and crops can be planted in the fertile alluvial soil of the riverbeds during drought; in these rich deposits crops commonly mature within three months. These and other humid zones serve as storehouses and suppliers of food for surrounding areas. Cattle raising predominates, as it did during the colonial days, but the area's prosperity, at its height in the seventeenth century, has vanished. The Sertão remains isolated, cut off from the coast, timeless.

The air temperature in this part of the hinterland varies according to altitude, not latitude. Triunfo, the highest town in Pernambuco at about 1,060 meters above sea level, has moderate temperatures and a reputation as a health resort. The few mineral resources found in the region include calcite, calcium carbonites, and graphite.[16] Beyond the caatinga region the vegetation is sparse, scattering livestock holdings and resulting in large concentrations of land. Full-sized trees grow on the high Sertão, in the north of the state, but at lower altitudes they shrivel to the size of a shrub. Only cotton is successfully grown for shipment from the region, though subsistence crops abound.

When drought does not strike, the sertanejo has a far less monotonous and more nutritious diet than his counterpart on the coast. Corn taken with milk in the form of curd cheese is the basic fare, supplemented by yams, black beans, manioc, coffee, and even onions, squash, and cucumbers. A local tuberous root, *macunã*, toxic if not carefully prepared, is rich in natural protein. Berries grow at higher elevations, as do guava and mangabeira. In addition, many sertanejos raise chickens, goats, or pigs. The majority, however, are moradores with no land of their own. For the sertanejos, as the anthropologist Allen W. Johnson has noted, land tenure is a matter of the right to use someone else's land.[17]

The People

The Brazilian Northeast accounts for only 10 percent of Brazil's land surface, yet among Latin American countries only Mexico surpasses it in total population. Most of these people, as I have said, are thickly crowded along the littoral. The interior has not only remained sparsely settled, but has steadily lost migrants to coastal urban capitals and the South.

Racial composition. Racial patterns vary little throughout the region. On the coast the upper and middle classes are composed mostly of whites and light-skinned mulattoes. There has been little large-scale European immigration. There were the Portuguese, of course, some numbers of whom were active in commerce and banking by the late eighteenth century. In addition, modest-sized communities of Englishmen, Germans, and other foreigners flourished in Recife between the 1880's and 1920, drawn there as employees of foreign-owned businesses and public utilities. However, though foreigners made up perhaps as much as 10 percent of Recife's population during that period, the foreign-born population in the state as a whole never exceeded the 1872 peak of 1.6 percent.

Thereafter the ratio fell to nine in 1,000 inhabitants in 1900 and only six in 1920. In 1940 more than a quarter of the *municípios* (counties) in the state did not have a single foreign resident.[18]

Slavery, the heart of the plantation system that dominated the regional economy for nearly four centuries, left its legacy in the ethnic composition of the population before and after legal emancipation. A typical engenho of the early nineteenth century owned about 40 slaves, though a survey taken in one município in 1857 revealed an average of 70 slaves and 49 free workers per engenho.[19] With the stagnation of the sugar economy during the nineteenth century and the simultaneous rise in demand for agricultural labor on southern coffee plantations, the sugar barons increasingly sold off their slaves to southern buyers. By 1872 only 89,028 Pernambucano slaves were enumerated by the national census, barely more than half the number estimated for the 1830's. At abolition, in 1888, only 41,122 were left. The traditional thesis that slavery in the sugar zone was benevolent owing to the paternalism of the master-slave relationship and to the sexual desirability of the slave woman has been discredited by recent scholarly research. Carl Degler and others have shown that the abuses were many and severe, especially before 1860, when slaveowners could easily obtain new chattel from the traders who plied the coast to replace those slaves who died from mistreatment or overwork.[20]

Though slave prices tripled in Pernambuco between 1850 and 1860 and runaway slaves became a growing problem for the sugar planters, most of them resisted emancipation. However, the abundant supply of free labor in the sugar zone eased the pain of abolition when it came. Newly freed slaves did not stream from the region as had been feared, though some migrated west into the Agreste from coastal plantations. Peter Eisenberg has shown that non-whites probably migrated less after abolition than whites, since the proportion of colored persons in fact increased slightly in the Mata during a period of relative population decline between 1872 and 1890; meanwhile, the percentage of non-whites in Recife remained constant, standing at about 55–56 percent. Former slaves merely joined the already helpless free workers, who by 1872 outnumbered slaves in all occupational categories by a ratio of three to one.[21]

Few full-blooded Indians survived the enslavement and decimation that followed on the Portuguese conquest. The Tupi and Guarani tribes that had once flourished throughout the Northeast, especially along the coast, all but disappeared. So did the Cariri peoples of the Agreste—the

Sucurús, Garanhuns, and Vouvês—and the Caraíbas of the Sertão. In part this was a matter of racial assimilation. Before emancipation most of the free laborers in the region were *caboclos*, persons of mixed Caucasian and Indian blood.[22] Eventually, blacks entered the caboclo melting pot, though some Northeastern scholars claim that the caboclos of the Sertão are free of any Negroid "influence."[23] At any rate, the term no longer has any racial connotation. In the twentieth century it has come to have a purely social meaning, used routinely for members of the (generally rural) lower classes, regardless of their ancestry.[24]

As Table 1.1 shows, the percentage of Pernambucanos classified as white increased substantially between 1872 and 1940. But we note also that the percentage of blacks (*pretos*) remained relatively constant in that period. It thus appears that what took place in Pernambuco was not so much a whitening process as a shift in the social definition of the mulatto, or *pardo*.

The attitudes of the elite toward the non-white ethnic groups have ranged from tolerance to racist opprobrium. But the perspective has always been that of the white society. In 1922, for example, the editor of Recife's *Commercial Directory* vigorously advocated European immigration, noting that Europeans would spread "better hygienic conditions" and create a new Brazilian racial type from which non-whites would be excluded.[25] Similarly, a quarter of a century before him, Manoel de Oliveira Lima, Brazilian diplomat and Pernambuco's leading historian in his day, attributed the Northeast's decline to "the almost complete absence of European elements," coupled with the "accumulated misery" and "hereditary instinct of uppityness" of the masses."[26] All the same, as Gilberto Freyre notes, though the women of the middle and upper classes disliked to employ *mamelucas* (caboclo women of pronounced Indian stock) because they were "lazy" and "disloyal," the men of the elite so prized *mulatinhas* (dark-skinned women with Caucasian features) as mistresses that the comely mulatta came to be the popular image of the ultimate sex object.[27]

On the whole, non-whites ranked low on the social scale. Though some individuals gained access to the highest levels of the elite (for example, the mulatto jurist and teacher Tobias Barreto), the white society effectively controlled all important facets of the state's economic and political life. As shown in Table 1.2, in 1940, at which time 45 percent of the population was non-white (compared with 12 percent for São Paulo and 11

TABLE 1.1

Racial Categories of Pernambucanos in the Censuses
of 1872, 1890, and 1940
(Percent)

Category	1872	1890	1940
Whites	34.6%	41.2%	54.5%
Pretos	14.9	11.5	15.5
Pardos	50.5	47.3	29.9

SOURCE: Instituto Brasileiro de Geografia e Estatística, *VI Recenseamento geral do Brasil: Estado de Pernambuco* (Rio, 1955), p. 1.

NOTE: Percentages in this table and the others that follow do not always sum to 100 due to rounding.

TABLE 1.2

Selected Male Occupations by Racial Category,
Pernambuco, 1940
(Percent)

Occupation	Whites	Pretos	Pardos
Professional	82%	4%	13%
Public administration	66	10	24
Commerce (employers)	87	2	11
Agriculture (employers)	71	7	21
Agriculture (employees)	44	21	34

SOURCE: Instituto Brasileiro de Geografia e Estatistica, *Recenseamento geral do Brasil (1º de setembro de 1940)* (Rio, 1950), pp. 6, 24–25.

TABLE 1.3

Educational Attainment by Racial Category of Pernambucanos
Above Ten Years of Age, 1940
(Percent)

Level completed	Whites	Pretos	Pardos
Primary	78%	4%	18%
Secondary	91	1	8
Advanced	96	<.5	4

SOURCE: Same as Table 1.2, p. 18.

percent for Rio Grande do Sul), whites almost monopolized the upper end of the occupational scale, filling most of the positions in the professions and the other similarly lucrative and prestigious occupations.

Even more striking is the disparity between the white and non-white groups in education (Table 1.3). In that same year, 1940, fully 91 percent of the persons with a secondary-school education were white, against just 1 percent for the blacks.

The urban population. Two worlds have in fact coexisted in the region ever since the sixteenth century: the genteel, frequently opulent world of the ruling elite, and the miserable, squalid world of the lower classes. It is true that over time social differentiation has blurred some aspects of what otherwise suggests the model of a two-class society, especially in urban areas. But that has not made the world of the lower classes any the less miserable. Indeed it is conceivable that the lot of the caboclo even worsened with the advent of the sugar factory and mechanized agriculture.

Until then, the caboclo had been tied to the land; even his name was often derived from the engenho or locality of his birth: Antônio Joaseiro; Manoel de Lagoa Grande.[28] But as modern agricultural techniques were adopted, more and more caboclos deserted the land. The flight began in earnest during the 1920's, when land prices rose, and wage labor replaced informal work exchange relationships between moradores and landowners, fostering what Manuel Diegues Júnior calls "nomadism" among family heads.[29] In addition, the sugar refineries in the Mata had by this time bought up most of the land around them, establishing their grasp on the economy and forcing agricultural wages downward. By the end of the decade and continuing into the 1930's, when wages fell sharply, thousands of workers poured out of the rural areas, migrating to Recife or south to São Paulo and Rio.[30]

There a sorry fate usually awaited them. The quality of urban life depends precariously on the capacity of a city to sustain the needs of its population. When social services fail to keep pace with rapid demographic growth, the lower classes suffer most. As historians have noted, the explosion of population in Paris between 1815 and 1848 plunged the city into the depths of social brutality, bringing in its train disease, indigence, criminality, and despair.[31] Recife, even though its own population growth was incremental, exhibited parallel symptoms almost from the start: idleness, malnutrition, prostitution, and beneath the thin veneer of seeming equilibrium, random violence and chronic apathy.

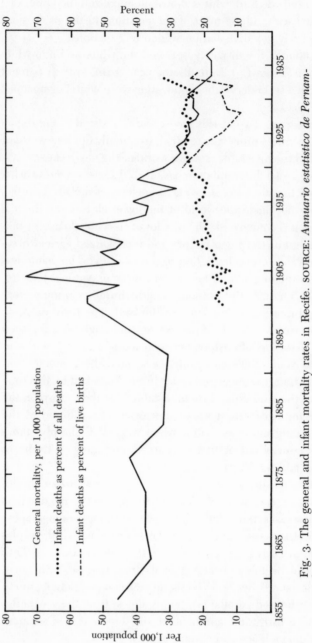

Fig. 3. The general and infant mortality rates in Recife. SOURCE: *Annuario estatístico de Pernambuco*, 1927, pp. 114–21; 1934, pp. 52–54; 1937–38, pp. 24, 26; A.J. Barbosa Vianna, *O Recife, capital do Estado de Pernambuco* (Recife, 1900), p. 205. NOTE: 1855–95 data are five-year averages.

In the nineteenth century the city's population increased substantially, and by 1872, the year of the first reliable census, 100,000 people lived within its boundaries. Since the urban death rate was higher than the rural one, the average annual growth rate during the century (2 percent) must be ascribed to in-migration.[32] The rate of infant mortality was also extremely high during this period, probably even higher than recorded levels; that, too, argues for the proposition that migration, not natural increase, accounted for Recife's growth.

Regional migration in the Northeast, as Bainbridge Cowell demonstrates, was influenced in part by short-run "push factors," most notably the periodic droughts in the Sertão. But it was primarily due to changes in the pattern of sugar production in the Mata. Refugees from the Agreste and Sertão tended to leave the Northeast altogether, whereas most of the migrants to Recife came from coastal plantations.[33] The single greatest impulse to cityward migration after 1885 was the arrival of the *usinas* (refineries), which began to amass large quantities of caneland, driving out the caboclos and former slaves who formerly subsisted as squatters. These migrants of the late nineteenth century did not make intermediate stops in smaller towns before reaching Recife, as Lacerda de Melo suggests was the case a half-century later.[34] The abolition of slavery, as noted, does not appear to have contributed significantly to the rural exodus in the Northeast, as it did in southern Brazil.

The migration from the sugar region swelled the lower-class "suburbs" of the city, as the *mocambos* (from an African word for cave) of the poor proliferated on the hillsides and swampy lowlands on Recife's periphery. Many districts rapidly deteriorated, losing their more affluent residents when the newcomers poured in. The baleful statistics track the changes. In 1930, for example, the rate of mortality in the transitional district of Afogados was seven times higher than in the less-crowded São José district in central Recife. By then most of the city's habitable stretches of dry land had been exhausted, forcing mocambos deeper and deeper into the adjacent mangrove swamps and floodplains.

Through 1920 the official recorded death rate in Recife exceeded the "wholesale slaughter" (to use the words of the historian Louis Chevalier) that marked the 1781–1810 period in Paris.[35] Though in the long term the mortality rate declined between 1856 and 1937, it rose ominously between 1895 and 1912 (see Fig. 3). This rise may in part reflect more accurate counting procedures, but there is little question that the death rate

genuinely rose as urban overcrowding put the population of the city at the
mercy of infection and disease. As Josué de Castro reminds us, the popular wisdom taught that Recife's infants were born in order to populate
heaven with angels.[36]

Even adults in the 30–39 age group had a mortality rate more than
twice the Brazilian average. Presumably the fact that the state's per capita
expenditures for health care were consistently much lower than in other
parts of the country played a role in all this. Nor did the federal system, as
later chapters will show, offer any relief. In 1937 Pernambuco's per capita
share of federal health revenue was three contos, compared with ten for
São Paulo and 90 for the Federal District of Rio de Janeiro.[37]

Disease, as one would expect, attacked the poor more than the rich.
Foreign residents of Recife fared quite well; a state official even declared
that Recife's healthful effect on foreigners constituted a "magnificent condition" that could be exploited to promote immigration.[38] Yet the truth
was known as early as 1909, when participants in a medical congress held
in Recife pointed to the heightened threat of tuberculosis among people
who lived in unhygienic accommodations, and even suggested that better
working conditions and wages might increase the workers' stamina and
reduce the number of strikes.[39]

But few heeded the physicians' advice. Recife did undergo major reconstruction after the 1850's, and a generous amount of money went to
public works. Yet on the whole the improvements benefited the affluent;
few of the city's blighted areas, save for the sugar-reeking warehouse region of the docks on the island of Recife, were helped.[40] The overall
mortality rate began to show a steady improvement from about 1920, but
even in 1939 the life expectancy in Recife was dismally low: 28 years for
men, 32 years for women.[41] Moreover, after a brief fall the rate of infant
mortality (infants under one year of age) climbed steeply through the
1930's and beyond (see Fig. 3). And the true infant death rate, as I have
said, was probably higher. In 1909 a city official noted that "well over a
third of the population" never bothered to have their children's births
recorded.[42]

Epidemics repeatedly swept the Northeast through the nineteenth and
early twentieth centuries, and particularly in the humid coast, leaving
thousands of dead in their wake. Between 1849 and 1920 Recife alone was
afflicted by 14 major epidemics. Smallpox raged through the city seven
times, and yellow fever and dysentery twice. The influenza epidemic of

1918–19 took an enormous toll. There were also major outbreaks of cholera and bubonic plague. More than half of the deaths in Recife in 1930 resulted from infectious disease. In normal years tuberculosis and various forms of dysentery were the leading causes of death; parasitic diseases, leprosy, and vitamin-deficiency ailments also took a fair share of victims. Tuberculosis caused 30,581 deaths in Recife between 1891 and 1918, mostly of children. The droughts added to the carnage by weakening their victims and driving them toward the disease-ridden cities. Nearly 57,000 people died in Fortaleza in the drought year of 1878 out of a total population of only 124,000.[43]

For the most part the authorities stood helplessly by. When yellow fever struck Recife in 1849 about all the city officials could do was establish a public cemetery, since Church burial grounds were filled to capacity. In anticipation of the visit of the emperor in the 1870's, the city authorities ordered that animal carcasses be collected and buried, and that slaves not be permitted to defecate in public.[44]

The 1918 influenza epidemic took 2,551 lives in Recife in three months. Politics interfered with calls for preventive measures. Opposition newspapers decried the growing epidemic, but the official *Diário de Pernambuco* insisted that no danger existed. When the epidemic hit full force, stores closed, hospitals overflowed, milk, lemons, and tea—the most popular home remedies—sold for ten times normal prices, and all houses of public entertainment shut down for a month until the epidemic subsided.[45]

Officials recognized the need for proper sewage facilities and other public health improvements in the more populous centers, but the state lacked adequate funds to keep pace with urban growth. Recife got a sewage system in 1873 that served well enough until the early 1900's; but small towns and rural areas received no improvements whatever. Disease prevention efforts before the early twentieth century were limited to warnings about health care in local newspapers—for those who could read. Public resistance to vaccination prolonged the survival of smallpox outbreaks until the 1930's. Even local officials termed public health facilities "abominable."[46] The general manager of the British-owned Great Western of Brazil Railway, a longtime resident of Recife, wrote in 1911: "The sanitary state of Recife has never, during my experience here, been so bad as at present, and there have been a number of deaths among the English community. Malignant fevers are now causing a large mortality amongst the native and coloured classes, which have previously been considered as immune."[47] Indeed, as shown in Figure 3, the mortality rate did shoot up in this very period. Ironically, the Great Western man attributed the rise in the death rate to the open sewers and polluted air caused by the work in process on an enlarged sewage system and improvements in the city's low-lying areas. But the flood of new migrants certainly contributed to the rising death rate, despite the reputation of the caboclo poor for resilience. Relative improvement came only in the mid-1920's and after, with increased efforts in public health by the state and federal mass inoculation programs.[48]

Urban Growth

In 1827 Recife was made the capital of Pernambuco, still further eroding the power of the rural-based aristocracy in Olinda. Between 1837 and 1865, under the provincial administration of the Conde de Boa Vista and guided by foreign technical missions, important improvements were made in the new capital. Bridges were built linking the island city's three principal zones; existing roads were improved; and two highways were built, one to Cabo, south of the city, the other west to Vitória.[49] Streetcar links were built to the suburbs of Apipucos and Caxangá in 1866, and to Olinda four years later. By 1900 the city had expanded to incorporate eight districts (freguesias), five of them urban and three suburban.[50] With the influx of in-migrants in the following decades, mocambos began to spread rapidly, accounting for one out of every two new dwellings erected in the city after 1920.[51]

Through most of this period the city's population grew steadily but not spectacularly. Indeed until 1920 its rate of population increase was outstripped by the state's (Table 1.4). But though the population then began to swell, until in 1938 Recife was Brazil's third-largest city (and its most densely populated one), its proportion of the state's population remained approximately the same (Table 1.5).[52]

This regional balance, however, disguised a clear and growing imbalance between Recife and the state's other urban centers. This was a relatively late development. Even in the nineteenth century the city had only surpassed the next-largest town in Pernambuco by a margin of something like three to one. By 1920, though, Recife, by any population estimate, was more than ten times the size of the second-most-populous city, Olinda, its own residential suburb. The third-largest center, the Agreste

TABLE 1.4
Comparative Population Growth, Pernambuco and Its Capital, 1872–1960

Year	Pernambuco		Recife	
	Thousands of persons	Index: 1872 = 100	Thousands of persons	Index: 1872 = 100
1872	842	100	117	100
1890	1,050	125	112	96
1900	1,178	140	113	97
1920	2,155	256	239	204
1940	2,688	319	384	328
1960	4,137	491	797	681

SOURCE: Pernambuco, Conselho de Desenvolvimento, *Demografia* (Recife, 1966), p. 3.

TABLE 1.5
Major Population Zones of Pernambuco, 1890–1935
(Percent of population)

Year	Mata			Agreste	Sertão
	Recife	Elsewhere	Total		
1890	10.8%	39.5%	50.3%	33.2%	14.9%
1920	11.1	40.4	51.5	34.6	13.9
1935	13.6	34.9	48.5	36.0	14.9

SOURCE: Directoria geral de Estatística, *Sexo, raca, e estado civil . . . 1890* (Rio, 1898), pp. 421–23; DGE, *Synopse do recenseamento realizado em 1 de setembro de 1920: população do Brasil* (Rio, 1922), pp. 26–27; *Annuario estatistico de Pernambuco*, 1934, pp. 43–44.
NOTE: Data based on município totals adjusted to 1895 boundaries.

town of Caruarú, had a population of only 24,000.[53] Pernambuco's lack of secondary cities and the bleakness and monotony of the urban landscape beyond the coast have led local historians to write of the state's "cities without history."[54]

Technically, each of Pernambuco's município seats is considered "urban"; but in 1930 only 30 of the 84 município seats had over 5,000 population, and 36 were under 3,000.* Only 39, or less than half, of these towns had more than 500 buildings at that time. A few boasted several thousand (Caruarú had 4,302 buildings, and Garanhuns, 2,878), but some of the sertanejo município seats had no more than 100, and one, Moxotó, had only 62.[55]

In that same year fewer than ten automobiles—and in many cases only one or two—were registered in most municípios, against 1,310 in the

*The term urban as I use it in this book always refers to towns with a population of at least 5,000.

state capital. The smaller município seats merely served as administrative
and commercial outposts for surrounding rural areas, offering few of the
services usually associated with cities. In 1930 Recife had 91 percent of all
the hospital beds in the state, 88 percent of all the secondary school students, 66 percent of all the persons employed in journalism, and 31 percent of all of the cinemas. Yet it contained barely 15 percent of the state
population and 15 percent of the electorate.[56]

Clearly, Recife is the heart of the state's life. Yet, as we shall see, in the
period of our study, however painfully and slowly, the city did finally
begin to reach out to and integrate its hinterland. But as we shall also
see, the interests of the Recife-based coastal elite did not always coincide
with the needs of the rest of the state or the desires of Pernambuco's
neighbors.

Rooted in an economically stagnant plantation society, the men who
inherited power after the fall of the Empire in Pernambuco were to some
degree both unable and unwilling to cope with the rural exodus from the
stricken agricultural areas of the Mata and the Agreste or with the influx
of people into Recife and other urban centers. Not that Pernambucanos
isolated themselves from the outside world: some of the initiatives taken
by state officials to revive sugar production and otherwise promote change
represented courageous efforts in an era of declining resources.

But that was hardly what was required. In São Paulo the dynamic expansion of the coffee frontier spurred the growth of the capital and
created the preconditions for national leadership. In Minas the elite attempted to create an economic base for political power within the state,
populous and stable despite subregional inequalities. As the center of a
region that was losing both skilled population and investments to the
South, Pernambuco could only expect to lose ground. Meanwhile, changing national circumstances acted to reduce the state's influence within the
Northeast. The federal structure of the Republic exacerbated the old
rivalry between Pernambuco and Bahia and encouraged them to seek advantage by intensifying their political and economic pressures on their
weaker neighbors—in Pernambuco's case, on the states of its satellite
bloc.

CHAPTER TWO

The Economy

PERNAMBUCO, described by the economist Celso Furtado as possibly the most profitable colonial agricultural enterprise of all time, reached the point in the nineteenth century where it could barely sustain its population. The economic slide began in the early 1800's with increased competition from foreign sugar growers that depressed market prices and cut the value of the Northeast's exports in half. At the same time gold was discovered in Minas Gerais, and the center of dynamic economic growth began to shift to the South. So rapid was this shift that by the 1850's the South had overtaken the Northeast in per capita income. Adding to the economic woes, cotton, the state's second major crop, was hit by a severe market decline in the next few decades. Sugar and cotton together had accounted for 50 percent of Brazil's export revenue as late as the 1820's; by 1912–14 they brought in a mere 3 percent. However, though both crops fell off badly, the decline of sugar caused far greater dislocations in the Northeast than the decline of cotton, since the life of the entire Zona da Mata depended on it.[1]

From Engenho to Usina

The early nineteenth century also saw the start of a trend toward land concentration as engenho owners, finding it inefficient to raise all their cane themselves, began to deal with tenant contractors. These suppliers, or *fornecedores*, cultivated small plots with the help of slave or family members and delivered the raw cane to the engenho's mill; many times they got no more than one-third of the refined product in payment.[2] In time, as sugar production became more mechanized, engenho owners themselves abandoned their water- or oxen-driven mills and themselves became fornecedores, supplying cane to the new centralized refineries and reducing their engenhos to the status of *bangües*, cane-producing farms. The steady decline of the sugar market as the nineteenth century progressed, together with the abolition of primogeniture in the 1830's, transformed most of the nearly 2,000 engenhos to bangües by the 1880's. Roughly half of the sugar output was by then monopolized by the surviving engenhos and the sugar refineries, whose owners increasingly removed land from cultivation in an effort to reduce costs as prices fell.

Rather than diversify and free themselves of their traditional dependence on cane sugar, the large planters opted to hold on; their spokesmen sought government aid to finance new machinery and to subsidize railroads and shipping facilities. But in the end the gamble failed, leaving the regional economy moribund and further weakening the Northeast's position in the national economy.

Labor patterns. Low profits weakened the hold of the slave system, which gradually yielded to a labor structure that made use of both slaves and free workers. In more prosperous times some plantations in the Mata had owned as many as 150 slaves, and slaves had once formed about three-fourths of the state's labor force; but by 1850 the free population outnumbered slaves in every município in Pernambuco. The majority of the rural poor were now the impoverished landless classes—the squatters, tenant farmers, and sharecroppers, collectively called the *agregados*. Many of the region's slaves had been bought up by agents of the southern coffee planters, who circulated in the Northeast offering high prices for slaves and encouraging smaller proprietors to sell them for needed capital; recent estimates suggest that the post-1850 interprovincial slave trade may have siphoned off as much as 22 percent of the sugar zone's slave population. Other slaves, many of them old or infirm, gained their freedom through public and private manumission as abolition neared.[3] But the increasing scarcity of slaves did not necessarily imply that they were valued the more, and so fared better. On the contrary, many planters concentrated their remaining slaves in mill-work, punishing them when productivity dropped, and turned to sharecroppers for field labor.[4] The presence of large numbers of free rural poor so softened the impact of abolition when it finally came that the event produced little or no major change in the structure of agricultural life.

The squatters were one of the first groups among the hapless agregados to be brought to the planters' heel. Traditionally allowed to erect thatched mud huts and grow subsistence crops on engenho land in exchange for occasional labor, as early as the 1850's they began to be forced to work for regular periods or face expulsion, a device by which the planters relieved themselves of the necessity of raising cash for wages and exchanged otherwise unproductive land for labor performed on their own terms. In general the upper classes considered all agregados idle and untrustworthy; and after serious revolts occurred in a dozen Pernambuco municípios in 1851–52, landowners took steps to see that vagrants and potential troublemakers were impressed into units of the national guard or provincial police.[5] Commenting on the insecurity of agregado life, the French cotton merchant Louis-François Tollenare noted that the senhores de engenho seemed to have a special predilection for their tenants' wives and daughters, and that landlords rarely left their residences without bodyguards to protect them against angry men seeking to avenge their personal dishonor or their indiscriminate eviction from engenho land.[6]

Disdain for the caboclo free labor force contributed to the continued preference among sugar producers for slave labor, even as abolition drew near. In addition, planters considered slaves a good investment.[7] When, after abolition, sugar prices continued to fall, a result of competition from the Caribbean and the introduction of beet sugar to the world market, the rural worker's life became even more precarious. For day laborers, their ranks now swollen by the newly freed slaves, real wages fell to nearly half of the mid-century levels.

Labor conditions varied widely from one part of the Northeast to another, and even within the Mata itself. The cotton boom of the early 1860's drew rural population to the Agreste, but with the decline of cotton farming toward the end of the decade and the eastward flow of migrants from the 1877–79 drought, the Mata's population density was soon back to the previous high levels of between 65 and 100 persons per square kilometer. Even before abolition, in fact, planters began to use daily wage laborers, a portent of things to come, especially since early experiments with the centralization of sugar production had already suggested that the use of labor could be made both more efficient and more profitable.

Wage labor allowed the planter to hire hands only when they were needed, mostly for cane harvesting and work during the milling season. In addition, this kind of employee-employer relationship, like tenancy, was a form of social control: wages could be kept at subsistence levels, and uncooperative workers could be dismissed at will. And then, too, a planter could always fall back entirely on resident agregados in bad years when low prices discouraged him from paying any salaries at all. Between 1880 and 1914 male agricultural laborers earned between 500 and 1,000 reis for a day's work, barely sufficient for a family's survival even during periods of regular employment. Unemployed laborers drifted to the towns, where they tried to find odd jobs, or wandered from engenho to engenho. Only the most destitute families migrated to Recife, since unemployment among the lower classes there ranged between 30 percent and 40 percent. The ability of landowners to keep a supply of cheap labor permanently available was the most efficient element in the noncompetitive agricultural system.

Wage scales for daily labor in the Mata show that the poor did not benefit from the modernization and centralization of sugar production; indeed, in most cases their ability to sustain themselves deteriorated over time. Even workers in the new refineries—technically industrial workers —fared little better. Usina workers got perhaps a fifth more than fieldhands, but this was frequently offset by the exploitative charges they were forced to pay for company-owned housing and in the *barração*, the usina store. Their wives and children were usually not employable, and families were no longer allowed to cultivate small plots of land for their own use as they had as squatters on sugar plantations.

Table 2.1 illustrates the fate of agricultural workers from the 1870's to the 1930's. Abolition and the sugar refineries both acted to drag down the already low rural standard of living. Wages rose substantially between 1896 and 1910 but failed to keep pace with the rising costs of living. Nominal daily wages climbed again in the 1920's, but real wages fell. Moreover, the sugar factories' increased efficiency and growing share of production limited opportunities for employment and depressed wages for unskilled workers at a time when wages for skilled workers—carpenters, masons, and the like—were gradually rising. Rural real wages fell still further after 1930, and by the middle depression years had returned only to pre-abolition levels in most of the sugar zone. Unrelenting population growth made conditions still worse: the state's rural population actually doubled between 1900 and 1940. If wages were low for full-grown men, women and children, who made up perhaps one-fourth of the work force, got a mere pittance, receiving half or less of what a man was paid.

TABLE 2.1

Agricultural Salaries of Adult Male Workers in Pernambuco, 1874–1935

(Milreis)

Year	Nominal daily wage	Real wage (1912 = base year)	Year	Nominal daily wage	Real wage (1912 = base year)
1874	1$000	$625	1920	1$500	$510
1896	$445	$436	1926	2$220	$670
1900	$800	$740	1931	1$000[b]	$350
1910[a]			1935		
Fieldhand	1$030	1$240	Fieldhand	2$000–2$500	$600
Usina			Usina		
worker	1$300	1$560	worker	3$000	$900

SOURCE: *Annuario estatistico de Pernambuco*, 1934, p. 416; Orris Barbosa, *Secca de 32* (Rio, 1935), p. 70; *Boletim de União dos Syndicatos Agrícolas de Pernambuco*, 1910, p. 48; Públio Dias, *Condições higiénicás e sociais do trabalhador dos engenhos de Pernambuco* (Recife, 1937), p. 1; Directoria Geral de Estatistica, *Indústria assucareira; usinas e engenhos centraes* (Rio, 1910), pp. 5–6; DGE, *Salários rurais* (Rio, 1927), p. 11; Peter L. Eisenberg, *The Sugar Industry in Pernambuco* (Berkeley, Calif., 1973), p. 192; R. Fernandes e Silva, *Notas econômicas sôbre a indústria pastoril de Pernambuco* (Recife, 1927), p. 13; *Jornal do Recife*, Jan. 22, 1926, p. 1; José Lins do Rego, "Usineiros e Latifúndios," *A Manhã* (Recife), May 18, 1935, p. 3; *A Província* (Recife), Feb. 26, 1926, p. 4; Jaime Reis, "Abolition and the Economics of Slaveholding in North East Brazil," University of Glasgow, 1974; Reis, "From Bangüe to Usina," University of Glasgow, 1973, pp. 23–24.

NOTE: These are all the average wage. Pay varied substantially from place to place and from season to season. Fieldhand wages in 1910, for example, ranged from $800 to 1$100 and usina wages from 1$125 to 1$733.

[a] In 1911 a fieldhand in Pernambuco received an average wage of 1$025, a usina worker 1$260. This compared to wages of 2$300 and 2$600 in São Paulo.

[b] By official statistics, wages at this time averaged 2$000–2$500. However, the fall of sugar prices after the onset of the depression caused an immediate drop in wages as well (courtesy of Gileno Dé Carli).

Land tenure. Industrialization renewed the trend toward land concentration, which had slowed after the middle of the nineteenth century with the stagnation of the sugar industry. By the turn of the century only 5–6 percent of the agricultural land in the sugar zone lay under cultivation; and the milling season lasted only 120 days. All but 4 percent of the engenhos in the region still relied on water or animal power, which limited their daily output to at best 10 or 15 tons of second-grade sugar. The hilly terrain and the heavy soil that caked in the heat discouraged the importation of modern iron and steel plows and harrows, which had been used widely in Cuba and Louisiana as early as 1840. In Pernambuco fieldhands used primitive hoes well into the twentieth century.

For individual planters, investment in expensive labor-saving machinery was risky. Engenho owners could count on a 5 percent annual return at most; new machinery cost ten times the typical annual profit of five contos; and to expand production required investments of as much as 200. Land exhaustion, scarcity of firewood, lack of credit, and high transportation costs forced many planters to abandon their mills and become simple suppliers of cane to the new usinas. Efforts to organize agricultural interest groups attracted few members. New methods developed elsewhere to improve cane yield were known throughout the sugar region but were dismissed as too risky or as prohibitively expensive.

In the 1880's the Imperial government embarked on a plan for government-aided large, mechanized mills (*engenhos centrais*). When that program failed, officials turned to subsidizing usinas, modern sugar refineries. But 1,500 economically marginal bangües still survived in 1910, and of the 40 new usinas, only three were turning profits.[8] One of the major problems faced by most usineiros was the inability to find enough cane, though they hungrily bought out adjacent engenhos and put the cane fields under overseers. The usina consortium of the Bezerra de Melo clan alone owned more than 70,000 hectares of land surrounding its four refineries in Pernambuco and Alagoas.

Low sugar prices, however, compelled many usineiros to rely on the still independent engenhos for most of their cane. Many of these suppliers (fornecedores) had to pay up to 30 percent of their yield in rent and in penalties for less than first-quality cane; and in the end they were driven to organize and to campaign bitterly for government relief. The collapse of the price paid to suppliers in 1929—to 8$092 a ton for cane that cost 18$000 to grow—finally led the state administration to commit itself to some form of aid.

Meanwhile, the trend toward land concentration continued unabated —to the point where by the late 1930's Pernambuco's 60 usinas had come to own nearly 60 percent of the caneland in the state. Similar trends to latifundia on one end of the scale and minifundia on the other characterized the Northeast as a whole. In Pernambuco latifundia (holdings over 500 hectares in area, following the census designation) accounted for just 2 percent of the agricultural units in 1940 but held 43 percent of the total agricultural land. At the same time small farms had proliferated remarkably since 1920. Most of this increase was in the Agreste and reflected the subdivision of family farms. Minifundia (holdings below ten hectares) accounted for 55 percent of the agricultural units but for less than 5 percent of the total agricultural land.[9]

By 1940 in the Zona da Mata alone 72 percent of the agricultural units together held only 5 percent of the agricultural land.* The opposite trend

*Application of the Gini coefficient $[1-2 \Sigma P_1 CumY_1 + \Sigma B_1 Y_1]$, which measures deviation (on a scale of 0 to +1) from a norm of equality in the distribution of variables, yields 0.7325 for the Zona da Mata and 0.7139 for the state as a whole.

was to be found precisely in those municípios with more than one usina—Cabo (5), Escada (5), Serinhaëm (4), Agua Preta (3), Ribeirão (3), and Ipojuca (2). In these six municípios minifundia properties totaled less than 10 percent; rather the usinas owned virtually every piece of land, though much of it was leased to fornecedores. Throughout the Mata absentee landholding accompanied the trend to land concentration, characterizing more than half the agricultural units in the zone by the end of the 1930's.

The usinas not only affected the pattern of land tenure and rural labor, but shifted the base of power among the agricultural elite. By 1910 usinas in Pernambuco and Alagoas accounted for half the refined sugar exported from the Northeast. But the ability of some of the senhores de engenho to survive by abandoning their mills and becoming cane jobbers limited what might have been a generally beneficial impact of sugar modernization, forcing government officials to subsidize both usinas and fornecedores, thus stretching the state's financial resources and hindering growth in other economic sectors. The political costs to Pernambuco of the survival of the traditional system of sugar production were great, as we shall see in a later chapter.

The Sugar Industry

Fernando de Azevedo has suggested that the conflict over political and economic hegemony in the Northeast took the form of a horizontal struggle between the landed aristocracy and the urban bourgeoisie, an angry feud whose climax came in the wake of the gubernatorial campaign of 1911, which brought the state of Pernambuco to the brink of civil war.[10] This hypothesis seems valid if the usineiros are assigned to the bourgeoisie; in other terms, the conflict may be said to have taken place between the rural planters and the rising urban commercial and agro-industrial groups. It is a testimony to the tenacity of sugar's hold on the region that not all senhores de engenho were driven to abandon their fields to the encroaching usinas; nor, as occurred in Rio de Janeiro, did surviving engenho lands become so subdivided that most fornecedores were reduced to destitution.[11] True enough, between 1910 and 1920, 400 engenhos succumbed, but nearly 1,100 remained, their proprietors forming an independent capitalist class with carefully forged links with Recife bankers.

The engenho, the source of much romantic nostalgia in northeastern literature, remained largely unchanged until the nineteenth century. Henry Koster, visiting Pernambuco in 1815, found that local planters were "astonished to learn that Brazil was not the only country in which sugar was made."[12] Improved otaheite cane, imported from Tahiti by the French to the West Indies and thence to Brazil in the early nineteenth century, as well as the development of railroads and a period of relatively easy credit during the 1850's, led to the expansion of engenhos south and west in the Zona da Mata. The result was an average yearly increase in sugar output of 4 percent up to 1890, when gumming disease, which had struck southern Brazil in 1860, spread north despite efforts to isolate it, reducing cane yields in both quality and quantity.

Tariff protection in the United States for sugar grown in Louisiana and Hawaii accelerated the Imperial government's plans for centralizing the refining process in large, mechanized mills. But only six of the 31 planned engenhos centrais were constructed. Control regulations proved too constricting, and the problem of obtaining a steady supply of cane proved insurmountable.[13]

Even the modern usina failed to stem the tide of unprofitability. David Denslow has impressively shown why the usinas of the Northeast fared so badly on the world market. In the first place, compared with Cuban refineries during the same period—1887–89—they paid nearly three times as much in transportation and manufacturing costs per ton of sugar, even though their day laborers earned only one-third the wages of the Cuban workers. Moreover, United States tariff policies, giving domestic growers an effective subsidy of 80 percent of the price of sugar, allowed Cuba to achieve a 20 percent price reduction. Finally, high profits in this and other sugar-growing areas protected by the United States encouraged the reinvestment of earnings and attracted capital, whereas Pernambucan sugar producers competed with interests in other Brazilian regions for support within an economic infrastructure barely able to meet minimal needs.[14]

Still, however relatively disadvantaged, 74 usinas came into being in Pernambuco between 1885 and 1933. Ecologically, they accelerated and expanded the circle of destruction fed by the need for firewood, fertile land, and water. Rural families were brusquely expelled from former engenho land or were reduced to day laborers and employed as needed. The forced dissolution of the old patriarchal planter-laborer relationship

ended the right of the sharecropper to raise food crops for his own suste-
nance and to sell any surplus to the feiras of nearby towns.[15]

By 1910 northeastern usinas (including six in Alagoas) produced a third
of Brazil's refined sugar. But uneven and unpredictable market demand
and the general distaste among foreign purchasers for usina sugar doomed
the prospects for long-term and fundamental improvements in the Northeast's economy. Brazilian producers exported 3,000,000 sacks of refined
sugar in 1901, or 60 percent of the total national sugar production; only
three years later, in 1904, foreign sales totaled just 131,000 sacks, or 4
percent of the year's harvest.[16] Exports recovered in 1906, only to fall
again in 1907. Sugar sales rose during and immediately following the First
World War, reaching their apogee in 1922, but by 1924 the boom ended
as abruptly as it began. By this time the northeastern sugar producers
sold the bulk of their output in the domestic market. Even in 1910, in
fact, a third of the sugar imported through the port of Rio de Janeiro for
domestic consumption originated at the port of Recife. But the old dependence on foreign markets was replaced by a no more satisfactory dependence on uncertain domestic markets, and the effect was the same: to
inhibit the growth of markets for manufactures produced within the
Northeast.[17]

The northeastern sugar planters were hurt severely by economic reces-
sion between 1890 and 1904, but efforts in 1905 and 1909 to cartelize
the national sugar industry failed when northeastern producers claimed
that southern usineiros were getting preferential treatment. A sugar-
valorization plan was rejected in mid-1911 for similar reasons, with the
added opposition of the cane suppliers, who foresaw the extinction of the
bangües under the proposal. Even without the program, though, the
number of bangües dwindled steadily. Hostility between the usineiros
and the cane suppliers increased in this period, exploding in violence
after 1930, when market prices for usina sugar fell below the cost of
manufacture.

As we have seen, wages in the northeastern states shrank to 1$000 a day
or less, returning to the 1874 level; and in terms of buying power, the
rural worker was now far worse off. The crisis peaked in 1931–32, when
cane suppliers and usineiros, brought to the point of open warfare by
armed violence and arson throughout the Mata, separately demanded
federal intervention to avert disaster. In response the Vargas administra-

tion set in motion legislation that awarded Pyrrhic victories to both sides. With the establishment of the federal Sugar Agency (Instituto do Açúcar e do Alcool, or IAA) in October 1933, a government-appointed board took control of national sugar production, setting quotas, guaranteeing to purchase unsold sugar at minimum prices up to the limit of the production allocations, and keeping the fornecedores alive by obliging usinas to purchase fixed quantities of cane from local suppliers. The state production quotas, established after intense lobbying, allocated about 60 percent of the subsidy-backed output to the Northeast; Pernambuco had the lion's share of this quota, filling 37 percent alone through the early 1940's.[18] By then the usinas were turning out most of the sugar (see Table 2.2), though the sugar value export index fluctuated widely, declining by 1937 to pre–World War I levels.

In the long run the imposition of federal controls perpetuated an untenable system, with the northeastern states unable to obtain federal support for local improvements in transportation and for the capital expenditures that were necessary to regain a competitive advantage. By the early 1930's smaller usinas in the Northeast had begun to falter, further depressing wages and increasing the influence of the surviving large usinas. Some of these, like Usina Catende and Usina Santa Terezinha, not only exercised near-feudal local domination, but wielded a disproportionate share of political influence statewide.[19]

Cotton and Textiles

Recife's growing importance from the eighteenth century onward owed as much to the rise of cotton as the Northeast's second export crop as to the continued role of sugar. English textile manufacturers purchased large quantities of high-quality Brazilian cotton during the American War for Independence, during which time Recife became the second leading port of cotton embarcation after São Luis, Maranhão. By 1796 the value of cotton exports from Recife had climbed to the equivalent of 1,623,800 ounces of gold, a fourth more than the estimated value of sugar exports in 1710. Not long after, in 1806, cotton overtook sugar as an export item, accounting for 56 percent of all exports from Recife, by then Brazil's second major port after Rio de Janeiro.[20]

The cotton boom not only relieved Recife's dependence on sugar, but introduced new patterns of land use and ownership, particularly in the Agreste. Cotton, grown on small and medium-sized plots, brought some

TABLE 2.2
Usina Sugar Production in Pernambuco, 1900–1937

			Value of usina production (000 contos)		Output	
Year	Number of usinas	Number of workers	Nominal value	Value deflated (1912 = base year)	State total (000 kg)	Usina share (Percent)
1900	21	—	—	—	138,181	25%
1907	46	4,887	27,947	30,377	97,000	25
1916	51	—	34,834	25,060	150,696	45
1920	51	6,487	81,245	—	—	—
1927	66	7,275	142,899	42,029	271,571	80
1933	74	6,420	159,263	59,649	188,028	87
1937	60	—	119,561	22,773	183,939	83

SOURCE: Annuario estatistico de Pernambuco, 1934, pp. 252, 348–49, 392–95, and 1939–40, p. 201; Boletim da União dos Syndicatos Agrícolas de Pernambuco, Jan. 1907, pp. 78–79; Banco do Nordeste, S/A, Estrutura da indústria pernambucana (Fortaleza, 1963), p. 9.

measure of economic health to the interior zone. But several factors worked to cut short prosperity: the land was poor, slash-and-burn techniques made things worse, and transportation was primitive and prohibitively expensive. In 1884 the railroad charges for hauling cotton from the Pajéu valley in the Sertão to Recife, a distance of only about 320 kilometers, were 25–30 percent of the value of the shipment.[21] Long-staple "Pernambuco cotton," grown in the region from the Paraíba River to the São Francisco, was considered the most desirable variety by the British textile manufacturers before the 1850's, but it fell into disfavor when they turned to lower-grade sources in the United States, Egypt, and the East Indies.

The first textile factories, run by slaves, were established in the mid-1820's to produce rough cloth and sacking for sugar bags, but none succeeded. No other major effort to establish a textile mill was made for another 50 years. One started up in 1876, but it was only in the late 1890's when government import-substitution policies stimulated growth, that the number of looms in Pernambuco rose substantially, from 60 to 1,783. Dividends fell off after 1896, and the industry declined during the subsequent decade. Virtually all heavy equipment as well as skilled personnel had to be imported from abroad. After 1907 or so the pace of the industry picked up, and by 1915 Pernambuco had 6,180 textile workers and 3,154 looms, with neighboring Alagoas and Paraíba together totaling half again as much in textile manufacturing capacity. The regional textile manufacture still produced rudimentary goods, mostly sugar bagging, gray cloth, burlap, and coarse cotton shirtings unadorned by print. In this industry, as Denslow notes, economies of scale in styling were significant.[22] New growth took place after 1925, with five mills founded in the greater Recife area; two of these were at some remove from the city, in Cabo and Escada, reflecting the advent of trucking, and with it the ability to take advantage of lower land costs outside of the capital. By 1934, 23 textile mills operated in the state, from Escada, 29 kilometers southwest of Recife, to Timbaúba on the Paraíba border.

Other Industries

Apart from textiles, industry came late and slowly to the region, and was largely confined to the coast. At the turn of the century railroads had barely begun to penetrate the Northeast. In 1900 the entire region had only 1,054 kilometers of public track, compared with the then nearly 323,000 kilometers (200,000 miles) in the United States, nine times as much per capita. There were only two iron foundries in the whole of the region in 1906; like most of the early factories they were located near Recife, and like many, they were foreign owned (British in this case).[23] Nearly a quarter of the early factories in fact were owned either by foreigners or by immigrant entrepreneurs. Most were small enterprises, as were the foundries, which had no more than 50 employees each. Fully half of the industrial workers in Pernambuco were employed in textiles alone in this period, and even in 1915 the total industrial work force in the entire Northeast, including laborers hired by usinas during all parts of the year, constituted less than 2 percent of the total population (compared with 7 percent in the United States).[24]

Sugar usinas and cotton textile mills together dominated Pernambuco's industrial output at relatively constant levels throughout our period, accounting for 77 percent of the production value in 1909 and 79 percent in 1934. The import-substitution boom of 1889–94 encouraged the start-up of several small industries, but many were forced to close by 1900. Some, however, did take hold, aided by state tax exemptions; most were in food processing or livestock by-products. The state's first modern tannery opened in Olinda in 1891, to be followed by competing establishments in Recife and in the central Agreste. The first factory of canned fruits and preserves, Fábrica Peixe, opened in Pesqueira in 1897, hand-producing goiabada, the sweet, jellied paste of the guava, a popular Brazilian dessert. Within a decade the company bought sufficient modern equipment to allow it to export its products to neighboring states and, by the 1930's, to all of Brazil.[25] Among the other manufactures were cigarettes, matches, gunpowder, and oils and resins.[26]

Though working conditions in the new factories were as bad as anywhere in the industrialized world, employers prided themselves on their charity. Industrialists recruited their unskilled laborers from orphanages, training schools for the destitute, and the indigent lower classes; industrial paternalism embraced workers' cottages, infirmaries, and chapels, not to mention company stores. By the 1890's incandescent lighting allowed employers to lengthen the working day. Machine operators, mostly women, worked from 14 to 17 hours; inflation-eclipsed wages eventually became so low that sufficient numbers of workers could not be found even in Recife's worst slums, and recruiters brought in women and children from Alagoas and other distant areas, where even Recife's poor industrial wages seemed attractive.

Low per capita income in the Northeast depressed the level of investment in the region. Low expenditures for education hindered the development of a skilled work force and encouraged elite youths to migrate south. When firms prospered, they often shifted their headquarters to southern cities, like the Casas Pernambucanas, a dry goods chain. The availability of cheap labor discouraged the use of more efficient capital-intensive methods. And the hilly terrain of the Mata—60 percent of the cane in Pernambuco was grown on slopes up to 25 degrees—hindered railroad construction and drove up costs.[27]

The major obstacle to development, however, remained the region's isolation and lack of autonomy. Within the Northeast, consumer markets were small, and purchasing power remained strikingly low. Pernambuco's dominance over its satellite bloc was incomplete, restricted largely to the coast, with commercial relations rendered unfriendly by the desire of each state to raise sufficient revenue to meet its needs. Pernambuco could consume only 15 percent of its sugar production before the First World War; and nearly the identical proportion of foodstuffs, textiles, and other consumer products had to be imported in the mid-1930's as a half-century before.

Local factories continued to be generally rudimentary and unsafe, and workers received no compensation for on-the-job injuries until the 1930's. Most industries remained small in scale and output. Only 95, or 27 percent, of the 347 establishments (excluding cotton factories and usinas)

surveyed in the 1920 census yielded more than 100 contos annually.[28]
Processed foods and textiles still made up the bulk of industrial output,
suggesting how closely intertwined agriculture and industry in the state
remained.

Commerce, Banking, and Investment

Industrialization on the scale just discussed could clearly not restore
the state to economic health. Mounting population pressure and the
growing disparity between the Center-South and the rest of Brazil
exacerbated the Northeast's dependency status. The northeastern states
sent raw materials and semi-finished goods to other regions in return for
more specialized manufactures, processed foodstuffs, and even, owing
to competitive advantage, some of the items produced locally, including
cotton fibers, beans, rice—and sugar. By the late 1920's the aggregate
value of Pernambuco's imports was four times the value of its exports.
And its chief suppliers were the other states of Brazil: domestic purchases
outweighed foreign purchases by a ratio of almost two to one in 1937. In
that year cotton cloth and jerked beef were the leading domestic imports,
and coal and wheat flour the leading foreign ones.[29]

Unproductive agricultural methods forced the state to import so much
food, in fact, that the total cost of the raw and processed foodstuffs it
received from other Brazilian states in 1933—85,864 contos—was within
1 percent of its total expenditures for the fiscal year 1934.[30] Outsiders
attributed the inefficient agricultural system of the Northeast to local in-
competence. The British consul wrote in 1889:

There is very little worthy of remark . . . on this subject. Beyond the cultivation
of sugar and cotton very little attention is given to any other product; and as to the
animal and vegetable production of this province they are in a very low condition.
Rice, Indian corn, potatoes, onions, and nearly every kind of vegetable will grow
luxuriantly; but such is the indolence and indifference to an improved mode of
existence that there is very little hope of any progress in this direction.[31]

Evidence of indifference and indolence notwithstanding, other factors
contributed to agricultural difficulties. It was unquestionably the failure
of planters in the Mata to diversify and the pattern of land tenure imposed by the usinas that necessitated the importing of foodstuffs that
might otherwise have been grown or produced locally. But the seeds for
the virtual institutionalization of this system were sown in the nineteenth
century. Before 1889 the single most persistent impediment to agricul-

tural development, faced by large and small landowners alike, was the nagging lack of agricultural credit and the refusal of banks to issue rural mortgages. Unable to plant without liquid capital, growers were forced to rely on a small but wealthy group of moneylenders, the *correspondentes*. These men, who themselves paid dearly for loans from Recife banks (at monthly interest rates of up to 1 percent after the 1850's), not only increased the rate sixfold for their clients, but charged commissions as selling agents in the bargain.[32] Even when the national legislature liberalized mortgage regulations in 1890 in order to stimulate the capital market, most northeastern planters preferred not to take advantage of the new opportunities, since all or parts of their properties were acquired through illegal or otherwise undocumentable methods.[33]

An 1860 Imperial law imposing centralized control over banks and limited liability companies also severely limited opportunities for capital expansion in the Northeast at the very time when the region's lack of modernized facilities for agriculture and shipping had become most evident. The new system, which discriminated against outlying regions, was subsequently modified by laws in 1882 and 1890. But though the newly forming usina consortiums, which were limited liability enterprises, benefited from the relaxed restrictions, the senhores de engenho and other planters continued to be hampered by a lack of credit.[34]

In 1886 the region's first mortgage bank was founded by a group of Recife merchants over the strident opposition of the correspondentes, but it was only modestly capitalized (500 contos at its opening). Only in 1889, when the Imperial government reluctantly granted the bank 3,000 contos for agricultural loans, was it able to help usina interests get under way. Meanwhile, the other banks in Recife, following the lead of the two English firms that were dominant in banking circles at the time, still refused to make loans for agricultural or usina use. Speaking for the English banks, the British consul attributed this policy to their director's reluctance to invest in "industrial native enterprises."[35] And indeed, in hindsight, their reluctance to underwrite the manufacture of sugar in Pernambuco does not seem ill-advised: by 1909 defaults on state loans to usinas made in the 1880's and 1890's so strained the state's financial resources that it was forced to borrow U.S. $7,000,000 from the Banque Privée Lyon-Marseille and then to float a second substantial loan (almost as large—$6,000,000) from White, Weld, and Company of New York.[36]

The fiscal difficulties of planters and industrialists were exacerbated during the wildly inflationary Encilhamento period of the early 1890's, a nationwide spate of speculation and currency issues that briefly afforded the illusion of prosperity but led to the devaluation of the milreis, thus increasing the cost of imported machinery.[37] Even more burdensome, after 1900, were the new levies imposed by states that in effect taxed domestic imports. In Pernambuco alarmed officials feared that the state's commercial growth might be irreparably damaged, with other states levying duties as high as from 80 to 100 reis per kilo of imported sugar, and 200 reis per liter of alcohol and rum.[38] Meanwhile, shippers complained of discriminatory rates—and with good cause: in 1903 a sack of corn transported from Bahia to Pará cost 4$500, when the same cargo carried from Recife to Belém, a shorter distance by nearly 800 kilometers, cost 7$700.[39] Planters continued to find it extremely difficult to obtain cash or mortgages, and the per-acre cane yield in the Mata remained the lowest in Brazil. By the early 1920's usineiros found themselves in stiff competition with factories and mills in the Center-South, where lower costs and better transportation facilities made northeastern usina sugar competitively disadvantaged even in Northeast markets.

This legacy of underdevelopment was made worse by the persistence of conflict in Pernambuco between the usina-commercial interests (Azevedo's "urban bourgeoisie") and the surviving planter class.[40] Neocolonialism also created a fair share of tension. The foreign influence in the economy was pervasive. Answerable to overseas stockholders and directorates, managers of foreign firms and utilities frequently set policies that were detrimental to the local interest. (Yet as individuals, the foreign administrators, engineers, and businessmen were usually admired by the local elite; indeed some married into the highest social circles.)

Despite a history of bad feeling between Portuguese and Brazilians, Portuguese merchants dominated retail trade throughout the Northeast until the end of the Empire. In banking they yielded to the English in the 1880's. London-based banks clearly dominated through the end of the First World War, but in the following decade five other foreign banks— German, French-Italian, Portuguese, Canadian, and American (the National City Bank of New York)—opened. In 1931 the total assets of the foreign banks in Recife slightly outweighed the total assets of the 13 domestic banks, but thereafter the trend became reversed, and by 1937 the domestic banks overshadowed the foreign ones by a two-to-one margin (see Table 2.3).

TABLE 2.3

Banks in Pernambuco, 1900–1937

	Domestic banks		Foreign banks		
Year	Active capital in contos	Number	Active capital in contos	Number	Percentage of total assets
1900	30,500	5	—	—	—
1909–12	44,112[a]	5	53,751[b]	2	55%
1927	328,119	13	314,269	7	49%
1931	424,638	9	433,651	6	51%
1937	681,939	11	333,409	6	33%

SOURCE: A. J. Barbosa Vianna, *O Recife, capital do Estado de Pernambuco* (Recife, 1900), p. 120; J. P. Wileman, *The Brazilian Year Book, 1909* (London, 1909), pp. 753–54; Reginald Lloyd et al., *Twentieth Century Impressions of Brazil* (London, 1913); *Annuario Estatistico de Pernambuco*, 1942, p. 214.
[a] 1909.
[b] 1912.

The foreign banks routinely denied loans to rural applicants (they concentrated on monetary exchange and discounting bills for goods on export), and their domestic counterparts, except for the few and mostly unsuccessful institutions chartered to offer commercial and agricultural loans, chose to follow suit. "The Banco do Recife," an official publication boasted in 1922, "administered by a Pernambucan elite, offers an example of how we have incorporated the banking traditions brought here by the branches and agencies of the English banks in our midst."[41]

Foreign firms controlled the capital's urban transport system, the Recife-based regional railroad network, the gas works, and the telephone system. Foreigners dominated such local industries as cotton and vegetable oil processing and the small mechanized fishing fleet, besides operating several usinas and the two largest textile mills in the state. Foreign brokers and shippers handled a substantial portion of Pernambuco's imports and exports, including much of the traffic in hides, cotton, machinery, dried cod and beef, cement, pharmaceuticals, sugar, alcohol, flour, and wax. Twenty-three of the 37 leading firms in 1912 were foreign or had been founded by non-Brazilians in earlier times.[42]

The Commercial Association represented the entire business community of Recife. Established in 1839 primarily by Portuguese and English merchants, the association reached the height of its local influence in the closing years of the nineteenth century as a vehicle for the propagation of English classical economic liberalism, low export duties, and local commercial-industrial development. Not a part of the planter-based political oligarchy that dominated the state, it chafed under what its members considered Pernambuco's excessive taxes and expenditures, and in 1911 it broke openly with the state political machine.

Foreigners were still prominent in the association's leadership as late as 1908–9, when an Englishman was elected to the presidency, though by this time the association had become largely Brazilian in membership.[43] It clashed sharply with a succession of grower interest groups created after the 1870's, and then with the political lobby they built in 1903 in response to worsening conditions, the União dos Sindicatos Agrícolas. Usineiros remained to some degree aloof from the association; though they worked closely with exporters and other businessmen, they occasionally allied with planter groups on issues related to government subsidies for sugar production. More than anything else, the association objected to the disproportionate share of the state tax burden borne by the business community; the land tax in Pernambuco, as the businessmen pointed out, yielded the lowest proportion of state revenue in the country.[44] After 1905, however, when the state administration moved closer to the planter position, the association found itself isolated from political influence and never again regained a major role.

Adding no little to the tension between the planters and the business interests was the Republican political machine's close control over the instruments of power. Political representation did not extend to true geographical constituencies; rather, officeholders served their districts only nominally, often not even residing in them. This weighted both the state legislature and the federal congressional delegation heavily in favor of the incumbent Republican Party's alliance between urban politicians and sugar-zone clients.* It excluded, for the most part, commercial groups (the Commercial Association did not place a single member on the Republican Party Executive Committee during the entire oligarchic period between 1896 and 1911), agricultural producers from the Agreste and the Sertão, and the mass of the population, though opposition organizers tried to recruit neglected members of the urban salaried class as well as those members of the laboring poor who held the vote.

The European war further clouded the situation for the Northeast, ushering in the beginning of the end of the phase of foreign investment, which had lasted since the previous century and which had contributed significantly to what measure of modernization had been achieved. To be sure, the war produced good effects nationally. It boosted industrial out-

---

* Significantly, four of the five governors who were elected in the state between 1908 and 1937 were usineiros or closely linked through family ties to usina ownership.

put by curtailing manufactured imports; it spurred Congress to enact laws guaranteeing workmen's compensation; and it speeded the birth of a climate of opinion that led to more direct federal intervention in the agricultural economy, namely coffee valorization in the South.[45] Total sugar exports rose, though usinas in Rio de Janeiro, São Paulo, and Minas benefited most, capitalizing on their proximity to shipping and markets.

But in the Northeast the war, far from bringing economic benefits, instead produced severe dislocations. The most serious of these were in transportation and notably involving the Great Western Railroad, which was unable to import parts to replace its overtaxed rolling stock. Firewood replaced coal as fuel in all trains but those carrying cotton and passengers, thus cutting operating efficiency and adding to the work of train crews. The new uncertainties of shipping caused some banks and warehouses to close, though sugar prices rose; the regional telegraph system, operated for the most part by the Great Western, was threatened with paralysis; and hundreds of workers were dismissed from factories that found themselves unable to secure replacement parts for broken machinery. Usineiros complained bitterly about the shipping crisis caused by the use of vessels normally assigned to coastal shipping for international traffic. As the end of the war neared, employers found themselves forced to pay higher wages, cutting into profits (according to their claims) as the prices of food and commodities soared.[46]

Though rural wages dropped to prewar levels in the Zona de Mata in the early 1920's, new times had clearly arrived. Labor militancy established itself, albeit somewhat shakily, as a force to be reckoned with. Foreign investment began to taper off. The German business community had melted away during the first years of the war (several establishments in Recife, including the Casa Allemã, a leading fashion and fabric emporium, were looted and burned by rampaging crowds); the English and other Europeans slowly began to liquidate their holdings, many of those able to remain in Brazil choosing to consolidate their capital and shift their emphasis to other regions, mostly to the South. Lack of immigration to the Northeast and the region's unpromising long-range prospects added to the growing lack of enthusiasm for investment.

Transportation

The fate of the Great Western Railroad, the largest foreign-owned enterprise in the region, is a case in point. Founded in 1881, the company had set up most of the existing lines in the Northeast, and by 1910 it had become a virtual monopoly, reaching across the Agreste and linking the satellite bloc with Recife, standardizing in the process the five different track gauges previously used in the region.* A few independent usina lines continued to serve the Mata, and an urban-suburban system, the Pernambuco Tramways, operated in Recife, but for all practical purposes the Great Western had a lock on the region's commercial transport. The impact of the expansion of the Great Western system was tremendous. The railroad transformed the town of Palmares, a modest dependency of Engenho Trombetas, into the most important urban center in the southern Mata, causing in turn the deterioration of nearby Agua Preta.

In 1911 the Great Western system controlled 12 formerly independent railroads in the Northeast, four of which were in Pernambuco and had (by World War I) 1,200 kilometers of track. Two of these turned especially handsome profits: the Recife–São Francisco line (£59,952) and the Recife–Limoeiro/Timbaúba line (£57,130). But equipment shortages and lack of capital brought the railroad to the point of bankruptcy by 1919, at a time when higher agricultural prices raised demands for better and more extensive railroad service. Increasingly, northeasterners began to view foreign-owned utilities as symbols of exploitation. Not surprisingly, the first serious labor troubles in the region in the early years of the century erupted between employees of the state-run Pernambuco Tramways and those of the Great Western Railroad. Repeated requests from company officials for the state government to honor its contracted guarantees of capital and to permit rate increases met with mounting political opposition.

For its part, the Great Western resisted demands for wage increases and shorter hours, firing workers indiscriminately and especially as retaliation for strike activity. It relied heavily on lobbyists in Recife and Rio de Janeiro to win behind-the-scenes concessions. To its stockholders the railroad management blandly reported the use of "discipline" to break strikes, and proudly noted, on one occasion, that the workers themselves "finally recognized that the Company could not possibly increase [its] expenses . . . and returned to work."[47] The Great Western managers complained that the government-regulated rates were "absurdly low," and charged that political jealousies and red tape prevented the construction of new lines over the most suitable terrain, causing the railroad great

* All track incorporated into the Great Western system was converted to one meter, the narrowest of the track widths.

losses in revenue. They also complained bitterly about the disastrous effects of falling exchange rates, especially in the late 1890's; when the line
planned large-scale expansion.*

The standoffish manners of the English officials and their willingness to
cooperate with police, who were allowed to infiltrate employee syndicates
to circumvent protest, aroused the ire of the press, which for its own
reasons often preferred to overlook similar practices employed by Brazilian firms. Recife's *O Pernambuco* constantly referred to the railroad
company manager as the "British dictator of the Great Western." On a
more sweeping scale, *O Leão do Norte* attacked the railroad's English
employees in toto as pugnacious and drunken, mere playboys who had
gathered in Pernambuco to accumulate sacks of sterling to spend back in
"foggy and corrupt Albion."[48] The attacks revealed years of pent-up bitterness:

It happens that the English employees of the Great Western, paid regularly in
gold, . . . come, dressed as nabobs, for a few minutes to their offices, whenever
they are tired of emptying whiskey bottles and cocktail shakers in the bars they
call their homes during working hours; . . . the Brazilian employees . . . receive
at the end of the month an absurdly tiny wage, barely sufficient to bring their
families a bit of moldy farinha and a dish of roach-infested beans, accompanied, on
rare occasions, by minuscule and foul-smelling portions of dried beef.[49]

In any case, the Great Western, one of the most prosperous enterprises
in the Northeast until the First World War, found itself forced to re-
negotiate its contract with the national government in 1920. By the
agreement worked out, the company was to remit 4.5 percent of its annual gross revenue to the government in exchange for subsidies for new
construction and the right to impose rates that would guarantee a 6 percent return on its investment. Once the contract was ratified, the company immediately raised its rates 70 percent, causing a furor among sugar
producers and general protests throughout the region. But a year later the
Great Western found itself with a debt of £250,000 and raised its rates
again. At the company's annual meeting in London the director reported
acidly that if the inhabitants of the North of Brazil could not afford the

---

*The English looked at Brazil as a whole with derision. The author of the Embassy's
annual report in 1909 declared that in his opinion, "with reference to the administration, the
confusion, and the ineptitude of the public offices is beyond belief, far worse than in any
South American country I have known, or in Persia" (Great Britain, Foreign Office, file
371/201, 1909 report, p. 55; see also *The Times* [London], June 5, 1901, p. 5, and June 22,
1901, p. 5).

luxury of the Great Western Railroad, they certainly should not enjoy it at the expense of English shareholders.[50] This tug-of-war persisted through the late 1920's and beyond. Hostility continued to rise. In 1929 the company challenged Brazil to appropriate its holdings at a cost of £4,000,000; that the government could accomplish this feat was unlikely, said the director, but the prospect opened "to local patriots in Pernambuco visions of self-sufficient plenty."[51] As this suggests, foreign-owned utilities loomed larger and larger as targets of rising nationalistic fervor, finding themselves caught in the crossfire between groups of the far Right and far Left.[52]

Foreign shipping firms, in fact, increased in number over the years of the federation—reflecting, if not increasing European demand for northeastern products, then the entry of smaller European nations into the trans-Atlantic trade. In 1930, 19 lines of ten nationalities offered regular cargo service to the port of Recife. Sugar was exported to six European and four South American countries (England represented over 80 percent of the market), though by this time foreign exports constituted only 10 percent of all sugar sales. The rest was shipped to ports in the Center-South. Unfortunately for the northeastern producers, the shipping rates to what was now their major market were distressingly high, and this despite the fact that nearly all domestic lines were government-subsidized and therefore could conceivably have lowered their tariffs. In 1927 coastal navigation companies charged 31$000 per cubic meter of cargo between Rio de Janeiro and Recife, more than the price of a sack of refined sugar, and the equivalent of the daily wages paid to 14 usina workers in the Mata.[53]

Transportation deficiencies, then, remained a major stumbling block to growth. The consolidation of control by the Great Western left transportation policy for the most part in the hands of foreign managers and stockholders, with the company itself badly crippled by World War I and almost continually locked into a wasteful conflict with government officials over alleged breaches of contract, as well as the right to raise rates beyond levels deemed tolerable by local standards. Private rolling stock and tracks accommodated individual usinas, but on the whole the fragmentation of railroad services into public and private categories served only to inhibit whatever leverage agricultural shippers might have gathered by acting in unison.

Other means of commercial transport were negligible or nonexistent.

The loss of the gateway to the São Francisco as punishment for regionalist insurrection during the pre-Independence period left the state with virtually no navigable waterways, depriving Recife of easy contact with the state's 322-kilometer-long common border with Bahia, the key to control of the vast backlands stretching south to Minas Gerais. Coastal shipping to other northeastern ports accounted for only a small portion of import-export volume (less than one-third in the 1880's and under one-tenth by 1910).[54] When roads were built, they tended to compete with the faltering railroads and to sap the lifeblood of the Agreste towns that were formerly hubs of intrazonal commerce. In 1937 animal-drawn carts and wagons still outnumbered motor trucks by nearly four to one; Pernambuco's 1,489 trucks represented only 2.7 percent of the national total. Of the state's 5,378 kilometers of roads in that year, 68 percent, or 3,653 kilometers, were of unimproved dirt. Pernambuco boasted only 27 kilometers of concrete, asphalt, or macadamized road surfaces, almost all of which lay within the Recife city limits.[55]

The Port of Recife

The mounting insufficiency of the port facilities of Recife compounded in no small measure the economic bottleneck posed by the lack of a modern, integrated, internal transportation network serving the region. By the 1870's it had become apparent that Recife's harbor was too shallow to manage the 300–400 ships that plied the Atlantic and the coast. Though the symmetrical, reef-protected harbor was of adequate length, its seven-meter high-tide depth forced large ships to anchor in mid-harbor, requiring the use of floating docks and ferries for the on-loading and off-loading of freight and passengers. Decades passed before a satisfactory blueprint for dredging and port expansion was drawn up and approved, and by then Recife had slipped from second to third among Brazilian ports in total shipping volume. The project was opened to public bids in January 1889, but what with several transfers of title, corporate failures, and unsuccessful attempts to win new contracts, construction was delayed for more than a decade.

A major contract for the improvement of the port was finally let in 1908 by the national government. This was transferred in the following year to a French company, the Société de Construction du Port de Pernambouc. Simultaneously, the state undertook a major urban reconstruction of the downtown and dock districts of Recife to give better access to the port, widening boulevards and leveling mocambos and other structures that had previously hindered traffic. But apart from lengthening the docks to nearly 1,200 meters, the French company managed to make only small improvements in the port facilities before it shut down, forced into bankruptcy by the First World War. Meanwhile, like the Great Western Railroad Company, the Société thoroughly angered Pernambucanos by paying its French employees more than double what it paid Brazilian workers for equivalent tasks.[56]

Construction at the port remained at a standstill until 1920, when the State of Pernambuco, finally heeding the strident pleas of shippers and commercial groups, took over the defaulted Société contract and provided direct subsidies for the construction of warehouses and modern derricks, subcontracting projects to private firms. But facilities continued to be inadequate. Most of the docks remained unpaved, night loading was hindered by dim lighting, and there were not even enough warehouses to store perishables and explosives.

A patronage plum, the administration of the port had wallowed in inefficiency and corruption since 1889 and before. Officials frequently destroyed records, especially at the conclusion of their terms.[57] State control of the port after 1920 brought little improvement, and in 1932 management passed wholly to the Union amid fears that federal authorities would channel aid away from Recife to rival northeastern ports.[58]

Economic Modernization and the Hinterland

Rather than replacing standing institutions, most of the new techniques and forms of economic organization introduced in this period came to coexist side by side with the old. Thus just as the donkey cart survived the motor truck, the bangüe survived the usina, keeping alive a burdensome economic class and drawing off capital from other needy agricultural sectors. Though the modernization of the sugar industry had a disastrous social impact, preserving and even worsening the hopeless lot of the rural laborer and strengthening the trend to land concentration and monoculture, it nonetheless allowed producers to keep pace, for the time being, with outside competition. Yet the failure of usineiros to extend technological innovation beyond cane processing to cane production contributed to the survival of outmoded agricultural methods.

Some economic activities and occupational groups were in fact displaced by modernization, just as growing industrialization and the expanding complexities of public administration led to social differentiation and specialization in the urban centers. For example, the twentieth-century pattern of agro-industrial sugar production and the advent of the railroads depleted the ranks of the *almocreves*, or muleteers, who, as many as 20,000 strong in the late 1870's, carried sugar and goods between Mata plantations and the capital. Skilled and semiskilled millworkers were similarly displaced, especially as engenhos began to extinguish their fires.[59]

Even so, the structure of the economy remained largely unchanged, even into the 1930's. The relative share of each of the three principal sectors (agriculture and mining; industry and construction; services) shifted only slightly between 1920 and 1940; according to the censuses, the primary sector fell from 82 percent to 75 percent, while services rose from 10 percent to 16 percent.[60] Such statistics, of course, present an incomplete view as far as the society at large is concerned; tens of thousands were unemployed and were therefore excluded from the official calculations of sectoral economic activity.

Neglect of the interior took various forms. The railroad did not penetrate the western Agreste until the 1930's, and even in 1933 the Great Western's now 1,695-kilometer-long network reached only halfway across the state. The company's insolvency and the low official priority given to the hinterland led to the railroad's cancellation of its commitment in 1920 to extend its track to Flores. Moreover, as late as the 1970's, the railroad still stopped 200 kilometers short of Pernambuco's western border with Piauí and Ceará, with serious consequences for the economies of the satellite bloc states, dependent as they were on transportation links to Recife. Banking facilities, as might be expected, continued to be clustered on the coast, though the Bank of Brazil maintained agencies throughout the state after 1920. Still, more than 90 percent of its loans were negotiated at the Recife office. Agricultural credit banks were established in eight Mata and Agreste cities in the mid-1920's, but their combined active balances represented barely 1 percent of the total bank balances in the state.[61]

On the whole, modernization tended to increase social distance. Improvements—electricity, street lighting, water supply—came to the capital and the larger towns long before they came to the rural areas. On the eve of the Second World War much of the state was still without railroad service. Telephones, the telegraph, and improved coastal shipping brought Recife in closer touch with outside places, but the backlands remained isolated.[62]

Federally sponsored public works projects in the rural areas followed no sustained pattern (indeed, they dwindled to virtually nothing between 1922 and 1934), and the social and labor legislation of the 1930's applied only to industrialized cities. Still, as early as 1900 a gradual influx of shopkeepers, innkeepers, pharmacists, schoolteachers, and immigrant peddlers from Recife and Natal had begun to stimulate activity as commerce imperceptibly increased. A steady stream of migrants passed through the backlands, though most eventually wandered on, taking the São Francisco River route to São Paulo and other points south.

A letter written in 1925 from a young agent of the Bank of Brazil newly transferred to Olha d'Agua dos Bredos (later renamed Rio Branco, then Arcoverde) typifies the reaction of outsiders to the changing urban world of the backlands:

[Olha d'Agua] is a village entirely given to matters of the stomach. No one mentions books; they talk of [the bandit] Lampião, of the lack of small change, of the dust, of the price of cotton, of Epitácio's latest speech. . . . The hotels, the streets . . . are continually filled with cattle traders and sellers of goods of every description. On market day, the village looks like a Levantine city. But this impression lasts only at a distance; at close range, the flavor of the backlands asserts itself, the leather hats, the *jagunços* [ruffians], the tight-jacketed cowboys, . . . the sticky yellow sugar, . . . the cheese in the sun.[63]

Growing backlands commercial activity after the First World War spurred banditry and increased the number of outlaw bands that roamed the Sertão seemingly at will. Though often portrayed as bandits with social consciences and even as folk heroes, these outlaw gangs rarely favored the poor over the rich in their plunderings. Rather, they freely put themselves at the service of the highest bidder; frequently they hired themselves as mercenaries to rural bosses (*coronéis*) or to local, state, and even federal agencies. The presence of several thousand bandits in the region between Maranhão and Bahia in the late 1920's prompted coastal authorities to act in concert against the threat, which meant in part treading on the traditional autonomy of backlands clans and political bosses.

The economic maladies that afflicted Pernambuco—the inadequate transportation system, the unprofitability of its major export crops, the growing inability to compete with southern producers—plagued the other states of the Northeast as well, not only Pernambuco's own satellite bloc, but the entire region, from Bahia to Maranhão. The decline of the sugar industry affected the engenhos of Alagoas and Sergipe as much as it did those of Pernambuco. The cotton planters throughout the Agreste, from central Pernambuco through Paraíba and Rio Grande do Norte into Ceará, shared a common fate. The Sertão was as remote and underdeveloped in one state as in another. The entire Northeast, in short, was deeply influenced by what the economist Nathaniel H. Leff has called the shift in Brazil's comparative advantage away from sugar and cotton to coffee.[64]

CHAPTER THREE

Society and Culture

BY THE END of the 1880's the transformation of the sugar economy, the continued urban growth of Recife, and the other modernizing currents that pervaded the Northeast challenged the traditionally dominant rural culture. At the end of the Empire the stamp of regional culture was still rural, rooted in the sugar culture of the Zona da Mata and in centuries of colonial and neo-colonial social relations. But the social complexion of the regional environment had begun to change. By now the cumulative effect of declining sugar fortunes had reduced the standard of living of the typical planter to a level well below that of his landowning counterpart in the prosperous coffee regions of the South.[1] The rural landscape had begun to change as well. The railroad drew the region toward the port and stimulated the growth of rural towns in its path; and on the engenhos the bulk of field labor was now performed by sharecroppers. Yet the changes were slow to take hold; even in 1920 unskilled fieldhands still outnumbered usina workers by a margin of 125 to one. Nevertheless, by then the usineiro had undermined the formerly unassailable social hegemony of the senhor de engenho.

Deteriorating economic conditions forced scores of sugar planters to sell their properties either to usinas or to city-based speculators. Some promptly moved to Recife, where they sought public employment; others migrated south, or to the Amazon. A general malaise afflicted the planters who refused to move or who were unable to sell. Many fell into poverty and material discomfort, forced to rely on wealthier relatives for their

support. Some became alcoholics, surrounding themselves, as José Maria
Bello describes, with their mulatinhas and their bastard children, having
acquired the dubious status of the "new poor whites" of the Mata.[2] Souza
Barros recalls a popular ballad of the 1920's:[3]

Pedro Velho, cadê o teu engenho?	Old Pedro, where is your engenho?
A usina passou no papo!	The usina swallowed it up!
E onde vais fundar safra este ano?	And where will you sow your seeds this year?
Na barriga da mulher! Na barriga da mulher!	In the wife's belly! In the wife's belly!

Life in the Interior

Traditionally, the engenhos had dominated rural life in all of its aspects. Around them grew towns; within them occurred the constant process of miscegenation.[4] Above all, the engenhos were, as the abolitionist
Joaquim Nabuco wrote, centers of agricultural exploitation, operating
solely for the well-being of the rural sugar elite.[5] Depressed by the persistence of bad times and low prices for their exports, even the planters
themselves adopted a pejorative and pessimistic attitude toward the
land, sending their sons to be educated in the law rather than to the
new schools of agronomy. Beneath this behavior lay a deeper reason for
not seeking sweeping change: any effort that might alter rural society
threatened the psychological equilibrium of the Mata itself, a world in
which affluent and destitute had lived side by side for generations.

The rural elite. Until the end of the nineteenth century the Imperial
nobility constituted the top echelon within the plantocracy. Most of Pernambuco's titled peers lived at their rural estates, at least nominally.[6] A
few of the wealthier planters, aided by government subsidies and corporate capital, constructed central factories and later usinas on their property. These included two usinas owned by the Baron of Suassuna, who, in
addition to being an extremely influential planter and sugar producer, was
a director of the Bank of Recife and a former member of the provincial
and Imperial legislatures.

Few planters could withstand the impact of sugar industrialization in
their midst, though some attempted to ignore the usinas and the other
factories that appeared as the city-based corporations and administrators
took over the estates of their neighbors. By 1920 what may be called the

sugar elite had shrunk to no more than 500 families, with only the usineiros and a few large planters in any state of prosperity.[7]

For northeastern society, the life of the rural planter represented the pinnacle of history, tradition, and order. Planter patriarchs saw themselves as enlightened classical liberals, thriving within a pragmatic political system that, under the Empire if not after, tended to absorb nonconformist thinkers and turn them into conservatives. The ability to accommodate themselves to change—as long as it did not threaten the traditional distribution of power—eased the rural elite into the twentieth century without upheaval. At the same time, the plantocracy vehemently opposed all threats to stability, especially urban politicians with populist tendencies. Félix Cavalcanti, scion of one of the leading families in the entire Northeast, scornfully derided fellow planter and opposition leader José Mariano Carneiro da Cunha as "deliriously liberal, . . . *compadre* and friend of annoying mulattos and celebrated thugs, . . . passing among the *pardos* for votes and stooping to take black urchins in his arms."[8]

Unusually outspoken, Félix Cavalcanti considered himself a watchdog protecting society against change.[9] A prestigious senhor de engenho who lived in Recife, he attended mass twice weekly, affected European elegance, and presided over his household in an authoritarian manner. His diary relates that as a youth he frequented Recife's docks to watch the ships and to pick up mulattas. Gilberto Freyre, writing somewhat later, reminds his readers that the sons of the usineiros preserved the habits of the older planters, supporting handsomely the prostitutes who crowded the coastal cities.[10]

Félix did change with the times in spite of himself. He permitted his children to choose their own marriage partners; he sent his sons to the university and his daughters to become teachers. For all this, like many of his peers, he died an unreconstructed monarchist, aware of the uselessness of his intransigence but still railing at the Republic as a "ridiculous comedy."[11]

The rural elite shared a common sense of place and hierarchy. Life tended to reflect stereotypic roles: the morose and domineering father, the submissive mother, the terrified son. Planter families imitated what they believed to be European modes of behavior; they included large quantities of fats and sugars in their diets, avoiding native vegetables and fruits. Senhores de engenho interested in cultural affairs generally considered themselves Francophiles, mistrusting the Germans, supporting the Boers against the English in 1898, and often revering the United States as the only "great Republic."[12]

As time passed, the reality of declining rural fortunes permeated the planter class. José Maria Bello, whose memoirs recall equally the cruelty and the exuberance of life in the Zona da Mata in the late nineteenth century, remembers that virtually every great family in the region suffered privations as sugar production became mechanized and centralized.[13] Yet even in the 1930's politicians still rose to defend "Pernambuco's noble class of senhores de engenho" against those who would suggest that this group constituted an obstacle to rural progress.[14] The bucolic memory of the Zona da Mata fixed itself inexorably on the regional memory.

The rural poor. At the mercy of the stratified and all-powerful social order, the northeastern poor coexisted with the rural elite, unwitting accessories to the quiet evolution of regional culture. Caboclos and blacks traditionally formed the Northeast's lower classes, though in the Agreste and Sertão the rural poor included whites as well.* On the whole Pernambuco's rural population "lightened" as one traveled westward from the coast.[15]

The installation of the Republic did little to alleviate the endemic illiteracy among the rural poor. From 1872 to 1940 the state's official rate of literacy rose only 5 percentage points, from 17 to 22 percent. As late as 1940, the rate of literacy fell under 10 percent in some rural municípios, with no clear patterns discernible on the basis of zone, predominant economic activity, or distance from the capital.[16]

Conditions rooted in local life tranformed the rural poor into social pariahs: excess population, passivity brought on by malnutrition, repressive forms of social control, and religious fatalism. A northeastern proverb declares: "The poor man's table is bare, but his bed is fertile."[17] Though the Northeast as a whole lost substantial population to other regions, the population of the Mata, itself the major source of migrants to the state capital, grew from 475,000 in 1890 to nearly 900,000 in 1920. Those who

*The census definition of "white" is a highly subjective one in Brazil. There is no ostensible reason for the extreme variation in racial percentages in adjacent municípios in Pernambuco, as, for example, Moxotó and Aguas Belas, 92 percent and 25 percent "white," respectively, in 1940. One suspects differing perceptions on the part of the census takers or município officials responsible for recording census findings.

did move to Recife found hardship and the threat of violence. Police periodically rounded up the scores of beggars who crowded the city's streets and bridges and expelled them or, at least according to local whispers, threw them in sacks into the swampy marshes of the Capiberibe and Beberibe rivers. Even so, Recife's demographic role as the urban nucleus of Pernambuco's satellite bloc continued to grow, with the proportion of cityward migrants from that region increasing from about 13–14 percent in the early nineteenth century to 39 percent in the period between 1890 and 1910.[18]

In the Mata superstition and necessity moved the caboclos to sell, not consume, what foodstuffs they could gather or grow. Kept at bay by the bodyguards of the senhores de engenhos, considered potential criminals by the ruling elite, threatened with military impressment, the rural poor only rarely exploded in mass violence. Instead, they reserved their frustrations for the weekend, when workers could purchase their raw cachaça rum—and thereby reinforce the stereotype of the rural caboclo as drunkard.

The intellectuals of the region lumped lower-class groups together, sometimes eulogizing the poor for their strength, sometimes castigating them for their helplessness and inertia.[19] But gradations did exist within the rural lower classes, based on jobs and circumstances and even geography, leaving for all but the very lowest on the socioeconomic ladder the prospect of sinking even further into the abyss of poverty. As Torcuato DiTella has noted for Mexico, "There were various sorts of masses . . . according to the stresses they were undergoing."[20] Upward mobility was thus possible—if not out of the lower class, at least to a higher occupational rung on the lower-class ladder. This possibility, heightened by the penetration of capitalistic institutions through the Mata and into the Sertão, served to divide the rural mass and gave employers and landowners the upper hand in dispensing status and wages within a matrix of competition and fear.

Rural towns supported an urban-looking middle sector of businessmen, administrators, and small entrepreneurs, as well as artisans, commercial employees, and what DiTella terms the "shifting proletariat"— prostitutes, street vendors, domestic servants, and odd jobbers, perhaps half or more of the town populations. In the Sertão occupational differentiation separated unskilled rural laborers from the vaqueiros, independent cowboys with extensive responsibility and commensurate status. Through the region wandered itinerant peddlers, traders, even school-teachers. In the Mata higher standing was given to refinery workers like boilermen, furnacemen, and turbine workers, as well as to sugar masters on the old engenhos, distillery workers, and skilled craftsmen.

But the majority of workers were at the bottom of the barrel. The rural birthrate exceeded the urban rate five to three, whereas the death rate stood about the same. Nearly half the rural population suffered from malaria, schistosomiasis, or Chagas' disease; virtually all were afflicted by lesser (but equally debilitating) parasitic ailments, and many showed the effects of rickets as well. A 1937 survey found that 63 percent of all girls were married or widowed by fifteen years of age, and that 87 percent of the rural workers interviewed wore no protection on their feet in the fields.[21] Travelers to the backlands frequently became transfixed by the impact of the environment on human life:

When the railroad ends [one wrote in 1937] the world seems to end with it. . . . The land lies ashen, the sky hangs sickly, a colorless blue. . . . The vegetation retains an artificial, yellowish pallor. The sun matures the girls early; . . . at eleven years they develop strong appetites, vigorous legs, good teeth, and good bone structure to facilitate frequent and crippling bouts with childbirth . . . but by their twenties they are pitifully shriveled. . . . The men, bronzed, leather-clad caboclos, spit streams of tobacco juice onto the blackened earth. They wander in circles, seeking work. A ferocious and dehumanized individualism is seared into them by the sun.[22]

Save for occasional outbreaks of labor violence (in the interior mostly directed at the Great Western Railroad) and the arson and cane burning of the 1930's in the Zona da Mata, the only known example of mass rural mobilization in the Northeast was the Quebra-Qilos revolt of 1873–74. This movement, a reaction to the Imperial government's decision to convert to a decimal system of weights and measures for tax collection purposes, spread panic through the rural markets of Paraíba, Pernambuco, Rio Grande do Norte, and Alagoas, and led to looting, destruction of the new scales, and attacks on município record offices, tax collection agencies, and legislative chambers. Repression was swift. Some commentators expressed sympathy with the frightened rebels, attributing their rage to rural economic problems and government neglect. But in the end the episode was forgotten, written off as "sedition" and relegated to the list of historical curiosities, along with such other movements as the Canudos uprising in the backlands of Bahia.*

The rural towns. As we saw in Chapter 2, rural areas were slow to be penetrated by the new coastal institutions. The first bank in the Sertão opened in 1921, in Crato, Ceará. By the early 1920's the Bank of Brazil had installed agents in more than three dozen Pernambucan municípios, including full-service branches in two interior cities, Garanhuns and Pesqueira. Pharmacies, often run by proprietors without the least formal training, were set up throughout the region. A few physicians established themselves in major towns; some were competent, but some were more like the notorious Dr. Félix, whose previous experience consisted of caring for Pernambuco Tramways mules in Recife. Four rural municípios were served by mechanized water supply systems by 1920; other places depended on wells, even towns where the water was known to be bad.[23]

The history of Canhotinho to 1922 illustrates the gradual change that affected rural towns. Situated in the southern Agreste about 160 kilometers from Recife, the town held its first trade fair in 1856. The railroad arrived in 1885; a year later a local cotton planter imported the first steam-driven motor. The town's first physician, a Protestant missionary from the United States, arrived in 1897 and met considerable hostility. Politically, violence between warring factions bathed the entire município in assassinations and led to state intervention in 1903, the year in which Canhotinho was elevated to the status of city. In that year, it paved its two streets. Bloody factional strife erupted again in 1911 (mirroring the state-level contest for political control) and persisted until 1917.

The 1920 census enumerated 54,251 inhabitants in the município. Modestly prosperous because of its location on the Recife-Garanhuns railroad line, Canhotinho strove to emulate the state capital in cultural style. In 1922 the município council organized a two-day public celebration to commemorate Brazil's centenary of independence. The high point came when the town's schoolchildren donned foreign costumes and paraded across a wooden stage in the town square in a "Procession of Nations." There, on the rural Pernambuco-Alagoas border, an enthralled crowd lis-

---

*The history of the Quebra-Qilos remains to be written. (See Flávio Guerra, *Lucena*, pp. 150–54; Henrique Augusto Milet, *Os Quebra-Kilos*; José Antônio Gonsalves de Mello Neto, "Por um história," pp. 56–57; and "Vocabulário Pernambucano," p. 618.) The Canudos uprising in the Bahian backlands in the late 1890's, a clash between well-armed government troops and the ragged followers of the religious mystic Antônio Conselheiro, was poignantly described by Euclides da Cunha in his 1902 classic *Rebellion in the Backlands*.

tened as children recited verses praising Pizarro's conquest of Peru, the "robust but immature" United States, and the greatness of Brazil, and deplored the atrocities being committed against innocent Africans in the Belgian Congo. It is worth noting that rich and poor alike attended the ceremony, demonstrating that openness of Brazilian social relations outsiders so frequently admire; the rigid, protective hierarchy of status offered security and comfort in a world unmarked by overt threats to the social order.[24]

The affluent residents of Canhotinho and other towns of the Northeast imitated their counterparts on the coast in a variety of ways. Prosperous landowners constructed comfortable wooden houses, furnished with utilitarian cabinets, heavy leather chairs, leather-covered beds, and walls adorned with portraits of departed loved ones. Families bought their linen, china, and furniture in Recife. Gentlemen wore National Guard uniforms or English coats; high collars, imported leather boots, and silver-tipped canes were great favorites. Women wore jewelry and large gold crucifixes. Some older rural customs survived, however: until about 1900 wedding festivities included the display of the required proof of the bride's virginity.[25]

The secular influences of modernization weakened Catholic observances among the affluent in the interior, though formally expressed piety remained a desired virtue. To combat secularization and such fanatic populist religious movements as those led by Antônio Conselheiro at Canudos and the discredited Padre Cícero at Joaseiro, the Church launched on a vigorous campaign in the early twentieth century to restore orthodoxy throughout the rural Northeast. The campaign succeeded in some ways. In 1925 Church statistics claimed a rate of 45.8 baptisms and 7.2 marriages per 1,000 inhabitants in the backlands diocese of Garanhuns-Pesqueira, a rate that exceeded even the achievements of the archdiocese of Olinda and Recife, where parishes vied with one another for leadership in scales of religiosity. Even if the Garanhuns-Pesqueira figures merely represent the victory of ecclesiastical zeal over accurate counting, it is evident that the Church was expanding its presence in the rural Northeast, importing new influences not only from Recife but from Rome.[26]

But the understaffed and mostly foreign-born rural Catholic clergy watched helplessly as traditional Catholic practices became adapted to more familiar, local conditions. Meanwhile, rural inhabitants quickly embraced such modern and secular practices as state and national patriotic holidays, public dances and festivals, and rowdy political campaigning.[27] Pre-Lenten Carnival clubs existed in the backlands as early as 1904; and newspapers, films, and radio broadcasts flooded the interior with their secular messages by the 1930's.

Life in Recife

The new urban values that accompanied modernization entered through Recife, its commercial life strongly influenced if not controlled by foreigners and its elite anxious to keep up with at least some of the new urban trends. For centuries Recife had overshadowed the lesser cities of the hinterland. Only Caruarú, Garanhuns, and Pesqueira within Pernambuco can be said to have had any degree of real urban life, yet each was closely dependent on Recife for economic reasons. Most of the state's 85 município seats, even by 1937, were sleepy villages; some contained less than 4 percent of the total population of their municípios.[28]

In these circumstances Recife stood out even more sharply as a cosmopolitan, urban oasis. Yet at the same time it remained jealous of the ways of the past and resistant to indiscriminate change. As a consequence, new arrivals to the city that one lyricist has called "the greatest urban center south of the equator in the world" and "the heart and source of all northeastern civilization" often felt encouraged to maintain dual emotional loyalties—to their birthplace and to Recife (but not, it is worth adding, to the state of Pernambuco, a reality that rarely transcended political considerations).[29]

Though elite out-migration after the late nineteenth century drained the Northeast of some of the most talented of its natives, Recife was a magnet not only for the poor and the displaced, but for thousands of middle-class whites, an illustration of what demographers euphemistically call "select stream" migration.[30] Recife's overall growth occurred less because of industrial development than because of the expansion of commerce and the sheer weight of its unemployed and underemployed lower classes. More than half the city's employed population officially fell under the "personal services" category, the inflation of which, as Paul Singer notes, is the most notorious way to hide unemployment.[31] This distinction was not apparent to Governor Agamenon Magalhães, who in his preface to the state's special 1939 mocambo census asserted that the results showed Recife did not need to create new jobs, but merely needed to raise the salaries of those already working.[32]

The urban elite and bourgeoisie. Two disparate groups produced the post-1889 urban elite: the old rural families and the urban merchants and bankers, many of foreign origin. This new upper class constructed a façade of cosmopolitanism and gentility. Just as the rural gentry strove to follow coastal fashion, Recife's elite in turn looked beyond its own bounds, to Rio de Janeiro and to Europe. The spacious townhouses of the upper class dotted the city's most prestigious sections—Boa Vista, Casa Forte, Casa Amarela, and Derby. The two- or three-story houses invariably were surrounded by high fences or walls, and were well tended by a permanent staff of workmen, gardeners, and other domestic servants, who maintained the house, the stables, and the grounds. The townhouse usually included a music salon, a chapel, a library, and numerous guestrooms. Household china and linens were imported from Europe, as were such amenities as English biscuits and tea and Portuguese lace tablecloths and wine.

Women rarely left the house. According to a nineteenth-century French traveler, the life of the Brazilian woman "alternated between the window and the hammock."[33] The upper-class woman's life was merely sheltered, however, not indolent. She typically supervised the household, handled day-to-day emergencies, and busied herself with music, embroidery, and other domestic activities. She was not permitted to go shopping, since stores were dark and unattractive; most purchases were left to black houseboys called *moleques* or other servants. A small minority of women achieved some degree of emancipation, but in Pernambuco during the Empire and early Republic that usually amounted to little more than the right to sew their own clothing and have a say in the choice of a marriage partner.[34]

Young children fared well in the family-centered upper class. Boys were given classical names or, in the late nineteenth century, names of hemispheric statesmen: Bolivar, Juarez, Washington. Girls were named after the saints or the pious (Maria da Penha, Maria da Conceição) but soon acquired such nicknames as Baby and Tété. Nursemaids and governesses cared for children until early adolescence. Age often brought a harsher life. School discipline was rigid, especially for boys. Youths released pent-up aggression by tormenting younger victims, plotting

against teachers, or mistreating the many half-witted beggars who frequented the streets. Occasionally the sons of the elite created more serious disturbances, leaving their schoolyard to pelt passing trams with rocks
or to perform other mischief, but the incidents were quickly forgotten.

After adolescence boys of the elite entered an exhilarating atmosphere
outside their homes, a world of sexual double standards and student cam-
araderie. Many upper-class secondary and university students, particularly those sent to Recife from rural engenhos or other cities, left the
comfort of their homes to live in shabby boardinghouses filled with prostitutes, gamblers, and other unsavory characters. Students followed full
schedules of parties and contributed breathlessly to here-today, gone-
tomorrow literary journals. Some students entered politics as aides to
party officials or officeholders, or took part-time journalistic work. The
heady life was capped by elaborate graduation ceremonies and balls, after
which the new graduates set themselves to enter public life.[35]

Below the city's social elite were the aspiring professionals, merchants,
and bureaucrats of the urban upper-middle class. The most successful of
this group married into the elite or built townhouses next to the more
exclusive neighborhoods. The middle class also encompassed families of
more modest means, well employed but bereft of luxury. All these people
patterned their lives after the elite and considered themselves *gente
bem*—good folk, responsible citizens of the Republic, modern and civ-
ilized.

The urban poor. As in all Brazil, nineteenth- and twentieth-century
society cast people into two categories: the popular, or common, folk; and
what during the Republic was called the *classes conservadoras*. This
rigid, twofold division, as Ruben Reina shows for the Argentine city of
Paraná, created a vast gulf between "people" and "respectable people,"
"women" and "respectable women." This view was carried over to the
city itself; it was merely an extension of one's self and one's household.[36]
Rich and poor coexisted but lived in separate worlds. To the gente bem
the masses remained faceless—not only the pathetic beggars, crabbers,
and other residents of the festering slums, but also the industrious artisans, commercial employees, and skilled workers, who put in long, hard
days in the city's shops and small industries, especially in the period before World War I.[37]

Fully 50 percent of Recife's inhabitants lived in mocambos. To be sure,
not all mocambo-dwellers suffered equal deprivation; some, for the most

part entrepreneurial types, managed to provide services for (or to exploit) others. The median monthly mocambo-family income recorded in 1939 was 133$000, about double the salary of a rural agricultural worker during a full month of daily work.[38] Urban families, of course, could not raise garden crops, and costs in the city—for public transportation, for example —were higher than in the countryside.

Some contemporaries observed the squalid conditions of the poor but chose to describe the urban proletariat as "joyfully agitated."[39] For those inclined to see, life in Recife presented mercurial contrasts between wealth and penury: silk-and-feather-bedecked socialites side by side with the burlap-clad poor scavenging for edible garbage.[40] Half the mocambos were owned by their inhabitants; the rest were typically rented for about one-fifth the average monthly family income. Descriptions of living conditions vary according to the bias of the observer. The state Mocambo Census Commission catalogued 63 percent of the city's mocambos as "livable," though it noted that many of them became uninhabitable during the winter rainy season.[41]

Salaried commercial and industrial workers lived in the city's declining neighborhoods, many in old houses of crumbling concrete, two to five stories high, others in low, barrack-like cortiços, situated on winding, narrow streets, airless and dark. Though Recife was one of the first cities in Brazil to install a modern sewage system (in the 1870's), the city was confronted with a crisis in 1903 when its disposal plant reached capacity, and gutters were flooded with fecal wastes.[42]

The Growth of Urban Culture

Nineteenth-century observers called Recife's streets "narrow, filthy, and disagreeable," and the city as a whole "old, moldy, and decaying."[43] But as the century drew on, officials set out, in various ways, to improve its physical appearance and its facilities. As noted, the city was well ahead of others in Brazil in building a sewage system. Incinerators, suburban streetcars, a civil registry, and a technical school all were in operation before 1906.[44] The state initiated a major renewal program for the capital in 1911 and another in 1932. All in all, Recife boasted as many improvements as any Brazilian state capital as the years passed, though its peculiar river-and-island configuration created special problems, especially in communications and traffic flow.[45]

To some extent the effort to Europeanize Recife and bring it up to date diluted the city's flavor, though a visitor noted in 1913 that the downtown district still reeked of sugarcane.[46] Other innovations, less obvious, perhaps, than urban reconstruction, contributed to a new urban climate and a new social complexity that ultimately spread to the hinterland, though on a reduced scale.

Clubs and associations. Central to the development of urban culture were the voluntary associations that began to proliferate in Recife as urbanization progressed. Several political groups were formed before the end of the nineteenth century, including a small Republican circle in the 1870's and some important abolitionist societies, notably the women's Ave Libertas and the men's secret Club Cupim, both founded in 1884.[47] Brazil's second Archeological and Historical Institute was founded even earlier, in 1862, and the state's Academy of Letters was established in 1901.

The social club became a prominent feature of elite life with the establishment in 1885 of the International Club; its success as the focal point for family social activities and recreation created many imitators. Clubs issued a fixed number of shares; candidates for membership had to buy at least one share, but many men bought several as investments, thereby adding to their influence within the club and reserving additional openings for their sons or other family members. Some of the clubs sponsored soccer teams, a sport introduced by the English, who also played cricket until the ranks of the English community dwindled. With the exception of Carnival societies organized among the poor, the lower classes (and non-whites) were summarily excluded from the clubs and organizations in the city.

Most of the foreign clubs became Brazilian as the expatriate colonies dwindled after World War I. By 1926 every member of the board of directors of the Jockey Club was a Recifense, all but one a descendant of a prominent sugar family. Other associations of foreign origin that ultimately became wholly Brazilianized were the Commercial Association and the Boy Scouts and Girl Scouts.[48]

The press. The periodical press was the very hallmark of regional urban culture in Pernambuco—the pride of the elite and an essential part of the political system. By 1899 a total of 1,239 periodicals and newspapers are known to have published at least one issue, and no fewer than 1,165 of these were published in Recife alone. The statistic attests to the vitality

TABLE 3.1

The Periodical Press in Pernambuco, 1918 and 1930

	Number of periodicals	
Year	1918	1930
Zona da Mata		
Recife	28	45
Other areas	11	26
SUBTOTAL	39	71
Agreste	8	30
Sertão	1	4
TOTAL	48	105

SOURCE: *Estatística de imprensa periódica no Brasil* (Rio, 1931), p. vii; Mário Melo, *A imprensa pernambucana em 1918* (Recife, 1918), pp. 5–20; *Annuario estatistico de Pernambuco*, 1934, pp. 104–5.

of Pernambucano enterprise if not to the quixotic nature of local journalism.[49]

In 1920 three Recife newspapers claimed daily circulations of above 10,000. The typical newspaper or journal averaged between 300 and 500 copies per issue; only nine publications had runs of more than 5,000 copies, and most of these were subsidized by private individuals or groups.

What is significant is that as early as the 1890's Recife newspapers were regularly distributed beyond their metropolitan area, reaching urban centers from Alagoas to Ceará. Clearly, they played a major role in creating a twentieth-century regional consciousness. Pernambuco ranked second among the northern states in 1916 (after Bahia) in total newspaper circulation, and sixth nationally.[50] After 1930 newspaper growth slowed, in part because of the appearance of new media (radio, national circulation magazines, and newsreels and motion pictures, the "newspapers of the poor") and in part because the literacy rate did not keep pace with population growth. Beyond Recife, newspapers were short-lived except when they were privately subsidized. Rural political bosses used newspapers to promote themselves and to lend legitimacy to their rule. Table 3.1 illustrates how journalistic enterprise spread through the state in the years between 1918 and 1930.

Education. Education in Pernambuco was decidedly a preserve of the elite, a means by which the upper classes sought to legitimize their own domination while controlling opportunities for upward mobility.[51] Few children outside the elite—and certainly outside the white society, as shown in Table 1.2—had access to even the public schools. In 1907, for example, only 92 school-age children in 1,000 attended school, compared with a national average of 137. Teachers were poorly paid—as they were bound to be, considering that during the period after 1900 the state rarely allocated any more than 1.6 percent of its revenues per capita (or 5 percent of its budget) to public education, the smallest proportion in all the country and pitifully little compared with the amounts spent by Rio Grande do Sul, Minas, and São Paulo. (As early as 1912, Rio Grande do Sul devoted 20 percent of its budget to education, and Minas and São Paulo, 15 percent.)[52] In addition, most of the teaching positions were filled by patronage, with the result that many children were taught by persons with no other qualifications than their own primary schooling.[53] In the states of the satellite bloc things were as bad or worse: in Alagoas, in 1921, only 6 percent of the school-aged children attended class.[54]

As interest in education increased, private schools proliferated at a faster rate than public schools. This trend continued until the mid-1920's, when administrators took steps to improve the state system (these measures are discussed in some detail later in this chapter). However, the state retreated to a more conservative elitist posture in the next decade, and on the eve of the Second World War the public educational system was still in a sorry state. During the 1930's the state emphasized new school construction—mostly in the larger rural towns—but budgetary allotments were kept low. For a good measure of Pernambuco's total effort we have only to consider the progress made in increasing the literacy of the population. As I noted earlier, even by official claims, the rate only rose from 17 percent in 1872 to 22 percent in 1940.

Few youths enjoyed the luxury of school beyond the first two or three grades. For those unable to aspire to private academically oriented schools roughly at the middle and upper secondary levels (the *colégios* and *ginásios*), the state provided little in the way of alternative public education apart from a school for the industrial arts, a few trade schools for indigents, and, after 1930, three institutions that offered training in secretarial, clerical, and domestic skills. Of Recife's 21 secondary schools in 1927, most were operated by foreign Protestant religious groups, the Catholic Church, or charitable organizations; only five were state run. All of the schools were small, with an average of 70 pupils, most of them boys. The editors of the state's own *Annuario estatistico* for that year

confessed their inability to obtain any data on secondary instruction beyond the capital.[55] Presumably there was little.

The only two secondary schools of consequence in the Northeast were
both located in Recife: the Ginásio Pernambucano and the less prestigious
Escola Normal. The Ginásio, which drew students from as far away as
Pará, took care to keep enrollment levels low to preserve its exclusivity.[56]
The Escola Normal was a teacher-training institute whose course of study
amounted to a watered-down version of the Ginásio's classical curriculum. In teacher education, Pernambuco, like the Federal District and
the states of Minas and Bahia, followed the elitist French model, whereas
São Paulo led a handful of other states in following the pattern of schools
in the United States.[57] But teaching was never given much importance as
a career, and with the Escola's conversion to a girls school in the mid-
1920's, it ceased to have any real influence.

What did count enormously, indeed stood at the very center of the
Northeast's cultural universe, was Recife's Faculdade de Direito, one of
only two schools of law in Brazil until 1891. A great majority of Pernambuco's leaders attended the Faculdade, which, for northern Brazil, paralleled in importance France's Ecole Normale Supérieure and Mexico's
National University. The *bacharéis*, or professional school graduates,
bridged the period between the early Empire, when the rural agricultural
elite had dominated the state, and the post-1930 years, when technocrats
joined (but did not entirely supplant) them in the political and administrative panoply.

Perusing an impressive list of bacharéis active in nineteenth-century public life, Gilberto Freyre suggests that the law degree virtually
amounted to a "title of nobility."[58] More accurately, the bacharel title was
the stamp of legitimacy awarded by a society willing to bestow its fore-
most esteem on the products of a ritualistic higher educational system,
with the Faculdade at the pinnacle.

The centers of bacharelismo in the nineteenth century were the law
schools of Pernambuco and São Paulo and, to a lesser degree, the medical
schools of Rio de Janeiro and Bahia. The law faculties were established in
1827 by the Imperial Court to lessen reliance on the homeland (mainly
the University of Coimbra). The two schools (São Paulo's was known as
the Law Academy) accepted boys at the age of fifteen and offered a five-
year program, with two optional additional years and a thesis required for
the title of *doutor*. Most students ended their studies with the bacharel

degree, since as administrative networks expanded with the growth of government services that was sufficient to ensure them immediate public employment.

Classes at the law school were archly formal, student and faculty absenteeism high, and faculty salaries irregularly paid. Professors taught a maximum of three hours a week, devoting the rest of their time to full-time careers in law, journalism, and, in many cases, politics.

The undergraduate style, reflecting the students' privileged origins, encouraged the gentlemanly attributes of revelry, wit, boldness, and romanticism. Those from declining planter families with insufficient income to pay tuition supported themselves by tutoring or other part-time jobs. Virtually every student who entered the university graduated. Once matriculated, the student considered his degree to be an immutable right. Brazilian society esteemed the degree more than the content of university training. [59]

Though the law school, like the other universities, may be faulted for its tendency to elegant superficiality, it cannot be denied that over the years the bacharel elite immersed itself in a wide variety of intellectual and political movements. These included republicanism, abolitionism, neo-Kantism, positivism, modernism, and the neo-orthodox Catholicism of the 1930's. [60] At its worst, the Recife Law School produced a kind of vapid intellectual mediocrity, responsible for the creation of what Vamireh Chacon calls the "bacharel prototype—pedantically erudite, aggressive, provincial, [and] alienated from concrete political and social problems." [61] Over the years, law school enrollment remained representative of an unrepresentative society. Women were admitted in token numbers—four to the end of the nineteenth century—and tended to seek entrance to the more progressive institutions when they began to seek formal higher education in greater numbers after 1930.

Some boys of "poorer" families attended the law school. The Ginásio Pernambucano even provided a few scholarships for orphans, and a handful continued on to the law degree. By 1900 a growing number of law students came from what might be termed the second-status level of the regional upper class—sons of ranching and farming families of the interior, of groups allied with the plantocracy (merchants, bankers, bureaucrats), of the coronéis. The large majority, however, wealthy or not, still came from the region's leading families—if only, as a Recife newspaper remarked, to pass the time of day. [62]

Some few men rejected the law school's claim to intellectual supremacy. The Pernambucan diplomat and historian Oliveira Lima, for one, refused a chair at the Ginásio and, holding Pernambuco's academic climate to be too narrow-minded, donated his personal library to the Catholic University in Washington, D.C., rather than to the Recife Law School or any other Brazilian institution. But in any case its role as a national institution diminished increasingly after 1890, when the establishment of law schools in nearly every state and the growth of new professional schools reduced the exclusivity of its appeal. Nevertheless, the Faculdade successfully resisted the federal government's attempt in 1933 to merge it with various arts and sciences faculties, and continued to exercise substantial influence over the new law schools in the region.

Religion

The Catholic Church contributed to the growth of regionalization by subdividing its internal organization, creating new bishoprics out of the old diocese of Olinda in Ceará (1854), Paraíba (1892), Alagoas (1897), Piauí (1903), and Natal and Aracajú (1910). As in the political sphere, the fulcrum of Church influence shifted from the North (the bishopric of Bahia) in the nineteenth century to the South in the twentieth century. The Church considered the vast majority of the population to be Catholics, but it lacked the manpower to shepherd this enormous flock, especially in rural areas, where much of the population saw priests only once in several years if at all. In Recife it was the priests of the various orders —most of whom were foreign-born—who played the most important role in religious life.[63]

From 1891 onward, the Brazilian Church concentrated on reunifying Church and State and on combating the twin challenges to its hegemony from Pentecostalism, introduced among the lower class by foreign missionaries, and Marxism, whose specter rose among urban intellectuals. The Church hierarchy long stood firmly opposed to the liberal state, then did an about face in the 1920's, to cast its lot with the Republic and against the latent power of the masses. The turning point came in 1922 at the National Eucharistic Congress in Rio de Janeiro; thereafter the Church relied increasingly on national and regional congresses as vehicles for mobilization and for access to those in power.[64]

The center for the revival of Catholic militancy in Pernambuco was the Congregação Mariana, founded in 1924 by the Jesuit Antônio Fernandes—a by-product of the renewed Church interest in creating institutional bases for influence among the intellectual elite. The Congregação assumed a major role in the 1930's, when its members led a vocal campaign closely following the neo-orthodox revival led by Rio's Centro Dom Vital and its mentor, Alceu de Amoroso Lima (Tristão de Ataide).[65]

Fernandes and his followers stridently attacked anti-Catholic values and the cosmopolitanism promoted by the forces of "international Jewry" and "atheistic Communism." During Carnival, the Congregação operated austere religious retreats, given to silence and prayer, to isolate youths from "the satanic world of sensuality."[66] The neo-orthodox movement gained influential support and was joined by several leading members of the state goverment.

Despite the hostility of the Church, both Masonry and Protestantism were well established in Pernambuco, though on a limited scale. Many of Pernambuco's Imperial elite were Masons, including the abolitionist José Mariano. Protestants had 14 missions in the state in 1899, all but one in Recife. The English colony maintained a Protestant cemetery, and some of the Protestant churches, as we have noted, ran their own schools, the most famous being the American Baptist School, attended by Gilberto Freyre and the author Graciliano Ramos. A small number of Jews immigrated to Recife from Eastern Europe during the first decades of the century; but the state's Jewish community remained relatively small, numbering only 800 all told in 1934.

Regional Stirrings

In the late nineteenth century Brazilians began to wrestle with the question of cultural identity, assigning to local populations attributes that reinforced popular stereotypes of personality and behavior. Pernambucanos were generally considered in a proud light as the heirs to their region's historical acts of defiance. The Pernambucano was regarded as complex, enigmatic, paradoxical; an individualist in a region that resisted change; an energetic man in a region that was in decline; an introspective stoic, idealistic and tenacious.[67] Of all northeasterners, he was considered the most aristocratic, in keeping with the favorable impressions made by Pernambuco's elegant and well-bred Imperial elite.[68] For the majority of Pernambucanos, however, the attribute of tenacity seems to be the single most accurate description, since this trait was a practical necessity.

Intellectual movements. Cultural and intellectual activity first reached significant proportions in Pernambuco during the Empire, as Recife's burgeoning cosmopolitan atmosphere began to engender supporting institutions. Out of this new milieu came a philosophical movement, born in the 1870's, the Escola do Recife, or Recife School. Its leaders, centered at the law school, rejected positivism in favor of an eclectic, open-minded "evolutionist modernism," chiefly typified by a deep interest in German philosophy. The Escola exercised considerable influence not only in academic circles, but in literary criticism. Thus even as the Northeast sank still more deeply in economic decline, it gave rise to a vital and dynamic school of social thought that made its mark on Brazilian intellectual life, and that played an important role in the promulgation, in 1916, of a new federal civil code.[69]

Along with the Escola do Recife and the modernist movement that swept Brazil in the 1920's came new local interest in regional themes. Essayists explored in classical form Pernambuco's origins, the influence of its rivers, its geographical settings, its indigenous peoples, its heroes. Poets composed poems to the sea, odes to the tropical sun, hymns to the regional spirit. On a more scholarly level, academic dissertations focusing on the backlands or on regional problems began to emerge. Some of the Northeast's cultural figures acquired national reputations: Castro Alves in poetry, Tobias Barreto in philosophy, Clovis Bevilaqua in jurisprudence. But at the same time many of the region's writers, artists, and poets migrated to Rio de Janeiro and São Paulo, where the less traditional intellectual environment encouraged experimentation and afforded greater opportunities for cultural expression.* At least a few complained about Pernambuco's provincial atmosphere, and chafed at the fact that the latest books took weeks or even months to arrive from the South.[70]

Yet most remained, and thanks to them the 1920's witnessed a flowering of regionalist expression. The moving force behind this development was Gilberto Freyre, who organized a Regional Congress in 1926 on the model of the Modern Art Week observed in São Paulo in 1922. Both events shattered tradition in the sense that their participants de-

---

*Among those who departed were the novelists José Lins do Rêgo, of Paraíba, and Graciliano Ramos, of Alagoas; the poets Manoel Bandeira and Jorge de Lima, of Pernambuco; the sociologist Manuel Diegues Júnior, of Alagoas; and the writer Gustavo Barroso, of Ceará. The historian and diplomat Manoel de Oliveira Lima lived abroad, as did his fellow Pernambucano Cícero Dias, a celebrated artist. On modernism's impact on bacharelismo, see João Luiz Lafetá, "Estética e ideologia," p. 21.

clared their independence from outmoded cultural strictures. But under
Freyre's direction the northeasterners took a middle ground, adopting
the modernists' stylistic experimentation while voicing their allegiance to
regional traditions and lamenting the deleterious effects of modernization
on the dominant sugar culture.

Freyre's own upbringing broke with local custom. After graduating
from the American Baptist School in Recife, he completed his undergraduate studies at Baylor University, then went on for his master's degree at Columbia University, where he did graduate work in anthropol-
ogy and history (including classes taught by the noted anthropologist
Franz Boas). From New York Freyre proceeded to Europe for a period of
travel before returning to Recife and joining the regionalists' circle.

The new regionalist, Freyre contended, sought neither the mystique of
separation nor regional chauvinism. Waxing lyrical, the enfant terrible of
northeastern letters—who would receive international recognition a decade later with the publication of his innovative *The Masters and the
Slaves*—challenged regional writers to embrace the most humble local
resources, such as the poetic names of Recife's streets, the Catholic fervor
of the nineteenth century, Sertão cotton, and even the "harmonic and
aesthetic" mocambo, which he described as a "human construction har-
monized with nature . . . adapted to hygiene, to the need for shelter of
tropical man."[71]

The tendency to idealize indiscriminately all aspects of northeastern
life was the Achilles' heel of the movement. Its message was not especially novel, since local cultural pride had existed for generations. The
press remained indifferent; and some bystanders attacked Freyre as a
hidebound conservative or a narrow provincial. A critic called the northeastern regionalists "a group of sorry mental reactionaries," pointing to
Freyre's regrettable tribute to Recife's mocambos (and his advocacy of a
restaurant offering Afro-Brazilian cuisine).[72]

Nevertheless, Freyre's initiative left its mark. His regionalist school
survived in the form of the Center for Regionalism during the 1920's.
Moreover, several new regional-minded cultural journals took up the
cause: *Região*, *Nordeste*, *A Província*, *Clã*, *Bando*, and *Planalto*. The
movement briefly sponsored its own theater company and encouraged the
production of local films. The regionalists maintained their defense of the
plantocracy, providing fuel for those who labeled them reactionaries, but

gaining additional support among the nostalgic and those who feared the encroachment of modernization. [73]

It is not so surprising, after all, that these men so strongly championed the plantocracy. Most of the Northeast's cultural leaders came from that class, though there were exceptions. The most outstanding example was Tobias Barreto, one of the principal figures of the Escola do Recife. Barreto was a mulatto from Sergipe, who lived in a poor district of Recife in near penury, supported by his meager teaching salary and by handouts from disciples. But despite this very different background, Barreto, like the others, avoided social issues and clearly adhered to the upper class in outlook if not in condition.

Even as nonrevolutionary adjuncts to the socioeconomic elite, the cultural rebels invariably clashed with the intellectual establishment, which Freyre once attacked as a group of "gloomy antiquarians."[74] Freyre's own awakening came in 1934, when he organized a second major regional congress in Recife, this time on the subject of Afro-Brazilian culture. But by the mid-1930's times had changed: the anti-liberalism and anti-intellectualism buried in the *tenente* movement had surfaced and hardened under the Vargas regime.* The regionalist movement of the 1920's had seemed a harmless intellectual exercise; but now Freyre's Afro-Brazilian Congress focused on the touchy subject of race. This thoroughly scandalized the local elite, but more important, it raised irrational fears of social upheaval, drew the wrath of conservatives and the newly militant Church, and brought to prominence opportunistic politicians who successfully linked the Congress in the public mind with the alleged permissiveness of the state administration.

Freyre invited the cream of the new generation of social scientists, writers, educators, and artists to Recife. A showman, he created a kind of sociological "happening," surrounding the conference with Afro-Brazilian dancers, cooks, fortunetellers, and cultists. African dances and other activities of the congress were spotlighted in public meetings throughout the city. Opponents decried the publicity given to "primitive fetishism" and demanded that authorities close the meetings. [75]

---

*The tenente movement, which takes its name from the young officers who participated in it, arose in the years 1922–26, when a group of nationalistic junior officers rebelled against the federal government. The tenentes were important supporters of Getúlio Vargas in the Revolution of 1930.

Physicians, psychologists, and anthropologists submitted papers on a wide array of subjects. One of the most important, by the prominent physician and reformer Ulisses Pernambucano, dealt with mental illness among Pernambuco's blacks. Other participants reported on the rates of mortality among racial groups, on racial typology, on crime and delinquency, and even on the use of marijuana among the lower classes in Recife and Maceió.

In the main, however, the congress focused its attention on Afro-Brazilian folklore and culture. A public health aide offered a study of his agency's efforts to interview cult leaders in depth about their community roles as priests, physicians, judges, and family counselors. Only a few papers touched on living conditions, notably one by the sociologist Edison Carneiro, who asserted that conditions generally were "deplorable" for Brazilian blacks, and that the authorities treated them like "animals." Though few of the congress participants could be described as militant, the involvement of representatives from the grass-roots Frente Negra Brasileira (Brazilian Negro Front) of São Paulo further upset local conservatives.

The enemies of the congress prevailed. Freyre and his collaborators were officially labeled subversives; many were fired from their jobs, some were arrested, and others were driven from the state. Groups that had supported the congress were persecuted or dismantled. In November 1937, on the eve of Vargas's imposition of the authoritarian Estado Novo on Brazil, Recife's *Diário do Nordeste* linked the congress with the Comintern's efforts to instill hatred of whites among blacks and attacked intellectual interest in Afro-Brazilian life as the product of weaklings, cowards, Jews, Bolsheviks, and assorted other groups that were similarly dedicated to the "destruction of Christian culture."[76]

Reformist efforts. The modernist movement of the 1920's encompassed a nationwide impulse toward educational reform, notably in Bahia, the Federal District, Minas, and São Paulo, demonstrating once again the trend toward national integration that began after the First World War. Pernambuco joined the movement in 1928, under the administration of Governor Estácio Coimbra, when a Paulista educator, José Ribeiro Escobar, was persuaded to come to Recife as Secretary of Education and Public Health. Escobar, who had made a considerable name for himself in his work in the South, was enticed to accept the job by the promise of a healthy jump in the school budget—to more than double the five percent typically allowed.[77]

Escobar plunged in with a vengeance, installing an inspection system in order to standardize and raise the level of instruction, and introducing the revolutionary principle that schools should educate pupils for participation in society. Some of the public schools began to offer preschool classes based on Montessori and other innovative methods, which a few private schools in Recife had introduced in 1927. The state authorized the expansion of the primary school curriculum to seven years and decreed that no school, not even in isolated rural areas, should offer less than four years. Escobar introduced visual aids, rhythm and dance classes, and hygienic and sex education, and urged teachers to create a "socializing class environment" in which children would learn teamwork and responsibility. His pedagogical handbook, published in Recife in 1930, cited most of the leading reform-minded foreign educators of the day.[78]

But Escobar was moving against the tide of a revived cultural orthodoxy. The efforts to implement the changes evoked a furor. The secretary was vilified as an outsider, a charlatan whose "courses in pornography threatened the sanctity of the Pernambucan family."[79] And the campaign succeeded: Escobar was forced to resign, and his programs were canceled. The state, through its Director of Education, officially rejected his 1928–29 reforms as "erroneous," "inflammatory," and "fallacious."[80]

Even more ugly was the case of Ulisses Pernambucano. Ulisses Pernambucano Gonsalves de Mello—his family chose to retain the old spelling of its surnames—was one of the most remarkable northeasterners of his time. Born in 1892 in Vitória, in the Zona da Mata, he took his medical degree at the age of twenty in Rio de Janeiro. On completing his studies, he returned home to practice surgery, then turned his interest to psychiatry and mental health. Pernambucano's family's ties to the Rosa e Silva political machine barred him from public appointments until 1918, when he was named chief resident of the state mental hospital. From 1919 to 1928 he held several posts in education and public health.

He proved to be an administrator of indefatigable skill and vision, rebuilding the state's mental health facilities, opening clinics for the poor, introducing the practice of allowing patients in mental institutions to make home visits, and expanding services to the criminally insane, the retarded, and the urban poor. He directed sociological studies of the state's mental health facilities, and in 1931 visited São Paulo as the head of a commission to study hospitals and clinics there. Reacting to the prevailing racist view among Brazilian biologists on genetic inheritance, he studied racial aspects of mental illness; with Freyre and a team of other social scientists, he also attempted to organize a regional study to examine the physical conditions of usina workers in the sugar zone.

In return, Pernambucano was pilloried as a Communist and finally ousted from his state posts. Hounded by the right-wing press, the now infirm physician was personally harassed by ruffians sent by his enemies in the state administration. The man who symbolized the capacity of the elite to produce social visionaries was destroyed along with his visions for change.[81]

It is inaccurate to speak of a single regional culture for the Northeast unless one means institutionally, where the regional culture of arts and letters was clearly "Recife culture" or "urban culture," closer to the world of Rio de Janeiro and Europe than to the rural interior. The rural hinterland remained a foreign place to Recifenses, as it was, to some degree, to the would-be cosmopolitan inhabitants of the larger towns and villages of the interior, with their four-page newspapers, horticultural clubs, and patriotic pageantry.[82] Sugar-dominated, the Zona da Mata maintained its own way of life; Agreste culture, rooted in the small sleepy towns and regional trade fairs, developed along different lines, as did life in the remote Sertão.

In the city, most of the population was excluded from the institutions of social mobilization that accompanied urban growth: the schools, the social clubs, even the labor unions, which were limited to the relatively small number of workers who were regularly employed, and which were carefully watched by the officials. The conservatism of the elite was reinforced by the threat of increased social participation by the lower classes and soothed by the reassurances of cultural romanticists seeking to preserve the past as a shield against an uncertain future. Cultural expression both allowed northeasterners to screen themselves from inrushing modern values and offered, to some, a means of dealing with them. The elite's firmness in preserving its regional identity—and with it, an emphasis on order and stability—fit the pluralistic view of region and nation that came to maturity under the political structure of federalism after 1889. The following chapters consider the federal system from this perspective.

CHAPTER FOUR

State Politics: Men, Events, and Structures

PERNAMBUCO'S political evolution under the Republic may be divided into four distinct phases. The first, from 1889 to 1896, saw a succession of short-lived repressive administrations imposed from Rio de Janeiro literally to restore order out of political chaos. During the second, which ended in federal intervention in 1911, the state's fortunes revived under the iron discipline of the Rosa e Silva machine. The third phase, 1911 to 1930, witnessed shifting alliances and a tenuous restoration of one-party rule. That ended with the coup of 1930, when decision-making power reverted to federal authorities, vested once again in Rio as it had been during the infancy of the Republic.

Men and Events

The first phase. News of the fall of the Empire arrived at Recife by telegram on Saturday, November 16, 1889. Politically conscious Pernambucanos were not surprised by the proclamation of the Republic, but most did not welcome it. As for the general population, they showed little interest; few public demonstrations took place, save for a crowd that gathered spontaneously at the French consulate to sing the "Marseillaise." On November 18 troops disembarked from a steamboat that had been dispatched from Rio de Janeiro and were deployed without opposition.[1] Orders from the provincial government delivered the state to a military administrator. Nevertheless, local Republicans, still mourning the death of their party leader, Maciel Pinheiro, remained expectant, especially since their new spokesman, José Isidoro Martins Júnior, was given the post of chief of police. But the devolution of leadership to the twenty-nine-year-old dilettante proved fatal to the party that would later call its members Historical Republicans, to differentiate them from the dozens of Monarchists who converted, at least in name, to the new order.

Even so, it might have been expected that the Republicans would come to power in Pernambuco as they did in most of the other Brazilian states. The Liberal Party had been split since 1874, and the Conservatives were weakened by the refusal of their leader, João Alfredo Correia de Oliveira, to support the federation. Yet of the major political blocs bidding for power after the events of November 1889, the Historical Republicans held the weakest hand. Drawn from the small urban middle class, the Republican Party of Pernambuco was hardly representative of the governing elite; only a few of its members were directly connected to the plantocracy, a group that had no use for them or their new leader, who was scornfully dismissed as a popinjay. Eventually, the conservative planters would rally behind the new party organized in 1893 by Francisco de Assis Rosa e Silva, formerly the second in command of the old Conservative Party. Of the same conservative bent as its predecessor, despite its name, the Federal Republican Party (PRF) also included dissident Historical Republicans, and was linked to the national PRF through Pernambuco's congressional delegation. Three years after its founding it came to include ex-Liberals as well, when Sigismundo Gonçalves, the son-in-law of one of the Liberal Party leaders, brought in a dissident faction. Even the abolitionist Joaquim Nabuco (who, like João Alfredo, remained an unreconstructed Monarchist) looked to Imperial politicians for leadership; writing to José Mariano, the Liberal Party leader, in early 1889, Nabuco called him the "positive hope" of the Republican future.[2]

The true Republicans failed because they shared neither kinship nor philosophical principles with the regional power brokers. Unable to absorb the stream of Imperial converts to republicanism into their own small political party, Martins Júnior and his followers found themselves upstaged by their powerful former antagonists, who simply usurped the Republican nomenclature. As a result, through all the First Republic (1880–1930) not a single Historical Republican was elected to the governorship of Pernambuco, in contrast, for example, to São Paulo, where nine of the first 11 governors were historicals.* The overwhelming major-

---

*Gov. Manoel Borba, who was elected in 1915, claimed to have been a Historical Republican, but he had only been a law student when the Empire fell and was never a member of the Republican Party.

ity of Liberal and Conservative party leaders brazenly and with perhaps indecent haste announced their adherence to republicanism, capturing two-thirds of the seats on the state's delegation to the 1890 Constituent Assembly and acting in concert to keep the "legitimate" Republicans as far from power after 1889 as before.*

Violent exchanges among the competing political factions, mostly centered in the press but occasionally spilling over into physical attacks and beatings by hired thugs, contributed to Rio de Janeiro's decision to withhold support from the local Republicans. Martins Júnior added fuel to the fire by impetuously demanding the control of patronage, which only earned him a stiff letter of reprimand from Rio.[3] Mediation efforts failed to curb the warring factions, leading in December 1891 to a takeover by a three-man junta imposed by the federal government.

For the second time the Historical Republicans seemed to be poised to take control; Martins Júnior, in anticipation, assumed the directorship of the law school and devoted his attention to political planning. In the 1892 state elections the Republican Party swept all legislative seats not reserved by law for the opposition. But the national chief of state, Floriano Peixoto, like his deposed predecessor, Deodoro da Fonseca, distrusted the unrepresentative Pernambuco Republicans and, amidst a gathering political storm in the state, named his own interventor.† His man, Capt. Alexandre José Barbosa Lima, a career military officer born in the Agreste, was a Historical Republican but had no links with any political faction. Floriano's laconic response to a list of four local prospective governors submitted by the junta, each acceptable to the state Republican Party, has become legend: "Captain Barbosa Lima accepts the nomination. Congratulations."[4]

As soon as he arrived from Rio, where he had been a federal deputy representing the State of Ceará, Barbosa Lima—an impetuous and iron-willed administrator with a strong authoritarian streak—revealed his intention to crush the Republicans. For their part, they naïvely believed that they would be able to dominate him. Striking quickly, the new gov-

---

*Historical Republicans accounted for only 21 percent of Pernambuco's political elite (as defined in Appendix A) after 1889, compared with 50.5 percent in São Paulo. The figure for Minas was 49.4 percent, but 8 percent of the Mineiros were "eleventh-hour" Republicans.

† In the 1890's and especially during the 1930's men were often named directly by the President to act as governor, bypassing (or overruling) the electoral process. Officially, such appointees bore the title interventor, though some preferred to stick to the title governor. This was true in the case of Barbosa Lima. I routinely refer to them as governors except in special cases.

ernor postponed local elections, suspended Recife's municipal budget,
and moved to redistrict município boundaries to the detriment of Republican incumbents. Martins Júnior lobbied in Rio de Janeiro to have Barbosa Lima deposed, and Republican partisans raised armed resistance
in the backlands. Neither effort succeeded. In desperation, Martins attempted to have Barbosa Lima impeached and placed under arrest, but
the federal military commander remained firm, and the governor weath-
ered the challenge.[5] In retaliation, he purged pro-Republican officials
from the state judiciary and harassed the Republican Party. Weary public
opinion fell behind Barbosa Lima, who early in 1893 stripped Martins
Júnior of his law school position over strong protests from the faculty
about the inviolability of academic tenure.

Barbosa Lima's acts left two groups in contention for control of the state
political machinery: the Liberals, led by José Mariano, and the allied
Conservatives and Historical Republicans in the PRF. The field narrowed
when José Mariano committed the fatal error of backing a naval revolt in
November 1893, an abortive anti-Floriano conspiracy that Mariano partisans claimed had involved Barbosa Lima himself. Unruffled, the governor
instituted a wave of police terror that culminated in the imprisonment or
flight of all persons implicated in the rebellion.[6]

As governor, Barbosa Lima earned high marks for his advocacy of hon-
est administration, his program of state incentives for the modernization
of sugar production, and his efforts to establish centers for technical training. But his strong-arm methods and personal aloofness alienated him
from influential citizens. He reportedly carried a pistol and frequently
sent police to smash equipment at opposition newspaper offices. Once he
allegedly forced an offending editor, at gunpoint, to swallow a hostile
editorial, washed down with a glass of water from the filthy Capiberibe
River.[7] In the words of one observer, his use of force "cannibalized" the
state. Lacking an effective political base, he in the end only deepened the
political vacuum that had existed since 1889. Floriano, who had sent him
to Pernambuco and who might have taken steps to assure a smoother
transition in the state, died in June 1895. Barbosa Lima exited soon after,
arranging for a seat in the federal Senate. The only remaining figure in a
position to inherit power in Pernambuco was Rosa e Silva, the president
of the federal Chamber of Deputies and the embodiment of the values of
the Imperial aristocracy.[8]

The second phase. Rosa e Silva reigned from 1896 to 1911, when federal intervention undermined his political empire. His PRF functioned on three interrelated but distinct planes. At the state level it oversaw all administrative, judicial, and legislative activities, centered in the state capital, Recife. On the local level it wove an intricate network of alliances with the coronéis, trading recognition of their quasi-feudal domains for the delivery of votes from their rural constituencies. And, finally, on the national level, in addition to majority control of the state's congressional delegation, it had links to the national PRF and to well-placed federal officials in other branches of government, giving Pernambuco a modest voice in national affairs, with Rosa e Silva acting as the political spokesman for the northern states.

His popular stance as the "Lion of the North" notwithstanding, Rosa e Silva, a wealthy, cosmopolitan autocrat who ruled in absentia from Rio de Janeiro and who preferred France to Brazil, despised the Northeast, which he considered uncivilized. He avoided Pernambuco for as long as two years at a time, even at the height of his power, returning only to mediate questions of patronage among subordinates on board ship in Recife's harbor as he passed through en route to Europe or to his home in the federal capital.

Rosa e Silva was born in 1857 in Recife, the second son of a Portuguese immigrant from the Province of Minho. His father had thrived in his adopted land, becoming a prosperous Recife merchant and an intimate of João Alfredo, and eventually acquiring the title of commendador and a seat in the Senate. Young Rosa e Silva entered the Recife Law School at sixteen and emerged as a bacharel at the age of twenty.* He returned a year later and took his doctorate, submitting a thesis on the divine origin of sovereignty in which he attempted to refute Rousseau's theory of the social contract. After a two-year sojourn in Europe, he returned to Recife and became affiliated with the Conservative Party and its newspaper, O Tempo.

In 1888, then only thirty-one years of age, Rosa e Silva joined the João Alfredo cabinet as Minister of Justice. Linked to the plantocracy through his wife, the daughter of the Viscount of Livramento, he defended northeastern sugar interests and demanded that equipment for the new sugar factories be imported duty-free. His older brother, José Marcelino,

---

*Even as a law student Rosa e Silva was called "menino de ouro" (golden boy) for his aristocratic mien and vanity ("O dr. Rosa e Silva e a sua formação," O Pernambuco, May 9, 1910, p. 1).

guarded the family's political and economic interests at home in Pernambuco. The Rosa e Silva clan differed from most of its local contemporaries
in one regard: though both brothers married into the aristocracy, their
fortune was based on the commercial investments and urban real estate of
their father.

Rosa e Silva, who had been decorated by the Emperor, adhered to the
Republic after a brief initial hesitation. Finding himself the favored champion of the Conservatives, he mobilized them to form the PRF. He rose
to the presidency of the Brazilian Chamber of Deputies a year later. In
1896 he entered the Senate, preserving absolute authority through a carefully controlled political network that extended not only to all parts of
Pernambuco but to neighboring northeastern political oligarchies as
well—to the Maltas in Alagoas, to Artur Reis in Bahia, to the Acciolis in
Ceará, to Justo Chermont in Pará. By this time he had become an ally of
Rio Grande do Sul's powerful senator, José Gomes Pinheiro Machado,
thanks to which he gained membership on the national PRF executive
committee. More important, he had also by this time established himself
as one of the most prestigious public men in Brazil.

Rosa e Silva's style separated him from other political bosses of his day.
He disliked unnecessary violence and rarely associated himself with men
of low standing. He dressed impeccably, always wearing a hat, silk hand-
kerchief, and Parisian cologne. He spoke in a measured voice, a nervous
facial tic contrasting with his precise words and carefully articulated
speech. On his rare visits to Pernambuco he received the honors afforded
visiting royalty. Only a handful of his closest aides ever called him by the
familiar *você*; even men who worked closely with him for decades used
the formal *o Senhor*. Opponents reviled him as an egotistical autocrat, but
he did not seek public acclaim. The journalist (and would-be politician)
Gilberto Amado hinted that Rosa e Silva displayed an air of inferiority
when he spoke in Europe: he addressed his audiences not with the customary "Messieurs," but with a servile "Excellences," as his voice qua-
vered and rose in pitch. Amado also noted that Rosa e Silva, a smallish
man, was always careful to stand erect, trying to appear taller than he was,
and favored shoes with built-up heels to add to the effect.[9]

Rosa e Silva was able to serve only briefly on the PRF national committee, for the party was hopelessly split by 1897 and disintegrated the next
year, shortly before the presidential elections. But he gained still more

power locally, when the new President, Manoel de Campos Sales, allowed the state machines to move to the center of the political stage under what was called the "politics of the governors." The system effectively ensured one-party rule, guaranteeing a local machine a free hand in its state and indefinite tenure in office in return for its loyalty and ability to deliver support to the national administration. In simple terms, the states traded their congressional delegations and their people's votes in presidential contests for local autonomy and the largess to be distributed after national elections. Whatever pretense at free and open balloting existed before the institutionalization of the new arrangement vanished in its aftermath.

In Pernambuco the state party machine extended its influence to all areas of the public realm. Rosa e Silva's ownership of the *Diário de Pernambuco* gave the party constant public exposure; the PRF so ubiquitously acted in the name of the state that it seemed to *be* the state's permanent and rightful voice. The line between party and state administration blurred. The PRF-dominated legislature changed the post of mayor of Recife from an elective to an appointive position, allowing the party to manage the seat of one-tenth of the state's population as if the capital (and its bureaucracy) were its own private preserve. PRF officials carefully scrutinized candidates for teaching chairs at the Recife Law School, using the coveted positions as patronage plums (and conveniently ignoring the results of the required academic competitions as it chose). The party controlled nominations to all administrative positions in the state: the faculty at the Ginásio Pernambucano; primary school posts in every município; appointments of medical examiners, police officials, port inspectors, and tax collectors. If a young law student unwisely became the protegé of an out-of-favor law professor, his petition for public employment would likely be denied. The PRF's links to neighboring oligarchies extended the party's arm and forced dissidents to migrate as far south as Rio de Janeiro or São Paulo to escape its wrath. Even in the federal capital a candidate for a bureaucratic job required a letter from the PRF incumbents at home before he could be hired.[10]

At the head of the state party machine sat the governor, elected in Pernambuco to a four-year term after having been carefully handpicked by the party chief. All of the state's governors from 1896 to 1911 were loyal party hacks. The first, a wealthy attorney and law school professor, married into the Imperial nobility. The second, also a law school professor, embroiled his administration in a fiscal crisis; as a result, he was returned to private life, and his sons were not granted public employment. His successor, a bacharel from a smaller northeastern state, married into one of the state's most aristocratic families; not by coincidence, his administration became known for its willingness to help reduce the debts of the sugar refinery owners. The next governor was a planter and usineiro himself, a close friend of Rosa e Silva and, even more than his predecessors, a political puppet. By the end of this man's term in office, opposition to the oligarchy had grown to the point where Rosa e Silva reluctantly moved to take personal control of the PRF and stand as its candidate for governor.[11]

In his exercise of political control Rosa e Silva never treated the PRF as an instrument of family power. Unlike other state bosses, he did not seek to groom a relative to succeed him. His own son always remained on the periphery of the party's leadership, and his son-in-law, Anibal Freire, a bacharel from Sergipe who had earned an impressive record at the Recife Law School, spent most of his time in the federal capital, assisting Rosa e Silva with legislative matters. Whether Freire would have been recalled home to succeed Rosa e Silva had the latter been elected in 1911, we cannot know, but others, including Estácio Coimbra, soon emerged as potential heirs to the dynasty, and Rosa e Silva did nothing to stop them, though he remained as titular head of Pernambuco's congressional delegation until his death in 1929.

The state's socioeconomic base presupposed that the PRF would staunchly defend agricultural producers, though individual planters and usineiros did not, for the most part, assume active positions within the political apparatus. All five civilian governors of Pernambuco from 1890 to 1911, however, had direct (or indirect) ties to sugarcane agriculture; between 1908 and 1937 five of the seven elected civilian governors were either usineiros or major planters, and one of the others was a textile industrialist whose relatives were senhores de engenho. PRF potentates occupied the directorates or held shares in the state's major utilities, banks, commercial houses, and usinas.[12] Yet the Commercial Association's relations with the PRF were at best strained, and in the end the association broke with the Rosa e Silva machine, helping to precipitate its defeat in 1911.[13]

Each of the four men chosen by Rosa e Silva to govern Pernambuco from 1896 to 1911 administered the state uneventfully, though José Mariano partisans and a handful of surviving Republicans raised token opposition, mostly before Martins Júnior's death in 1904. Some former dissidents enlisted in the Rosista ranks, the way made easier by the fact that few ideological distinctions separated political factions. The elite, in short, agreed on how the system should operate. Artur Orlando, a one-time Liberal Party stalwart and advisor to José Mariano during the Barbosa Lima period, abandoned his colleagues in 1896 and became editor-in-chief of Rosa e Silva's *Diário de Pernambuco*. In 1911 he switched allegiances again, to Emídio Dantas Barreto, Rosa e Silva's challenger in the gubernatorial race. Nevertheless, his stock in political circles remained uniformly high, an illustration of the fluid nature of partisan politics under a system in which members of the elite were interconnected by common education, family ties, and social perceptions.

The third phase. In 1910 all pretense at national political unity fell apart in a bitter presidential election campaign between the establishment's candidate, War Minister Hermes Rodrigues da Fonseca, and a reform-minded senator from Bahia, Rui Barbosa. The contest reverberated at the state level and broke the hold of the incumbent machines across northern Brazil. Though Rosa e Silva had backed Hermes, he had balked at joining the alliance of satellite political parties that Pinheiro Machado had forged in support of the new President. The impasse set off a chain of local events, leading to the formation of a coalition of anti-PRF politicians, aided and abetted by Recife businessmen and spokesmen for the emerging urban middle class. With the blessing of the Hermes administration, the coalition chose War Minister Dantas Barreto, a Pernambuco-born hero of the Paraguayan War, to challenge Rosa e Silva for the governorship in 1911. The Dantistas waged a heated seven-month-long campaign marked by extensive violence on both sides. Though Rosa e Silva's control of the political apparatus produced an electoral majority (Dantas carried Recife, but Rosa e Silva won lopsided margins in the interior), both sides claimed victory, and with Recife and some interior municípios on the verge of civil war, Rosa e Silva was forced to yield under pressure from the Army.[14]

Despite the stated rationale behind the Hermes-Dantas Salvacionista campaign—to dislodge "the greedy and corrupt oligarchies" of the North—the new administration and its successors differed very little from

their predecessors in style.* There is no question that the Dantas administration did make more concessions to Recife's commercial interests than
the Rosa e Silva regimes, along with brief if substanceless overtures to
urban workers, but it governed in much the same manner and according
to the same politics as Rosa e Silva's PRF. When, in 1913, Dantas broke
with Pinheiro Machado, he effortlessly curtailed his bitter public feud
with the Rosistas; Rosa e Silva's price was the return of his Senate seat,
which he continued to hold until his death.[15]

As a military man foisted on the state by the federal government, Dantas, like Barbosa Lima before him, exercised no lasting personal influence
beyond his own administration, though he did manage to handpick his
successor, Manoel Borba. Moreover, the Dantas Barreto interlude clearly
marked a transition, if not a turning point, in the political balance of the
state. The changes took several forms. First, the Dantista coronéis who
rose to power with the ouster of the PRF in 1911 generally acquired an
iron grip on their fiefdoms, which they held until the coronel system itself
began to weaken after 1930. Second, the sugar planters and their bacharel
surrogates who had dominated the governorship lost ground to the
usineiros, who entered state politics in a real way in 1911 and controlled
the governorship after the Dantista intervention.* Third, the bitter electoral campaign of 1911 and its aftermath revealed the urban electorate as
a new force to be reckoned with and saw the emergence of interest groups
heretofore excluded from the narrow base of the ruling political parties.
Dantas recognized the change in offering seats in the state legislature to
two labor spokesmen, João Ezequiel and Santana de Castro.* The modernization of the sugar industry, the expansion of government at the state
and local level, the slow but steady development of industry in and

---

*The anti-oligarchy interpretation is widely cited, though it overlooks the manipulative
role played by Pinheiro Machado and the cynical context of electoral politics under the
federation. The then British ambassador accepted the definition of the salvações as an anti-
oligarchy measure, which had "the merit of replacing the old state administrations, if not
better in themselves, at least better controlled by the central power and thus more amena-
ble to the pressure of foreign states in support of their interests." (British Foreign Office
Archives, file 371/1052/4002, Ambassador W. Haggard, Rio, to Foreign Minister Edward
Grey, London, 1911 annual report, p. 11.)

*Hercolino Bandeira, the last Rosista governor (1908–11), was a planter when he started
his term and a usineiro when he left, having bought a usina in his last year of office.

*Neither man was especially militant, in contrast to the Pernambuco-born José Elias da
Silva, who returned to Recife in 1914 after a brief career organizing Rio's dockworkers,
organized several labor unions, and helped precipitate the 1919 general strike. José Elias
was *not* courted by Dantas or any other politico.

around Recife—all contributed to increasing occupational specialization and the fragmentation of interests, complicating political life and adding to its potential instability.

Growing economic differentiation, the necessity that the PRF choose among increasingly competitive groups related to the sugar industry— cane suppliers, brokers, usineiros, local planters' syndicates, bankers, and exporters—and the beginnings of labor consciousness exploited by Dantista partisans in the 1911 campaign undermined the PRF's efforts to remain in power. Yet the substitution of one faction for another did not guarantee that the old politics would fade away. On the contrary, the years after Dantas Barreto saw a revival of the old political factionalism. Dantas himself broke with his own man Borba in 1917—a year that also saw the first citywide labor strike. The death of the Borbista incumbent in 1922 provoked an angry succession crisis, unfolding a crazy-quilt patchwork of new political alliances resolved only by the renewed threat of federal intervention and the imposition of a non-aligned candidate, Sérgio Loreto, as governor. Loreto surrounded himself with his relatives and looked aside while they helped themselves to the spoils of office. As governor, he maintained order through mediation with politicians and the use of repressive measures against labor organizers. Meanwhile, the Rosistas, led by Estácio Coimbra (then Vice-President of the Republic), organized quietly for their return to power at the end of Loreto's tenure.*

But by the 1920's new political winds were sweeping the nation. Politics had become more specialized. National-level members of the state elites increasingly spent their careers outside of their home states, and many became removed from local issues. As political recruitment expanded, the patriarchal form of the state oligarchies began to be diluted; new economic groups (bankers, industrialists, professionals) began to displace the more homogeneous interests that had traditionally made up the state political elite. Though Estácio Coimbra was a usineiro and depended on the old Rosista coalition to win the 1926 gubernatorial election (which he took with 98 percent of the vote), an unprecedented crack appeared in the political façade a year later, with the establishment of a viable opposi-

---

*See Manoel Borba, *Sérgio Loreto*; and Carlos de Lima Cavalcanti, *Pernambuco saqueado*. The 1922 impasse over succession was directly related to the national crisis between Hermes and Epitácio Pessôa, and according to at least one historian (Souza Barros, *Década*, pp. 93–95), created the atmosphere that led to the tenente revolt at the fort of Copacabana on July 5.

tion party. The Democratic Party of Pernambuco (PD), organized by Carlos de Lima Cavalcanti, not only had links with dissident groups in other states, but was backed by a strident newspaper chain, anchored by the *Diário da Manhã*, which Lima Cavalcanti edited. The PD recruited support from the same interest groups that sustained the Rosista majority; but Lima Cavalcanti was able to exploit the tide of revolution that swept Getúlio Vargas into power in 1930, stirring up local unrest as a pretext for the intervention of units of the rebellious Liberal Alliance.

The plan succeeded admirably. A month after the rebellion began with the outbreak of fighting in October 1930, the alliance's northeastern military commander, Juarez Távora, took control of Recife.[16] Incredibly, the Coimbra administration was caught unprepared—even though it had been put on notice many months earlier, in July, when the defeated vice-presidential candidate, João Pessôa, had been assassinated in Recife, an act that grew out of a struggle for control of neighboring Paraíba and related to state politics in Pernambuco. Ignoring this and other evidence of unrest, the administration did not concern itself with the gathering crisis until September, when it cabled the War Ministry for emergency supplies of ammunition.[17] By then it was too late; Távora took Recife with only brief street fighting and installed Lima Cavalcanti as interventor.

The fourth phase. Lima Cavalcanti, like Coimbra a usineiro, was a man of the same social background as the members of the "old order" who were ousted by the Liberal Alliance. Indeed, he had been a member of the Rosista majority until his defection in 1927. Now, at the head of the "revolutionary" state administration, he governed by decree; he had the mails and the press censored, prosecuted former officials for alleged corruption, and enthusiastically declared his intention to carry the spirit of the Liberal Alliance to every município.

The new centralization of authority under Vargas left the states with little say in their own affairs. Each interventor took orders directly from Rio de Janeiro. New federal agencies imposed control in areas formerly free from government prerogative. The tenente "viceroy" Juarez Távora was given administrative authority over the entire region from Bahia to Amazonas, but in Pernambuco he left the state administration alone from the outset, perhaps as a reward for Lima Cavalcanti's strong support during the 1930 coup.

Paralleling the experience of Getúlio Vargas on the national level, Lima Cavalcanti had to defer to two mutually antagonistic groups during his early days in office. On the one side were the liberal constitutionalists, elite politicians who, like Lima Cavalcanti himself, had belonged to the political "outs" until the Liberal Alliance victory. On the other was a diverse group of political novices, not unlike the Martins Júnior circle of Historical Republicans in the days immediately following the fall of the Empire. These men, and especially a small reformist bloc in their midst, were bitterly opposed by the more seasoned politicians who had supported the PD, and also, as one would suppose, by the Rosista loyalists, who though silenced by the 1930 coup, viewed the reformists as troublemakers and Communists.*

Caught in the middle, Lima Cavalcanti attempted to integrate both factions into his state administration. As a result, his support splintered; his own aides jockeyed for influence and battled against their enemies. Hindered by political inexperience, Lima Cavalcanti's seven-year regime amounted to little more than a revolutionary façade behind which the interventor struggled in vain to secure control as competing interests fought to retain their share of the political spoils.

Lima Cavalcanti's party, renamed the Social Democratic Party (PSD), began to fragment as early as 1931. In Rio de Janeiro a federal deputy from Pernambuco, Agamenon Magalhães, a belated convert to the PD and a personal adversary of Lima Cavalcanti's, was made Minister of Labor in 1934 and given virtual veto power over requests from Recife for political favors. Refusing to be humiliated by this rebuff from Vargas, Lima Cavalcanti stubbornly persisted, asserting himself as the leader of the northern interventors and lobbying ceaselessly to regain Vargas's confidence. The state's delegation in the Constituent Assembly split as soon as the body convened, dividing Pernambuco's voice and undermining Lima Cavalcanti's ability to use the state's large voting bloc as leverage in political negotiations.

The federal Constitution of 1934 required immediate state elections and made incumbent interventors eligible to run for four-year gubernato-

---

*The liberal constitutionalists included João Cleofas; Luis Cedro and Francisco Solano Carneiro da Cunha (both related to the Lima Cavalcantis); and Oscar Benardo Carneiro da Cunha, a distant cousin and a very powerful member of the plantocracy. Prominent among the reformers were Nelson Coutinho (active in education, agricultural administration, and public health) and Paulo Carneiro; both were accused of Communist sympathies and dismissed in 1935, in the wake of the uprising against the Vargas regime. Others in the reformist bloc were Josué de Castro, the architect Luis Nunes, and Ulisses Pernambucano. (Courtesy of Nelson Coutinho and Gileno Dé Carli.)

rial terms. When Lima Cavalcanti declared his candidacy, an opposition coalition of PSD dissidents and former Rosistas rallied behind their own candidate, João Alberto Lins de Barros, hero of the Prestes Column, a guerrilla band of tenentes that had roamed the backlands in the 1920's, and the man whose unsuccessful interventorship in São Paulo had contributed in no small way to the outbreak of civil war there in 1932. But what perhaps counted more with the conservative elements than João Alberto's past role was their conviction that they could easily manipulate him to their own ends; a locally born career soldier like Barbosa Lima and Dantas Barreto before him, João Alberto offered neither concrete program nor ideology.[18]

João Alberto attacked Lima Cavalcanti's record, emphasizing the interventor's alleged inability to secure federal aid, his angry public feud with Public Works Minister José Américo de Almeida over the minister's refusal to provide Pernambuco with drought relief funds, and his "flagrant disregard for the sane principles of liberal democracy," code words for Lima Cavalcanti's unwillingness to make peace with his pre-1930 enemies and his tolerance of moderate reform.[19] Alarmed at the prospect of a João Alberto administration infiltrated by holdovers from the overthrown Old Republic, the supposedly neutral Vargas promptly dropped that pose and offered his support to Lima Cavalcanti, who maneuvered the state legislature into voting him into office as constitutional governor in what proved to be an atypical display of political acumen.[20]

Ignoring the fact that his victory over João Alfredo was due to Vargas's intervention in behalf of the more controllable of the two candidates, Lima Cavalcanti chose to see it instead as a vote of confidence and accordingly encouraged his reformist aides to press their controversial programs. These programs in themselves were enough to anger the traditionalists. But three other projects that became identified with the state administration though they were only indirectly linked to it especially drew their wrath: the Afro-Brazilian Congress; a planned commemoration of Recife's founding as the Dutch capital by (the Protestant) Maurice of Nassau; and the proposals for a series of studies of rural social conditions. In addition, at least one member of the Lima Cavalcanti cabinet participated briefly in the National Liberation Alliance (ANL), a small anti-Fascist popular front organization active nationally in mid-1935. Oddly, despite increasingly heated attacks from conservatives, Lima Cavalcanti

decided to take an extended vacation from the state.* He left his administration in the hands of Andrade Bezerra, a lay Catholic leader and a militant conservative, who fed the fire by attempting to punish left-leaning
state officials.

The outbreak of left-wing revolts in Natal, Recife, and Rio de Janeiro in
late November 1935 found the governor traveling in Europe. Recife's
three-day uprising was crushed when the defending forces succeeded in
isolating the rebels outside the center of the city, where they were
finished off by federal reinforcements sent from neighboring states.[21] The
would-be revolution sealed Lima Cavalcanti's political fate. Conservatives
castigated the administration for permissiveness and leftward leanings,
demanding (and receiving from interim state officials) guarantees that
Communists and progressives would be rooted out of the government.
Vargas turned again to Agamenon Magalhães, installing him as a watchdog over the state's affairs and setting him to document the anti–Lima
Cavalcanti case.[22]

As soon as the governor returned, the right-wing military commanders
of the State of Siege Commissions, which had been established in the
aftermath of the 1935 insurrections, began to harass him unmercifully,
undercutting his constitutional powers and forcing him to plead personally with Vargas for relief. Lima Cavalcanti seems to have been singled
out for punishment because of his inability to avoid the label of leftist
sympathizer and his stubborn habit of playing Old Republic–style gubernatorial politics, like Rio Grande do Sul's José Antônio Flôres da Cunha,
with whom Lima Cavalcanti and Juracy Magalhães of Bahia) frequently
conferred.

On November 10, 1937, the day of the promulgation of the Estado
Novo, Vargas formally removed Lima Cavalcanti from office. Shortly
thereafter he named Agamenon Magalhães as interventor. Magalhaes
contrasted sharply with his predecessor. Where Lima Cavalcanti was a
warm and courteous man, an elegant product of the plantocracy, his successor, with a reputation for ruthlessness, was called "the Mongol" by his

*Some opponents, including the editor of the *Jornal do Brasil*, Alexandre José Barbosa
Lima Sobrinho, referred to Lima Cavalcanti as "Carlos Cavalcante," a slur on his ancestry
(the Cavalcantes were allegedly an illegitimate branch of the Cavalcanti clan). (See, for
example, *O Estado*, April 6, 1934, p. 6.) The Left, meanwhile, attacked him as reactionary.
(See "O Estacismo redivivo," *Folha do Povo*, Nov. 19, 1935, p. 1; and *O Homem Livre*,
Sept. 15, 1934, p. 1.)

adversaries and "my political hatchet man" by Vargas.[23] Magalhães governed tensely, instilling fear among his subordinates. Of the Sertão lawyer (whose father had been a federal deputy in the early Republic), it was said that he never removed his hat, even when working, and that he boasted that he never forgave an enemy.

During the late 1920's Magalhães built a following as a defender of unconventional causes. Even before his defection to the Liberal Alliance from the Rosistas, he had attacked the Great Western as an instrument of economic exploitation. Though personally authoritarian, his early career reveals a decidedly populist strain, something that was to be found in no other Pernambucano politician save for José Mariano, a patrician with a devoted following among the less-affluent members of the Recife electorate. But unlike Mariano, Magalhães cared nothing for personal popularity. As a reward for his loyalty to Vargas and his distaste for traditional state politics, he was entrusted with Lima Cavalcanti's political execution as Brazil moved to the Right.

Magalhães recruited a number of political novices to his administration, few of them directly linked to the old elite. Many, however, were closely linked with the neo-orthodox wing of the Catholic Church. Indeed, it has been noted that probably nowhere else in Brazil was a state government so well identified with this group. Magalhães himself had prepared for the priesthood, and a strikingly high percentage of his aides belonged to the Congregação Mariana, and were influenced deeply by what has been called the "clerical fascism" of prewar Portugal, Spain, and France.*

With legislatures closed, partisan activities ceased. Moreover, where the political process had been relatively open before 1936, heavy censorship and the replacement of politicians by less-flamboyant bureaucrats served to withdraw the state government from public view. To some extent Magalhães used the weakened but surviving coronelismo structure to deal with interior municípios, but as the decade drew on, relations between the capital and the rural municípios became more and more regularized as the lengthening arm of government reached out to curtail the worst abuses of the coronéis and the depredations of the bandit gangs.

---

*Among them were some of his closest aides: Nilo Pereira, João Roma, Manoel Lubambo, Apolónio Sales, and Luis Delgado (*Arquivo da Congregação Mariana*). For the views of the Congregação's leader, the Jesuit Antônio Fernandes, see his *Jacques Maritain*.

Family clans continued to exercise strong influence, but the power that formerly accompanied control of local offices diminished as moderniza- tion shortened the effective distance to Recife.[24]

Political Structures

The Republic cast the new states adrift, forcing each to rely on its own tax base for revenue. Soaring income gave the State of São Paulo virtual autonomy from the central government until the Vargas era, but the other states were hard pressed to squeeze out income from their economies, though revenues did rise during the 1920's. In this context, Pernambuco's internal political battles might seem inconsequential given its limited ma- neuverability. But political hegemony within the state still brought with it control of patronage and such perquisites as the power to grant tax exemptions, determine railroad routes, and regulate fiscal and commer- cial affairs. The major structures of politics during the Republic—the po- litical parties, the electoral system, coronelismo—provided the vehicles through which this power was maintained.

A certain sameness underlay local political life under the Republic. For one thing, though the states adopted modern democratic structures, the closed nature of the political system served to mold the borrowed struc- tures into forms wholly different from the institutions of the countries from which they had been borrowed.[25] The limited flexibility built into the system of elite recruitment acted as a filter of sorts, and in the long run it preserved traditional values. Despite efforts by individuals to rec- ognize and treat social ills, an entrenched conservatism permeated politi- cal life, hostile to outside influences in spite of passing attention paid by intellectuals to foreign philosophical trends. This fear of change surfaced with a vengeance in the 1930's, but it had never receded far beneath the surface in earlier years.

Perhaps the most characteristic institution of the Republic was the free-wheeling state political party. But though Rosa e Silva's PRF, the strongest of all the state's political groupings, compared in terms of hierarchy and discipline with its southern counterparts, it was always de- pendent on a system of personal linkages. The small state police force, moreover, and the capacity of rival landowners and coronéis to raise pri- vate armies, weakened the state administration's control over the interior (and its needed ballot boxes). As a result of such obstacles, even Rosa e

Silva's machine survived only 15 years. The PRF no less than its several successors—the short-lived Dantas coalition, Estácio Coimbra's neo-Rosista bloc, and the opposition PD—was but a pale shadow of the machines in Rio Grande do Sul, São Paulo, and Minas. Like Bahia, Pernambuco was unable to achieve internal political stability, the prerequisite for a monolithic and successful state party.

The officeholders. Bacharéis in law or medicine filled most of the appointive and elective administrative posts of the late Empire and early Republic. On graduation, the young (twenty to twenty-two) bacharel received a nomination as public prosecutor (*promotor público*) or municipal judge. Before the end of the Empire it was quite normal for a young Recife law graduate to be appointed to a post in Santa Catarina, or Maranhão, or Amazonas. He usually returned home after several years, his apprenticeship having prepared him for entry into the political elite. Some bacharéis voluntarily followed the traditional pattern. Such was the case of Sérgio Loreto who, after graduating from the Recife Law School in 1892, went to Rio and then to the coastal State of Espírito Santo, where his brother's marriage ties gave him access to various political positions, and where eventually he was elevated to the federal bench. In 1922 he was brought back to Pernambuco as governor by President Artur Bernardes, who allowed him to transplant various relatives from Espírito Santo to local administrative posts.

Another well-traveled path to office reveals an important characteristic of the political environment of Pernambuco: cultural prestige, usually achieved through publication in newspapers or in one or more of Recife's many literary journals, often provided a stepping-stone to a political career. Recife's newspapers lionized cultural creativity, even in the most unsophisticated form. Membership in the state Academy of Letters or a law school chair guaranteed access to public jobs for writers, poets, historians, and educators. At worst it produced literary-political hacks. On the other hand, cultural figures in politics, if no better than others, were demonstrably no worse. To some degree the practice was a harmless variation of the patronage mechanism on which the public bureaucracy rested.

The electoral system. For voting purposes the state was divided into three electoral zones. (There were five to begin with, but they were consolidated in 1896 in order to allow the state machine to manage the vote more easily.) The first zone encompassed the capital and the northern

Zona da Mata to the Paraíba border; the second, the rest of the Mata and part of the Agreste; and the third, the sparsely populated western half of the state. The zones were divided into wards, or districts, each containing a roughly equal number of electors.[26] Recife's total number of wards grew from nine in 1882 to 37 in 1911 and 43 in 1930.

In the Old Republic, as in the late Empire, the franchise was limited to adult literate males (though as we shall shortly see, the literacy requirement was honored more often in the breach than in the observance, especially in the rural areas). Under the Empire a negligible 1 percent of males over twenty-one voted between 1881 and 1889; by 1930 the figure had risen to only 6 percent. Even after the vote was extended to women, the level of participation remained low; in 1945, for example, only 13 percent of the state's adult population cast ballots.

The impetus for women's suffrage in fact came from the Northeast, and more specifically from Rio Grande do Norte, whose gubernatorial candidate in 1927 included the vote for women in his platform. Since this violated the federal Constitution, his campaign promise may have been a purely cynical political move, but in any event, on winning the race, he had the state Constitution amended accordingly, and 15 women voted in the congressional elections held the following year. Though these votes were quickly annulled by the federal Senate's Electoral Commission as inconsistent with federal law, the rebuff provoked a national campaign that culminated in Vargas's granting women the vote in 1933.[27]

Since the key to political power under the Republic was electoral control, the state machine concentrated its efforts among eligible voters, paying scant attention to the disenfranchised mass of the population, urban and rural. The mechanics of the voting system fostered manipulation, though a semi-secret ballot was introduced by the 1881 Saraiva Law. To vote at all, a citizen's eligibility had to be certified by an election board, or *mesa*, a body invariably controlled by the incumbent political machine, which offered rewards for votes (in the form of small payments) and threatened partisans of the opposition with bodily harm. The would-be voter, moreover, was required to obtain the signature of the president of the local município council, to attest to three continuous years of local residence, and to show that he had paid local taxes. The federal Rosa e Silva Law, passed in 1904 under the patronage of the Pernambucan leader and later adopted by the state as well, ostensibly reformed the election-board procedure, but the old way of thwarting the opposition

TABLE 4.1
Voting for Governor and President in Pernambuco, 1894–1930

Year[a]	Governor	President
1894–95	27,400	20,735
1898–99	25,421	31,057
1902–3	35,521	37,334
1906–7	27,112	21,590
1910–11	31,568[b]	31,751[b]
1914–15	—	34,287
1918	—	28,311
1919	32,465	21,176
1922	39,916	40,846
1926	44,967	33,865
1930	58,507	72,082

SOURCE: State. Pernambuco, *Imprensa oficial; Jornal do Commercio* (Recife), June 6, 1922, pp. 2, 5; Lemos Filho, *Clã de Açúcar* (Rio, 1960), pp. 162–64. National. *Diário do Congresso*, 1894–1930.

[a] Until 1919 the state elected a governor a year after the presidential elections.

[b] Disputed results.

TABLE 4.2
Contested National and State Elections in Pernambuco, 1894–1930

Year	Office	Candidates	Official vote count	Percentage of vote
1910	President	Hermes da Fonseca	31,577	99%
		Rui Barbosa	174	1
1911[a]	Governor	Emídio Dantas Barreto	17,047	54%
		Francisco Rosa e Silva	14,521	46
1919	Governor	José Rufino Bezerra Cavalcanti	23,050	71%
		Emídio Dantas Barreto	9,415	29
1922[b]	Governor	José Henrique Carneiro da Cunha	25,093	62%
		Eduardo de Lima Castro	14,823	38
1922	President	Nilo Peçanha	39,624	98%
		Artur Bernardes	1,222	2
1930	President	Júlio Prestes	61,832[c]	87%
		Getúlio Vargas	10,015[c]	13

SOURCE: See Table 4.1.

[a] After federal intervention. These are the figures awarded the candidates by the federal authorities. Both camps claimed victory, but Rosa e Silva probably had the electoral majority by virtue of his machine's control of rural election districts.

[b] Sérgio Loreto imposed as governor by the Bernardes administration.

[c] Incomplete data.

parties was merely replaced by a new scheme to divide them by guaranteeing them token legislative representation. The measure had the desired effect. On the whole opposition leaders seemed content to accept the few seats offered to them rather than to contest the larger hold of the incumbent party on the political machinery.

Pernambucan voters cast their ballots for President of the Republic and for governor every four years, and periodically in between for three federal senators, 17 federal deputies, 15 state senators, and 30 state deputies. Between 1895 and 1922 about one-third of the state's registered voters went to the polls, and thereafter the figure rose to approximately one-half (see Table 4.1). The incumbent party supervised elections, counted ballots, and dominated the state's Electoral Court, the body with the final authority to validate or invalidate contested votes. When two or more candidates vied for office, each faction customarily issued detailed sets of statistics purporting to show a clear-cut margin of victory for its candidate.[28] Table 4.2 confirms that only a few elections were meaningful, and that contested gubernatorial elections were likely to end in federal intervention.

The coronéis. Since rural districts outweighed Recife in the total number of eligible voters, control of the rural vote virtually guaranteed electoral victory. Nearly every rural population center in Pernambuco was controlled either by a dominant family clan or by a single coronel. In contrast to various other states (such as Bahia and Ceará), Pernambuco's coronéis seem to have been satisfied with a limited political role. Once entrenched locally, a Pernambucan coronel rarely broke with the incumbent state political machine, though a prospective change in the state administration often set off violent struggles for succession between rival local factions.[29] Contested state elections, then, provided the most fertile stage for challenges to local power. In 1911 at least 23 Rosista coronéis were ousted by rivals riding the coattails of Dantas Barreto. But it took some doing in at least one case: the ousted chieftain led a band of several hundred armed followers into the backlands, where he waged pitched battles with the militia over a period of months before he finally accepted his fate.[30]

Urban politicians bestowed on the coronel personal patronage, the right to rule unchallenged within his domain, and political legitimacy in return for votes on demand. Through the 1920's government influence remained largely restricted to the coast. In this sense, the state party needed the coronel more than the coronel needed the politicians. The fact that Pernambuco's elongated shape and poor transportation network forced the various state administrations to concede near total license to their coronel surrogates may explain in part why its coronéis never united to challenge the ruling political machine.

As Eul-Soo Pang has shown for Bahia, not all coronéis were rural men-on-horseback, though the image of the rough-and-ready backlandsman who preferred (in the phrase of a famous Pernambucano coronel, Chico Heráclio of Limoeiro) his firearms and women "in virginal condition" still survives in Brazil to this day.[31] Some Pernambuco coronéis were merchants or bacharéis or even bureaucrats (like Honorato Marinho Falcão, of Ouricuri, who was a state tax agent). Many rural fiefdoms were controlled by kin groups (like the Vilelas in Bom Conselho) rather than one strong-armed individual. In Recife urban political bosses carried out the same functions as rural coronéis, though they were subject to closer scrutiny. After 1930 some coronéis allowed themselves to be awarded federal posts as new regional agencies reached into the interior. Publicly, the coronéis seemed to be content with the favors and show of affection they got from state party officials, who occasionally honored them at boisterous political banquets in the capital. The obituary of an Agreste coronel in 1902 hints at the nature of his relationship with the PRF. He had been, the newspaper said, "very much of a party man, but not much of a politician."[32] Behind the scenes, however, the coronéis and their clients fought tenaciously for economic concessions involving patronage, public works, tax exemptions, and financial aid.

The coronel manipulated electoral activity in his own município; often, local electoral boards received petitions for enfranchisement in the coronel's own house.[33] If tallies proved disappointing, ballot boxes were lost or burned; coercion and bribery were the order of the day. Under coronel rule, voter lists lengthened far beyond what the most credulous could expect the rural areas to yield in the way of legally qualified voters. By 1910 most municípios had between 400 and 1,000 electors; since only some 5,000 voters all told cast ballots in Recife, the balance of victory clearly rested with a dozen or so key municípios.[34] In 1911 fraud produced such lopsided margins as 610 to 0 for Rosa e Silva in Triunfo, and 934 to 18 in Aguas Belas—and no results at all in Bom Conselho and Belmonte, where the coronéis' henchmen shot up the town and prevented balloting from taking place.[35]

By the 1920's the increased complexities of rural economic life, fueled by improved transportation links, produced changing conditions to which the coronéis had to adapt. No longer could one coronel or clan hope to wield sufficient influence to maintain the traditional kind of local domination. Some coronéis adjusted to the times, sending their sons to law school or to the state Senate, or acquiring respectable businesses in order to forge a new power base. Others, in more remote regions, lost their grasp on power with the virtual federal military occupation of the backlands after 1930. On the whole, only a decade after northeastern coronéis had helped pursue the Prestes Column and sent contingents of jagunços to fight for the coronel Horácio de Matos in Bahia against the coastal-based state government, coronelismo as an institution lost most of its traditional trappings, though it remained a major element in rural life.[36]

Political violence. The violence that permeated the political system was not limited to the backlands, but overshadowed urban life as well. By 1900 the capital of the state had earned the label "bloody Recife," recalling the brutality of the 1890's and foreshadowing the bloodshed of coming decades. The level of violence was linked to political instability, subsiding during the stable Rosa e Silva period, and peaking again in 1911 and during the second half of the 1920's.[37] A high level of civil disturbances and violence, as Peter H. Smith notes, does not necessarily imply that a system is breaking down. In the case of Pernambuco, as elsewhere, it may suggest that it was functioning well.[38]

From the earliest days of the sugar economy senhores de engenhos employed mercenaries for protection and intimidation. As time passed coronéis and landowners adopted the practice.[39] In the cities men of influence employed *capoeiras*, black or mulatto bodyguards so skilled in dispatching their victims that their deadly form of brawling evolved into a ballet-like form of folk art.[40] Governors used the police and the civil guard to protect themselves, punish opponents, and neutralize the potentially hostile federal troops. Police brutality persisted throughout the Republic; after the electoral defeat of an incumbent administration, more than one police chief fled the state to escape retaliation.

The first governor of Pernambuco to use more than the customary amount of force was Barbosa Lima. Soon after he was installed, he postponed scheduled elections, dissolved the município councils, and stood by while cavalry troops savagely beat unruly student protestors. Opposition leaders—who themselves were known for their use of capangas—

were set upon mercilessly. An anti-Floriano uprising in the interior of the state was put down with bloodshed by a battalion of militiamen.[41]

National political events in 1893 gave the governor a pretext for intensifying the repression. Barbosa Lima himself toyed with the idea of falling in with the plan of the anti-Floriano forces to lead the northern states in secession, but he changed his mind; once he had picked his side, and conceivably to divert suspicion from himself, he turned on his would-be collaborators and arrested them for treason, sentencing them without public trial.

When genuine threats to his own rule developed, Barbosa Lima dealt with the miscreants harshly. Even the leaders of the political opposition were not immune from imprisonment; others were driven into exile. José Maria de Albuquerque Melo, the former president of the state Chamber of Deputies, cowered in hiding for more than a year, maintaining a desperate and anguished correspondence under assumed names with friends on the outside. In some of his letters he prophesied his own death at the hands of Barbosa Lima.[42]

José Maria was murdered shortly after he emerged from hiding under the promise of a general amnesty. His assassins, three police officers, were absolved by a state court despite fierce protests from dissidents. Further violence followed, including assaults on journalists, beatings, alleged torture, and murder. In the end, Barbosa Lima went so far in his strong-arm methods that he alienated even his allies, with the result that on leaving office he was politically finished in Recife, and spent the rest of his long career as a federal senator.[43]

His successors, Rosa e Silva's puppet governors, resorted to less blatant tactics and left repression to the police.[44] But the heated 1911 election campaign saw extensive terrorism on both sides. Recife fell under martial law for several days as businessmen closed their stores, the port shut down, troops searched pedestrians for hidden weapons, and federal reinforcements entered the city.[45]

Even after the return of one-party control in 1915 incidents of political violence continued. Victims insulted one governor by charging that he deliberately sent his capangas to attack his enemies' houses when he knew that the head of the family would be absent.[46] The 1922 gubernatorial campaign repeated the pattern of 1911, bringing federal intervention after widespread disorders in Recife, which included the dynamiting of public buildings. Opposition newspapers ran lists of politicians earmarked for assassination, even naming those who should be held responsible if the murders actually took place.[47]

A specialized vocabulary emerged out of all this: the *voto de cabresto*, or "halter vote," the vote of the herd, replaced after a time by the *voto-mercadoria*, a vote exchanged for a pair of shoes, a jacket, or a bottle of 180-proof cachaça; the *fecha-comércio*, a hired brawler and provoker of fights; and the *veado*, among other connotations, a candidate for murder.[48] Through the entire Republican period, normal practice included the beating of suspected lawbreakers to obtain confessions, political kidnapping, preventive arrests without charges, unannounced searches for arms, and the intimidation of political opponents, including the burning of homes and newspapers and the smashing of presses and printing machinery.[49]

In Recife political violence mostly affected members of the opposition and dissidents. But in the backlands violence encompassed daily life. It appeared with suddenness—without warning and without mercy. Most rural caboclos remained stoical, learning by necessity to move slowly to anger. But conditions pushed some men into the brigand bands that roamed the Sertão during the entire period of the Republic, terrifying local populations until officials mobilized sufficiently against them to hunt them down, one by one.

Already by the 1850's the devastating impact of the droughts on the growing population of the interior had begun to transform some of the free rural poor into bandits. In the beginning any bands that formed usually dispersed after the drought conditions eased. But Republican politics gave impetus to the formation of permanent *cangaceiro* bands. Local bosses hired their leaders, and competing family groups kept them on their payroll to enforce their control over marketplaces and to intimidate the caboclos who lived on their land.[50]

Coronéis frequently took advantage of their control of patronage to appoint capangas as police officials. This cynical practice, as well as the fact that militia troops were usually impoverished jagunços, contributed to the brutality of rural law enforcement. So many atrocities were attributed to soldiers supposedly in pursuit of bandits that some courageous town officials asked for the garrisons to be removed.[51] One rural inhabitant around 1930 is quoted on the matter: "I much prefer dealing with bandits than with the police, . . . a bunch of 'dog killers' who came from the capital with the idea that all the backlandsmen protect criminals. They think we know all the escape routes. So their chief object is to get confessions at all costs. If we say we don't know, they beat us. If we tell them, they still beat us, because that proves we have been tied up with the bandits."[52] After the 1930 revolution, tenente-led police detachments were paid daily wages and kept in line under tight discipline to placate fearful rural inhabitants.[53]

Individual cangaceiro leaders became, to use E. J. Hobsbawm's term, "ambiguous heroes," feared for their cruelty but respected for their boldness, secretly admired for their ability to flaunt their independence from government authority. Popular legends enveloped the most notorious: Antônio Silvino, the scourge of the sertões of Pernambuco and Paraíba between 1896 and 1914, who acquired a reputation for social justice; and Lampião (Virgolino Ferreira da Silva), the unredeemable, who took over where Antônio left off and was said to be motivated by the devil himself.

When not employed as mercenaries (Lampião himself was granted temporary amnesty when federal officials commissioned him to pursue the Prestes Column), cangaceiros systematically raided towns and ranches, sometimes opening jails and punishing landowners, but mostly attacking indiscriminately, sacking homes and stores. During Lampião's 20 years as a cangaceiro leader, he and his men were said to have murdered some 1,000 persons and to have fought more than 200 battles in six states.[54]

The cangaceiros knew the backlands intimately, using it as their base for forays against towns not 100 kilometers from the coast. In the end, their daring proved their undoing, impelling the northeastern state governments, normally jealous of their prerogatives and isolated from one another politically, to cooperate in hunting them down. Lampião, the most elusive of all the cangaceiros, was finally captured and killed in 1938 after a relentless pursuit from Ceará to Bahia.

Few of the inhabitants of the coast would have blamed urban lawlessness on social causes; most would doubtless have ascribed it to shiftlessness among the lower classes, or a like reason. But some northeasterners viewed the rural banditry in a more charitable—and more perceptive—light. João Pessôa, the Liberal Alliance's ill-fated vice-presidential candidate, reminded a Recife newspaper interviewer that the "great majority of bandits exist as a result of local political conditions, buffeted by calamity." "Banditry," he warned, "arises from the long-standing vices of the political system itself."[55]

Not only did banditry arise out of the violence of northeastern life; in the long run it acted as a catalyst for the decay of the "long-standing vices" of the patriarchal system in the rural interior. In fact, little of substance distinguished cangaceiro violence from the "legitimate" forms of coercion associated with rural life in Brazil. The problem of Lampião and his ilk was not that their values clashed with those of their enemies, but that their enemies were able to use the machinery of justice against them, since society branded them as outlaws.[56] The decline of coronelismo after 1930 accelerated the monopolization of violence in the hands of the state apparatus. The cangaceiro bands themselves acted as shifting poles of armed power within the sparsely populated wastelands from Ceará to Bahia. Organized as clans (Lampião rode with three of his brothers, his brother-in-law, and assorted compadres, along with all their wives), the cangaceiros were a distinct elite, in contrast to the mass of individual desperados who were recruited as the need arose. But the capture and death of Lampião and his band marked the passing of the heyday of the cangaceiro. As in other spheres—the eclipse of the coronéis, for example—the increasing complexity of rural life and the penetration of state and federal authority shrank the effective distance between the coast and the interior.

Two principal hypotheses emerge from this overview. First, a layer of society that was internally divided but essentially similar in outlook remained in power continuously for several reasons. These included, most conspicuously, the failure of political divisions to alter the social or economic structures that preserved the cohesiveness of the elite. Yet internal tensions remained sufficiently strong to block the formation of a resilient state machine, a circumstance that hindered Pernambuco's national role. Elite positions may have been interchangeable, but the residue of bitterness prevented political unity.

Second, the high level of fraud, intimidation, and violence should be seen not as evidence of political instability, but rather as a sign of the system's capacity for survival. The manipulation by officials of the constitutional façade—the campaign oratory, the rhetoric, the pomp and ceremony as substitutes for substantive ideological issues—provided window dressing for outside consumption, though the Brazilians would have been dismayed to learn that foreign diplomats ridiculed their electoral behavior and its accompanying "chicanery and violence."[57]

These two facets of the system were in fact simply interdependent parts of the same whole. The elite's ability to keep power out of the hands of those who might have genuinely threatened the social order, and its reliance on force to block legitimate dissidence and unorthodox political behavior at once suffused society with political conflict and made the system work.[58] The equilibrium broke down only briefly when cleavages within the elite set one faction against the other.

For the population at large, the presence of institutionalized violence posed an ominous deterrent to the organization of militant associations or other socially dangerous activities. Apart from the sporadic attacks on journalists, the mistreatment and arrest of opposition politicians during the pre-PRF period, and the occasional political assassinations, most violence was not directed at members of the elite but rather took the form of day-to-day coercion and generalized police brutality. The system tolerated opposition as long as it remained harmless. To be sure, the lack of libel laws and the intensity of personal feuds prompted mercurial exchanges. An editorial in the venerable *Diário de Pernambuco* in 1910 called State Senator Gonçalves Ferreira Júnior a "coward . . . a human feces . . . an alcoholic, a defective epilectic."[59] Yet factionalism itself threatened no functional change. Most political opposition remained ritualistic. Politics provided rewards: public jobs for the well connected; shoes, clothing, cash, and liquor for the poor who could vote.

Lawrence Stone reminds us that social stability is often "an illusion created by the slowness of change and the extraordinary stability of class character."[60] Conditions in the Northeast did change as the Republican era progressed, as society became more complex, differentiating into an urban, commercial world ever more dependent on the larger world outside. But the genius of the regional elite was its ability to absorb rising and talented individuals into its ranks—lawyers (the bacharéis), merchants, successful administrators—without damage to its traditional value system.[61] The growth of federal power, moreover, benefited the state elite by tightening the reins of social control, especially in the rural interior, where the twin phenomena of banditry and millenarianism played lesser roles after the late 1930's.[62] Even the Estado Novo, blandly authoritarian in its corporatist form, did not redistribute power. It merely spurred the elite to alter the form, but not the substance, of the political process.

The photo collage contains the following labels:

- 1891 — Dez.ʳ José Antonio Corrêa da Silva
- 1915 — 1919 — Dr. Manoel Antonio Pereira Borba
- 1892 — 1896 — Dr. Alexandre José Barbosa Lima
- 1911 — 1915 — General Emygdio Dantas Barreto
- 1919 — 1923 — Dr. José Rufino Bezerra Cavalcanti
- 1896 — 1899 — Dr. Joaquim Correa de Araujo
- 1908 — 1911 — Dr. Herculano Bandeira de Mello
- 1900 — 1904 — Dr. Antonio Gonçalves Ferreira
- 1904 — 1908 — Dez.ʳ Segismundo Antonio Gonçalves

1. Governors of Pernambuco, 1891–1923. Counterclockwise from top left: José Antônio Correia da Silva, Alexandre José Barbosa Lima, Joaquim Correia de Araujo, Antônio Gonçalves Ferreira, Sigismundo Gonçalves, Herculino Bandeira, Emídio Dantas Barreto, and Manoel Borba. Center: José Rufino Bezerra Cavalcanti. Correia da Silva (1891) was only an acting governor; he filled in for the Baron of Lucena, who was removed from office by Marshal Deodoro da Fonseca. José Rufino Bezerra Cavalcanti, whose tenure is shown here as 1919–23, died in office, in March 1922. The lighthouse at the top was the official state symbol for a time.

2. Recife, c. 1900. One of the iron bridges linking the Santo Antônio district with the mainland.

3. The *casa grande* of a Mata sugar plantation.

4. Francisco de Assis Rosa e Silva, the dominant figure in Pernambucan politics in the first two decades of the Old Republic.
5 (above right). Epitácio Pessôa, the only northeasterner to be elected to the presidency of Brazil (1918–22).
6 (opposite). "Coronel" José Pessôa de Queiroz, a usineiro, merchant, and banker who played a major role in Recife society and in opposition politics.

7. Carlos de Lima Cavalcanti (center), interventor of Pernambuco from 1930 to 1937. He is flanked by his brother Caio (left) and President Getúlio Vargas.

8. Offices of Lima Cavalcanti's *Diário da Manhã*, the state's leading opposition newspaper in the late 1920's.

9. The Recife Law School, alma mater of most of the Northeast's officeholding elite until 1930.

10. A family home of the type commonly found in the rural Zona da Mata and Agreste. The walls are mud poured over a wooden frame.

11. The sociologist and historian Gilberto Freyre.

12. Doctor Ulisses Pernambucano.

13. Sons of agricultural workers. The three dark-skinned boys are *caboclos*, the group of mixed African, Indian, and European origin that forms the mass of rural workers in the Northeast.

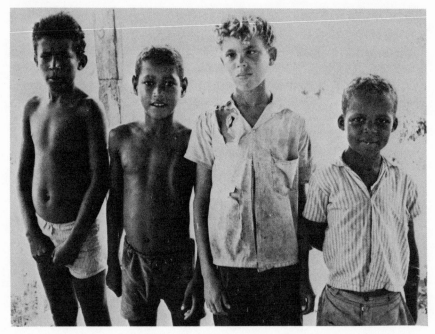

CHAPTER FIVE

The Political Elite

UNDER THE Empire the rural aristocracy routinely treated political offices as their personal domain. The old-line colonial dynasties—the Cavalcanti de Albuquerques and a few dozen other family networks—filled a fair share of the important positions themselves and saw that the rest were filled by men of their persuasion.[1] Typically such surrogates not only shared the convictions of their patrons but made their way to political fortune through marriage or business connections with them. For example, João Alfredo, the last Conservative minister of the Empire, first attained political influence through marriage into the Rego Barros clan; and as we have seen, Rosa e Silva's political star ascended after he married the daughter of a viscount.

As the Empire drew to a close, the tendency of the aristocracy to let others shoulder the duties of office became more pronounced.[2] In their retreat from personal participation, however, they took care to see that power did not fall into the wrong hands, demanding degrees from institutions of higher education that were deliberately kept small and select. The bacharel system thus became the means by which political recruitment was kept under tight control. At the center of this process, the single most important source of political recruits, was the Recife Law School, through whose doors passed seven of every ten members of the state's political elite between 1889 and 1937. These men, in turn, fully understood and accepted their role, satisfied to preserve the status quo and to operate under a system in which the plantocracy continued to exercise seigneurial power but not seigneurial responsibility.[3]

Composition of the Elite

Under these circumstances, though the base from which the political leaders were drawn was gradually broadened, the Pernambucan elite remained, like the elite of Minas, homogeneous and closed.* Kinship continued to be an important key to position. Fully 45 percent of the personnel on whom information was available ($n = 192$) were related either directly or by marriage to at least one other member of the state's elite, to the political elite of another state, or to the more narrowly defined Imperial elite. †

Pernambuco's relatively high percentage (12) of parentela ties to other states graphically illustrates the closely knit web of northeastern clan politics; Minas and São Paulo, in contrast, registered only 4 percent and 1 percent, respectively, in such ties. In the upper echelons of the elite, parentela links were even more visible. Excluding those men who were imposed from outside through federal intervention, nearly all of Pernambuco's governors shared identifiable clan links within the state. Furthermore, almost half of *all* of the governors boasted kinship with Imperial figures, nearly twice Minas's percentage, even though both states yielded close to identical results for the family-tie variable.

The interlocking nature of the elite becomes even more striking if one also takes into account close business associations. On the double criteria of service on the board of directors of the same firm and kinship, for example, I have found at least 60 men interlinked in one network.[4] Many more ties undoubtedly existed between individuals, particularly in the area of business connections, where prudence called for discretion.

An even more vivid measure of the homogeneity of the elite is found in the level and type of education of its members. Fewer than 6 percent ($n = 193$) lacked university degrees in a state where even by official claims at least 80 percent of the population was illiterate in 1940, and most of these men were of the generation born before 1869. Table 5.1

* The elite is here defined as in the parallel studies on Minas and São Paulo by John Wirth and Joseph Love. Details of our quantitative study are discussed in Appendix A, "A Note on Elites." A brief list of the almost 100 variables used to record the elite's characteristics, including values by state and the composite values, also appears in this appendix. The analysis was based on the use of an SPSS program (version five).

† Republican-era elite ties are defined as kinship through first cousin (consanguineal or affinitive). A tie to the Imperial elite (limited to senators or titleholders of the status of baron and above) takes in both relatives through first cousin and direct descendants through grandson.

TABLE 5.1

Education and Occupations of the Political Elite of Pernambuco

(Percent)

Category	Generation 1 (born before 1869)	Generation 2 (born 1869–88)	Generation 3 (born 1889 and after)
EDUCATION			
Bacharel degree	88%	86%	64%
Law	85	74	53
Medicine	3	12	11
Other university degree [a]	10	3	31
Secondary education or less	2	11	5
OCCUPATION [b]			
Liberal professions	81%	77%	73%
Commerce and industry	18	28	24
Military	5	2	8
Engineering	6	0	22
Clergy	1	2	5
Agriculture	17	21	19

[a] Men whose university careers stopped short of a degree are included in the secondary-education category.
[b] Multiple careers account for totals above 100%.

shows how thoroughly the bacharel system fed the political system with leaders. We observe also that the overwhelming majority of the bacharéis were lawyers. As I noted earlier, a remarkably high proportion of the elite—71 percent—came out of the Recife Law School; another 5 percent had law degrees earned either in part or entirely elsewhere. The brightest graduates of the Recife Law School competed for the school's coveted teaching chairs, creating in effect a selection process based in part on patronage but also on merit, a *carrière aux talents*. More than one-fourth of the elite population had taught at the law faculty itself or at one of its preparatory schools in the course of their careers.

Many physicians also gravitated to public employment, sometimes dividing their time between their medical practices and their public posts, sometimes abandoning medicine altogether. A few, including Amaury de Medeiros and Ulisses Pernambucano, forged careers in the field of public health—a field, as we have seen, in which the state deserves credit for innovation despite generally low per capita health expenditures.

As the table shows, some non-bacharéis did manage to make their way into the elite, especially as time went along. But locally the law school remained the premier training ground for the would-be politician. Pernambuco's agronomy school, for example, was always treated as an educational stepchild, and the engineering faculty graduated only 327 students between 1894 and 1937, 97 of whom came from neighboring states.[5] For much of our period, men in these specialties were largely closed out of the elite. Nor did persons trained in out-of-state institutions fare much better, and in this case time did not bring any improvement: roughly the same percentage of officeholders in the third political generation were schooled in Pernambuco as in the first.[6]

As this suggests, geography also contributed greatly to the elite's homogeneity. It is not just that the majority of officeholders were born in the state; 15 percent in fact were not (making the Pernambucanos slightly less insular than the Mineiros, with 13 percent out-of-state births, and slightly less open than the Paulistas, with 19 percent). What is significant is that most of the native sons were from the Mata. The Agreste and the Sertão, with almost half of the state's population, furnished less than a tenth of its political leaders.* This, plus the fact that most of the out-of-staters were from the satellite bloc, demonstrates the extent to which recruitment continued to draw on regional family clan networks. The coastal plantocracy, after all, spread its dynastic presence as far away as Maranhão and Pará.

Not a few sons of well-established families in the Northeast entered political life via Recife. For some the city was merely a way-station on the road to position. A notable example is Epitácio Pessôa, President of the Republic from 1919 to 1922, who came to Recife as a secondary school student and began his career as a public prosecutor and professor at the law school before moving on to Rio de Janeiro in the early 1890's. Those who remained typically found their success by drawing on their existing ties with the leading families or by forging new ones through law school contacts or advantageous marriages.

Where a man came from, then, played a considerable role in his political prospects. Another equally important credential was nationality. Only eight of the 276 officeholders in my group were from immigrant families (including those with just one foreign-born parent), and only two were naturalized Brazilians. Indeed, there were only a few men (4 percent) with non-Portuguese surnames (compared with nearly 10 percent in the Paulista elite). The small list included the journalist Thomé Gibson; lawyer João Peretti, who, after serving in Estácio Coimbra's state cabinet,

---

*The dominance of Recife is striking. After Recife (72 percent) came Barreiros (4 percent), Caruarú and Escada (3 percent each), Nazaré and Goiana (2 percent), and a handful of different municípios, mostly with only one or two members.

moved to Paris, where his father had studied medicine; and the Lundgren brothers, sons of immigrants who became, in effect, urban coronéis, carving their own município, Paulista, out of Olinda in the 1930's. Others on the list were Manoel Lubambo, who took his surname from Zona da Mata slang, and Samuel Hardman, presumably from a family of German descent, who married into the Cavalcanti de Albuquerque clan.

As might be expected, the political elite included no one from the working class, though two workers were sent to the short-lived national congress in 1934 as "class" deputies. It is true that the system was flexible enough to absorb a few sons of shopkeepers and even orphans granted scholarships to the Ginásio Pernambucano, but these were clearly exceptions. Probably at the most a dozen members of the political elite had risen from relative economic hardship. There were no women in the group and no men publicly identified as mulattoes or pardos, though some whispered behind Lubambo's back that his physiognomy matched his African-sounding surname.

In sum, the political elite was hardly more representative under the Republic than it had been under the Empire. Despite the broadening of the base from which the leaders were drawn and despite outward signs that the political system was opening (viz., a more responsive electoral system, growing newspaper circulations, urban social differentiation), it is clear that the plantocracy retained its control of the reins of power.

Yet were the political leaders of Minas and São Paulo so much more representative, after all? An examination of the composite elite ($n = 754$) from the three states certainly reveals more similarities than differences. Its members were almost invariably Brazilian-born; few were sons of immigrants, and virtually none had foreign wives. Kinship ties were fully as important in the South as in Pernambuco; 49 percent of the composite elite were related to at least one other member of the same or a parallel political elite, with virtually no variation among the individual state populations. Three-quarters of the (adjusted) composite elite were bacharéis, and the occupational breakdown in the three groups was roughly the same, with lawyers proportionately far out front, followed by journalists and educators. Of course, in this case as in many others, we do find disparities. Five members of Pernambuco's elite, for example, were priests, whereas São Paulo's had none. Similarly, this elite included more military men than the elites of the Center-South. But on the whole the composite elite was essentially as homogeneous as the separate state elites.

Career Patterns

In an earlier chapter we discussed the reasons for the failure of the state's Historical Republicans to take political power after 1889. The following figures, comparing the political affiliation of the elites of Pernambuco, Minas, and São Paulo, are a good explanation of that failure in themselves.*

Affiliation	Pernambuco	Minas	São Paulo
Monarchist	77.6%	50.6%	49.5%
Historical Republican	22.5%	49.4%	50.5%

Pernambuco's political elite, as we see, included many more holdovers from the Empire than the elites of the other two states, contributing to the Northeast's reputation for conservatism and resistance to change.

The three elites also differed in other important ways. For example, a far greater proportion of the Pernambucanos held office outside the state (17 percent, compared with 7 percent for the Paulistas and 6 percent for the Mineiros). This was due in good part to Pernambuco's close ties to the states of the satellite bloc. The Pernambucanos tended also, as did the Mineiros, to have established their professional careers in the Federal District: almost 18 percent of the Pernambucanos and 15 percent of the Mineiros had done so, compared with a mere 1 percent of the Paulistas. The Pernambucanos and the Mineiros likewise tended to follow a similar career pattern in their legislative service in the Federal District, as the following figures show:

Legislative experience	Pernambuco	Minas	São Paulo
Federal	55.7%	51.2%	31.7%
State	30.9%	47.4%	48.6%

Once again, the Paulistas followed a decidedly different pattern. One possible explanation for the divergency is that state service may have been given greater importance in São Paulo because the stakes were higher there.

For all three of the elites, however, the state capital was the principal political base. In the case of the Pernambucanos, 67 percent ($n = 199$)

---

*The tabulation covers only those officeholders who were at least age 20 when the Republic was proclaimed. Historicals include eleventh-hour Republicans (see Appendix A).

operated out of Recife. Most of the rest, as we might guess, had their base in other parts of the Mata; only 8 percent of the men stood for election or otherwise served somewhere in the Agreste or the Sertão. Still more evidence, if any is needed, of the unrepresentative nature of the political system.

The system was also peculiarly unrepresentative in quite a different way. From the occupational breakdown presented in Table 5.1, we see that in a predominantly agricultural and export-oriented society, the overwhelming majority of the political leaders were drawn from the liberal professions, not from the state's principal interest groups. The Pernambucan group had fewer representatives from the state's economic elite than São Paulo, and in the case of the industrialists and bankers, fewer even than Minas.

Analysis of the data on office groupings by the sequence of positions held turns up some other interesting differences between Pernambuco and the states of the Center-South. In Table 5.2 we see that three-quarters of the Pernambucanos held only one elite position during their careers, as opposed to about half in both Minas and São Paulo. In part this reflects the tendency in the early years of the Republic for youths from the satellite bloc and other northeastern states to commence their political careers in Pernambuco upon graduation from the Recife Law School and then move on. Also, the often abrupt changes in political fortunes in the absence of a strong state machine before and after Rosa e Silva encouraged turnover in office. It is possible, too, that Pernambucanos were more prone to seek public posts as sinecures, since opportunities in the private sector were presumably more limited than in the dynamic South.

Looking at the careers of the 25 percent of the Pernambucanos who did hold two or more jobs (Table 5.3), one finds no clear pattern in the sequence of the posts held except that appointment to federal-level ministerial positions tended to come only after a man had served in at least one other, ostensibly less prestigious office; few Pernambucanos were plucked out of the private sector and rewarded with high-level federal patronage. The comparable data from Minas and São Paulo indicate that in both places state cabinet members tended to move on to the governorship or federal service, whereas in Pernambuco a position in the state cabinet was something of an end in itself. In all three states senior politicians were more likely to hold top positions in their state legisla-

TABLE 5.2
Percent of State Elite with Tenure in More Than One Post

State	First post	Second post	Third post	Fourth post	Fifth post	Sixth post
Pernambuco	100	25	8	3	1	1
Minas	100	42	21	11	6	3
São Paulo	100	46	22	14	9	6

TABLE 5.3
Office Groupings of State Elite by Sequence of Positions Held
(Adjusted frequencies in percentages)

Office group	First post	Second post	Third post	Fourth post	Fifth post	Sixth post
State						
S1	4.0%	5.7%	4.8%	0.0%	0.0%	0.0%
S2	26.1	28.4	28.7	22.2	25.0	0.0
S3	15.6	18.6	19.1	11.1	0.0	50.0
S4	16.0	17.1	14.3	11.1	25.5	0.0
S5	4.0	4.3	4.8	0.0	0.0	0.0
S6	19.0	14.3	14.3	44.4	0.0	0.0
Federal						
F1	0.0	0.0	0.0	0.0	0.0	0.0
F2	2.0	4.2	9.6	11.1	0.0	50.0
F3	4.4	1.4	0.0	0.0	25.0	0.0
F4	4.0	1.4	0.0	0.0	25.0	0.0
F5	4.0	4.3	4.8	0.0	0.0	0.0
All federal	14.4	11.3	14.4	11.1	50.0	50.0
All state except S6	65.7	74.4	71.3	44.5	50.0	50.0
Absolute number in each group	276	70	21	9	4	2

S1. Governor.
S2. Secretaries.
S3. Other state executive posts (prefect, police chief, top administrator, bank president, lieutenant governor).
S4. State legislative posts (president of the senate, president of the chamber, majority leader).
S5. President, state court.
S6. Political opposition.
F1. President of the Republic.
F2. Minister.
F3. Other federal executive posts (president of the Bank of Brazil, etc.).
F4. Congressional posts.
F5. Supreme court.

tures, though senior Mineiros more often attained top federal legislative posts. In Minas and São Paulo the upper-level judiciary posts usually went to men with little or no past history of high position; most of the presidents of their state courts were first-time officeholders, and most of the Supreme Court justices from those states came to the court in their second post. In Pernambuco, by contrast, these positions were as often as not the appointee's third post, possibly indicating a more politicized judiciary there.

There is no great disparity among the three groups in the age at which elite status was attained. The Mineiros and Pernambucanos, at about forty-two, were slightly under the combined median (43.3), with the Paulistas lagging behind at forty-five. However, in Pernambuco the chances for early political success were considerably better. A full 38 percent of the officeholders had attained their elite status by age forty, and almost 80 percent by age fifty. The very young man also had a better chance of entering the elite in Pernambuco; 17 percent of the group had achieved high position before reaching the age of thirty, compared with 5 percent for Minas and only 4 percent for São Paulo. One Pernambucano had joined the elite at the age of nineteen, and two others at the age of twenty.

To a great extent, however, political success in Pernambuco owed as much to changes in the political climate as anything else. In times of relativer calm there was little turnover in the upper levels of government, and the chances of an appointment to an important post were considerably reduced. Thus, whereas a relatively high percentage of newcomers entered the elite in the turbulent first decade of the Republic, the rate fell off sharply with the restoration of order in the Rosa e Silva period. This same pattern was repeated in the subsequent years, with the rate rising and falling in keeping with the march of political events.

Once admitted to the elite, officeholders were likely to be as economically insecure as they were politically insecure, for the state was far from being a generous employer. Like France, where in 1900 civil servants earned little more than laborers,[7] Pernambuco paid all its public employees poorly, officials and administrators included. A police *delegado* in 1898 earned only twice the annual wage of his building's doorman (1:500$), and the chief of police only six times as much. A *juíz de direito* in Recife made 7:200$, 20 percent more than his rural counterparts but only 70 percent more than a scribe in the office of the state Supreme Court.[8] But unlike France, the state never developed a full-fledged civil servant class that became a refuge for security seekers. It was the power afforded by public office, not job security and certainly not the salary, that encouraged men to seek public employment even at high personal cost.

Many members of the elite, in consequence, had to scramble to support their families, dividing their time between outside jobs and their government post. Some were forced to carry on a frenzied schedule of remunerative activities, teaching or practicing law or medicine on the side, writing articles for a local newspaper, and perhaps sitting on a corporate board or two as well. Others were less hard pressed, but few could live on their governmental salary alone. On average the Pernambucanos held two positions besides their government post; the average for the Mineiros was even higher, though not by much, and the Paulistas' average approached three. The most commonly overlapped careers were law, journalism, and education.

The Three Generations

Though in broad outline Pernambuco's elite remained largely consistent over time, Table 5.4 shows that the years did bring a few significant changes; the eclipse of bacharelism, for example, as evidenced in the gradual decline in the proportion of magistrates and the increased representation of the engineers. Such other groups as industrialists, priests, and career military officers also made gains at the expense of the bacharéis.[9] There were also some geographic shifts over time. As we see, Recife's domination as a political base dropped off slightly, though barely enough for statistical significance. More important, though the interior continued to be grossly underrepresented, the share of officeholders from the Agreste and the Sertão increased by 14 percentage points, from 5 percent to 19 percent.[10]

Some of the cross-generational data suggest a modest tendency toward insularity and provincialism, notably the continuing low percentage of officeholders born outside the state, and more strikingly, the dramatic drop in the percentage of men with out-of-state career experience.[11] The last, however, is easily explained by the significant number of holdovers in the first generation, who by Imperial practice would have been rotated routinely from one province to another. Furthermore, the proportion of

TABLE 5.4
The Three Generations of the State Elite by Select Variables
(Percent)

Variable	Generation 1	Generation 2	Generation 3	Statistical significance
Out-of-state career experience, professional or political	62%	22%	16%	.0030
Foreign ties, including birth, study, and career experience	23	41	46	.0152
Foreign residence alone	13	22	37	.0091
Commercial agricultural interests (*fazendeiro*)	18	21	19	.0841
Magistrate	29	16	5	.0063
Bacharel degree (law or medicine)	88	84	64	.0065
Engineer	6	0	22	.0004
Recife base	72	64	57	.0527

men with foreign ties doubled, so that in this respect, at least, the elite was in greater touch with the outside world.

Despite the relatively constant level of the fazendeiro group, the general trend points to a shift of the region's economic locus from the Mata to the capital, and from a simple plantation agriculture to a more complex agro-commercial-industrial base.

The events of 1930 brought some modifications in the state political elite but few substantial changes.[12] There were fewer bacharéis in the post-1930 group, and, as might be expected given the nature of the Liberal Alliance revolution, more career military officers. The Mata, as noted, lost some ground to the interior. The most significant change was that substantially fewer of the men had served in the state or federal legislature: in the Vargas era legislative experience during the discredited Old Republic was considered a liability.

The Officeholders: Real and Hypothetical

In earlier chapters we studied the careers of some representative Pernambucan political leaders, and we shall look at a few more in due course. But first let us fit together all the characteristics we have been examining to construct a hypothetical member of the state's elite. Assuming he has just gotten his first elite post, we are talking about a man in his late thirties or early forties. By birth or by marriage he is a member of a "tra-

ditional family"; if by birth and if his mother's family is particularly prestigious, he has probably modified his name to emphasize his pedigree.*
He is a Catholic, though probably not a practicing one. His father, a
senhor de engenho, a coronel, or if our man was born after 1900, perhaps
a judge or law professor, had him educated by private tutors or sent him
to a small, exclusive primary school. He had then gone on to the Ginásio
Pernambucano (or after the First World War, the Colegio Salesiano) and
finally to law school. After earning his degree he had practiced law and
dabbled in journalism—probably for one or another of the Recife dailies
that served as political party mouthpieces.[13]

After one or more minor posts, our man's career could have taken one
of several paths that typically led to high position. He might have won a
spot on his party's delegation in the state Chamber of Deputies or Senate.
If he had set his sights on a particular position, he would have cast about
for a post or work that would best serve that aim. To gain the prestigious
judicial title of *desembargador*, for example, he would have accepted a
law professorship or served as a *juíz de direito* long enough to become
eligible for nomination to the state Supreme Court. If prestige was not
the only reward he sought, he might have looked instead for a stepping-
stone post to positions in the state cabinet, some of which—in particular
the secretariats of the treasury and agriculture—were especially lucrative. If he was notably loyal, he might have been rewarded with a seat in
the Federal Senate, winning himself both a life of relative leisure and
high social status. But whether by this path or another, our officeholder
has come to his present position only because he had been in the right
party or faction at the right time, or had the wit to switch when change
loomed on the horizon.

Our subject probably has to divide his working day between his office
duties and other business pursuits, but the demands on his time are not
such as to cut into his leisure-time activities. If prominent socially, he
belongs to one or more of the several exclusive clubs in Recife, probably
the ones that were founded by foreign residents: the Jockey, Inter-
nacional, and Sport clubs. If he has held a federal-level post and lived in

---

*As did Rosa e Silva, whose paterfamilias was a Silva. Similarly, the children of José
Camilo de Sá and Adriana Luisa de Albuquerque used their mother's name, and so did the
Lima Cavalcanti brothers. The historian José Antônio Gonsalves de Mello Neto used his
grandfather's name, disdaining to adopt the invented name taken by his father and
uncles—Pernambucano—when that practice had been fashionable before the turn of the
century.

Rio in the course of his career, he probably joined the Centro Pernambucano do Rio de Janeiro, an influential association that functioned in part
as a social club and in part as a political lobby. In the manner of his peers,
he spends most evenings away from his family, at a café, at his club, or in
the company of his current mistress—a young woman from a nonpromi-
nent family or a mulatinha. He is a polished man, able to punctuate his
conversation with illustrations from the classics and to demonstrate a
passing knowledge of French, English, and perhaps even German or Italian. Like his counterparts in other states, his life-style is set firmly according to the standards of his own society. As a northeasterner, this means
especially that he will publicly champion the virtues of morality, family
unity, chastity (for his wife and daughters), and religion.[14]

During slack times like the rainy season and at Christmas our man
retires with his family to some rural retreat in the Zona da Mata: his
own engenho, or his or his relatives' usina, or perhaps, like so many
businessmen and other affluent city dwellers, a property he has purchased outside the city. If, at some time in the future, our officeholder
should be elected to the federal legislature or named to a national post, he
will probably first go to Rio de Janeiro by himself, leaving his family behind. As many did in these circumstances, he may later move them permanently to the South, where some of his sons and daughters will marry
or take up their careers, thus broadening the base of the family clan and
perhaps achieving new status as a part of Brazil's national elite.

Few men, of course, fit this prototype down to every last detail. An
examination of typical biographies reveals not only many similarities but
also many subtle differences among the generally homogeneous political
elite. In Chapter 4 we looked at three "types" among the Pernambucan
elite: the political boss, Rosa e Silva; the frustrated reformer, Ulisses Pernambucano; and the Vargas-era bureaucrat, Agemenon Magalhães. Here
we shall look at three others: José Mariano, the minority politician; and
two outstanding examples of the "establishment," Estácio Coimbra and
José Maria Bello. We shall also look further into the checkered career of
Carlos de Lima Cavalcanti, the "out" politician who became a political
"in" with the Revolution of 1930 and headed the state administration until
his unceremonious ouster in 1937.

José Mariano Carneiro da Cunha, the principal opposition spokesman
from the 1880's through his death in 1912, was a Recife Law School bacharel, a newspaper editor, and a slaveowner who had come around to

the abolitionist cause late in his career. His father was a lieutenant-colonel in the National Guard, a senhor do engenho in the Zona da Mata, and a stalwart of the powerful Carneiro da Cunha clan. A leader of the Liberal Party, José Mariano was an adamant monarchist until 1889—as late as mid-year his capangas had attacked and dispersed Republican rallies in Recife—but after the fall of the Empire he rallied immediately to the Republic and served as a deputy in the national Constituent Assembly. He also hurried to create a new party, the Partido Autonomista, formed mostly around the old Liberals. Rosa e Silva himself was a member of José Mariano's party until he broke away to form his own party in 1893.

To his enemies, José Mariano was pure and simply a demagogue. Aided by his wife, an abolitionist and backer of humanitarian causes, he cultivated support from the less affluent members of the electorate, mostly urban shopkeepers and artisans in the less fashionable political wards. Thanks to this he was called a "compadre and friend of annoying mulattos and celebrated gangsters."*

For his loyalty to Deodoro da Fonseca after the Floriano Peixoto coup, he was imprisoned for several months on Rio de Janeiro's notorious Ilha das Cobras. Though this made him a martyr—he won election to Congress from Recife's first district from his jail cell—he spent the remainder of his career in the role of ineffectual leader of the opposition. Never did he overcome the charge that he had been a reluctant adherent to the Republic, though the majority of the post-1889 political elite in Pernambuco were no less belated in their conversion. A brief period of vindication came in 1911, when the Salvacionalista movement ousted Rosa e Silva and sent José Mariano back to Rio as a deputy. When he died a year later, some 80,000 citizens of the federal capital were said to have filed past his casket.[15] His identification with Recife's urban population notwithstanding, José Mariano was preeminently a patrician—a member of the social elite who had more in common with the aristocratic Rosa e Silva than with even the bacharel Historical Republican leader Martins Júnior, whom he disliked and with whom he never allied politically. If things had been turned around and José Mariano had achieved power instead of Rosa e Silva, it is unlikely that the ex-Liberal's style would have differed substantially from the ex-Conservative's.

*Félix Cavalcanti de Albuquerque Mello, Memórias, pp. 26–27. José Mariano also defended merchant interests and was made an honorary member of the Commercial Association.

Our next subject, Estácio de Albuquerque Coimbra, was born in 1872 in Barreiros, in southern Mata, about ten kilometers from the coast on the Una River. His father, João Coimbra, was a distinguished provincial politician during the Empire and the owner of at least seven engenhos in the Barreiros–Rio Formosa region. The son took his mother's name, Albuquerque, rather than his patronymic, Bello. An excellent student, he was elected president of his class at the Recife Law School. He graduated at age twenty and entered the state legislature three years later. He soon dominated the body, holding the floor more than any other deputy in spite of his youth. Though his family had belonged to José Mariano's Liberal Party, Estácio switched in 1893 to Rosa e Silva's PRF, as did his politically powerful cousins, the Bellos. Under the eye of the state machine, Coimbra rose to majority leader and president of the state legislature, then to the federal Chamber of Deputies (between 1900 and 1911).* After a short exile following the ouster of Rosa e Silva's party, he returned to national politics, becoming majority leader, then Agriculture Minister, and finally Vice-President of the Republic. When his term expired in 1926, he returned to Pernambuco as governor and PRF leader, the logical heir to the aging Rosa e Silva.[16]

Throughout his political career Coimbra staunchly represented Pernambuco's sugar interests. An important usineiro and cane grower himself, he also owned the most modern cattle ranch in the southern Mata. With the Vargas coup he fled to Europe, but two years later he returned to private life in Rio, where he remained until his death in 1937. A tall, handsome man, as elegant as Rosa e Silva but more outgoing and sociable, Coimbra played a central role in society both in Recife and in Rio.

His cousin José Maria Bello was chosen to succeed him in 1930. Unlike the Albuquerques, who had the singular luck (or acumen) to acquire the only usina in their município, his family's fortunes declined. His father, in fact, sold his engenho to Estácio Coimbra and took a public job in Recife. The boy attended rural public schools and was privately tutored by a mulatto woman his family had managed to find in Maceió. Ultimately, his father—at a considerable sacrifice—sent him to school in the capital. Bello later remembered that at that time in his life he faced what he considered to be a melancholy future: a law degree, marriage, a large family, and a dull and dispiriting career.[17]

* As the president of the legislature, he was briefly elevated to the post of acting governor during the federal intervention crisis of 1911.

Bello attended law school in Rio, holding part-time public jobs obtained through his cousin Estácio's connections. He joined the local literary circle, became a journalist, and spent nine months in Europe as an aide to the Brazilian delegation to Versailles. Bello was the first to admit his debt to Coimbra, who treated him like an "older brother" and arranged better and better public sinecures for him so that he could pursue his cultural interests. With no strong identification with any political faction and with kinship links to the planter and usina interests, he was considered an attractive candidate for political office. He was named to the state's congressional slate in 1926 and later became a senator. With his election to the governorship nullified by the 1930 coup, Bello happily left politics and pursued a career in law and letters. Later he was named to a number of ambassadorial posts.[18]

Bello's replacement, Carlos de Lima Cavalcanti, came from a background much like Estácio Coimbra's. Born in Bonito, 65 kilometers from Barreiros, he too was a lawyer, a pillar of society, and a member of a leading sugar family. He was sent to law school in São Paulo, but returned after graduation to become a state legislator as a member of the Rosista bloc. Coimbra was a close friend of Carlos's father and often stopped at the family's usina for meals on his way to Barreiros. But that made no great difference when, during Coimbra's tenure as governor, Lima Cavalcanti's name was omitted from the official slate for the federal legislature, a post that he greatly coveted. The founder of the opposition PD thus broke with the incumbent administration for purely personal reasons.[19]

The elite's high degree of homogeneity offers at least a partial explanation of why so few groups came together to challenge the prevailing system. The elite permitted growth but distrusted social change. We have seen that political life could be dangerous—and even deadly. Only a handful of the state's political leaders ever publicly embraced unpopular social causes. Some broke with the federal government and were punished for it, but this was due more to the state's own inability to maneuver and thus help its politicians maintain their position than to any genuine ideological differences. Indeed, the "out" group that seized power in 1930 and the men they ousted differed less in outlook and composition than had the Dantistas and Rosistas two generations earlier.

It should not be surprising, then, to find that career advancement was almost invariably accomplished under the protective umbrella of the ruling political party or faction. Only the most secure could dare switch factions in midstream, and many political careers, particularly in the interior, were doomed by links to the wrong family clan or warring coronel. But political differences rarely carried over into social life. The system co-opted into the status quo all those who were willing to keep their opposition within the bounds of gentility.

CHAPTER SIX

State and Nation: Political Dimensions

LIKE MINAS GERAIS, São Paulo, and most of the other states of regional influence, Pernambuco attempted to deal with the federation as an extension of its own region, vying with Bahia for the leadership of the North and seeking to tighten its hegemony over its immediate neighbors—the states of its satellite bloc—in an effort to strengthen its bargaining position. At the same time, events left Pernambuco itself a satellite of the federal government. Being relegated to the periphery frustrated the Pernambucanos, with their long historical memories, and not only compelled them to plead for special-interest aid (which usually was not forthcoming), but forced them, as well, outside the spirit of the federal Constitution, leading them to decree unconstitutional taxes and to clash with other states caught in the same dilemma. In this sense, it fell within the interest of the northeastern states to seek a greater degree of federal responsibility, but few politicians were able to translate this goal into realistic steps, and most were blinded by loyalty to their own states.

The National Balance of Power

Until 1911, and especially during the heyday of Rosa e Silva's PRF, Pernambuco exercised considerable influence in national politics, just as it had under the Empire. Rosa e Silva himself, as we have seen, managed to rule his state like a private fiefdom and was also able to play a leading role as a power broker in the federal Congress. But not even the Lion of the North, as the press liked to call him, could preserve Pernambuco's freedom of action once the presidential system became stabilized under the "politics of the governors" and essentially under the control of Minas and São Paulo. The major watershed came with the 1909–10 presidential succession crisis, a campaign that toppled Rosa e Silva from power and placed the state under the renewed threat of federal intervention.

To observers within the state, it often seemed as if political maneuvering could restore some or all of Pernambuco's vaunted national influence. For a time, Rosa e Silva was rivaled only by Rio Grande do Sul's Pinheiro Machado in congressional prestige, but in the end the Gaúcho's ability to align himself with the Mineiros and other disciplined state machines settled the contest. The turning point probably came in 1906 over the issue of federal participation in the Convention of Taubaté, a legislative battle in which Rosa e Silva found himself squarely on the losing side.

The Taubaté convention, a price-support program for coffee, had begun as a simple agreement among the three principal coffee-growing states, São Paulo, Minas, and Rio de Janeiro, negotiated and signed by the governors of those states without federal support or approval. President Rodrigues Alves, though himself a coffee planter and a Paulista, opposed the arrangement, arguing forcefully in Congress against the changes in monetary policy that it would require; and Rosa e Silva, leading a coalition of northeastern deputies and representatives from the Federal District, lined up on his side. Less concerned than the President about the government's money problems, the congressional opponents railed against the unfair disparities between the stronger and weaker states, Paulista hegemony in the Republic, and the arrogance of the demand for the support of coffee while other agricultural commodities and the needs of manufacturers were consistently ignored.[1]

But they persuaded few to their cause, and in the end the opposition effort failed miserably. Rodrigues Alves's Mineiro successor, Afonso Pena, backed and signed the measure, which passed by an overwhelming majority in both houses, 107–15 in the Chamber of Deputies and 35–4 in the Senate. The new President was not about to forget that he had met with open hostility from Recife business and labor associations on a visit to the Northeast before his inauguration. Now, with Rosa e Silva on the wrong side of the issue, with the southern powers united after Taubaté, and with Pernambuco embroiled in a bitter tax war (see below), the stage was set for the state's political humiliation.

By rights, Pernambuco should have been able to joust successfully in Congress on the strength of its 17-member *bancada*, or delegation, the fourth-largest after Minas (37), São Paulo (22), and Bahia (22). But the numbers do not tell the whole story, for Pernambuco's delegation, like Bahia's, was invariably divided along factional lines, even under Rosa e Silva, giving a still-greater edge to the bloc-voting states of the South. Moreover, the relative political weight of the weaker states was even further reduced as the years passed and the electorate expanded, since the franchise continued to be based on literacy, and the have-not states invariably lagged in educational resources. By 1930 Pernambuco, with 7 percent of Brazil's population, was able to cast only 4 percent of the votes in the presidential election.[2] (See the table on the North's electoral strength in the next section.)

Minas, the leading political power by virtue of its large voting population and disciplined congressional delegation, dominated Brazilian politics until 1930, usually in alliance with São Paulo, the economic giant. The Paulistas were content to keep a comparatively low profile in Congress, reserving their muscle for the federal policy matters that affected their own interests, such as the exchange rate, guarantees for state-negotiated foreign loans, and tariff and immigration policies. The key to congressional control lay in the domination of the major committees and ministerial posts. As an indication of how complete was the North's fall from power, we observe in Table 6.1 that whereas in the 20 years between 1891 and 1911 Pernambuco and Bahia chaired one or another of the four most influential congressional committees—Public Works, Finance (or the Budget Committee through most of these years), Credentials, and Justice—24 times, they held only five of those chairmanships in the 20 years following. Bahia was even more shabbily treated than Pernambuco, getting only one of the five coveted posts. In consolation for the loss of the control of these powerful committees, which supervised the budget, patronage, and electoral certification, among a host of other important matters, the lesser states received such ceremonial throwaways as the vice-presidency of the Republic and minor committee chairmanships. But until the Congress was closed by the 1930 Revolution, its real power rested with the big three states.

State and Region

Pernambuco's federal strategy was rooted in the belief that if it could unite the congressional delegations of the northern states, it would have enough leverage to make itself heard. But economic rivalry and mutual

TABLE 6.1

Pernambucano Chairmen of Key Committees, Chamber of Deputies, 1891–1930

Year	Public Works	Finance	Credentials	Justice
1891	Rio Grande	São Paulo	Bahia	Bahia
1892	Minas	São Paulo	Bahia	São Paulo
1893	Minas	São Paulo	Bahia	Rio de Janeiro
1894	*Pernambuco*	Ceará	Bahia	Rio de Janeiro
1895	*Pernambuco*	Ceará	Ceará	Minas
1896	*Pernambuco*	Ceará	Maranhão	Minas
1897	*Pernambuco*	Minas	Bahia	Minas
1898	Minas	Minas	Bahia	Bahia
1899	*Pernambuco*	São Paulo	Minas	Bahia
1900	Minas	São Paulo	Bahia	Bahia
1901	Minas	Bahia	Minas	Bahia
1902	Minas	Bahia	Paraíba	Bahia
1903	Minas	São Paulo	Paraíba	Bahia
1904	Minas	São Paulo	Maranhão	Bahia
1905	Minas	São Paulo	Maranhão	Bahia
1906	Ceará	Minas	Paraná	Minas
1907	Ceará	Minas	Paraná	Minas
1908	Minas (?)	Minas	Paraná	Ceará
1909	Rio Grande	Minas	*Pernambuco*	Ceará
1910	Rio Grande	Minas	Maranhão	Ceará
1911	Minas	Minas	Maranhão	Ceará
1912	Minas	Minas	Minas	Maranhão
1913	Minas	Minas	Minas	Maranhão
1914	Minas	Rio Grande	Minas	Maranhão
1915	Minas	Minas	Minas	Maranhão
1916	Minas	Minas	Minas	Maranhão
1917	Minas	Minas	Minas	Maranhão
1918	Minas	São Paulo	Minas	Maranhão
1919	Minas	São Paulo	Minas	Maranhão
1920	Minas	Minas	Minas	Maranhão
1921	Minas	*Pernambuco*	*Pernambuco*	Maranhão
1922	Minas	Minas	*Pernambuco*	Maranhão
1923	Pará	Minas	Minas	Minas
1924	Pará	Minas	Minas	Minas
1925	Pará	Minas	Minas	Minas
1926	Pará	Minas	Minas	Minas
1927	Rio Grande	São Paulo	Minas	Minas
1928	Rio Grande	São Paulo	Minas	Minas
1929	Rio Grande	São Paulo	Minas	Minas
1930	*Pernambuco*	São Paulo	São Paulo	Bahia

SOURCE: Culled from *Annaes do Congresso* and *Diário Oficial*.
NOTE: The Finance Committee was called the Budget Committee until 1905.

distrust among the potential allies worked against such efforts, and no northern or northeastern bloc ever jelled, though intellectuals, as we have seen, repeatedly appealed to what they considered to be a common regional identity. Politically, little glue held these states together. Moreover, Table 6.2 shows that even if Pernambuco had been able to unite all the states from Amazonas to Bahia, what would have represented an invincible majority under the Empire would have shrunk to a minority under the Republic. Pernambuco and its satellite bloc (Alagoas, Paraíba, Rio Grande do Norte, and Ceará), commanded just 43 congressional votes, only 20 percent of the total in the Chamber of Deputies. On the other hand, the combined delegations of Minas and São Paulo more than doubled from Empire to Republic, from 29 to 59.

Still, considering the data in Table 6.3, we might suppose that Pernambuco and its satellite bloc, taken as a unit, would have been politically influential even without the votes, given their combined economic strength. It will be noted that they were surpassed only by São Paulo in such important categories as gross agricultural and industrial production and total state revenues. But statistics in isolation are misleading; in any case, a closer examination of the table shows that in the years after 1920 both the state and the bloc declined in every economic category. In the critical sector of refinery production, moreover, Pernambuco's long-standing domination of the sugar industry shrank sharply in the face of the proliferation of sugar factories in the South: between 1907 and 1937 its share of the national production of usina sugar dropped from 41.5 percent to 25.2 percent.[3] The entire coastal economy of the satellite bloc was adversely affected by this decline.

In the nineteenth century the Northeast's role paralleled to some degree the role assumed by Rio Grande do Sul as supplier of raw materials for the domestic market. But as Paul Singer has noted, conditions in the two regions differed significantly, with the Agreste, the Northeast's counterpart of the far South's small landholding zone, being bordered by a hostile outland that inhibited the formation of an interior market.[4]

After the failure of several mortgage institutions in Recife during the depression of the 1890's, northeastern planters noted bitterly that the Imperial government had offered credit to southern growers, and demanded that European-style credit banks, like Bahia's state Banco de Crédito de Lavoura, be established nationwide and backed by federal guarantees. Sugar growers' associations called for tariff protection and subsidies on the order of the coffee valorization programs, but they failed

TABLE 6.2
Comparative Electoral Strength of the North and the Center-South

| | Number of congressional seats | | Population, 1933 | |
Region	Empire (1885)	Old Republic	Total (millions)	Percent registered to vote
North				
Pernambuco	13	17	2.8	2.13%
Plus satellite bloc [a]	33	43	7.6	2.44
Plus other northern provinces/states [b]	68	91	16.0	2.25
Center-South [c]	57	124	23.9	4.70
NATIONAL TOTAL	125	215	39.9	3.69%

SOURCE: Ministério da Justiça e Negócios Interiores, Arquivo Nacional, *Organizações e Programmas Ministeriais: Regime parlamentar no Império*, 2d ed. (Rio, 1962), pp. 383–88; Tribunal Superior da Justiça Eleitoral, *Boletim Eleitoral*, ano 3, no. 26 (March 1934), p. 388; Ministério das Relações Exteriores, *Brazil* (Rio, 1937), p. 34.
[a] Alagoas, Ceará, Paraíba, Rio Grande do Norte.
[b] Amazonas, Bahia, Maranhão, Pará, Piauí, Sergipe.
[c] Including territory of Acre (two seats) in Republic.

TABLE 6.3
Comparison of Political Units by Selected Indicators
(Percent of national total)

Indicators and year	Pernambuco	Satellite bloc states	Minas	São Paulo	Rio Grande do Sul	Federal District
Area	1.16%	4.19%	6.97%	2.90%	3.35%	.01%
Population						
1890	6.67	19.01	18.72	15.26	6.81	3.90
1940	6.48	19.09	16.36	17.42	8.06	4.29
Gross agricultural production						
1920	6.89	14.77	19.85	27.54	10.60	.04
1928/32 average	5.28	9.98	13.54	44.45	10.98	—[a]
Total sugar production (value)						
1920	22.18	38.32	17.24	8.38	0.57	—
1937	17.83	28.87	18.10	18.83	0.83	—
Gross industrial production						
1920	4.71	8.80	5.94	31.20	12.06	23.11
1938	4.20	—	11.30	43.20	10.70	14.20
Total bank assets						
1920	3.46	4.96	2.38	26.04	11.12	25.28
1937	2.81	4.73	7.28	29.50	10.48	40.90
Total state revenue						
1919	6.09	12.25	14.92	27.23	9.38	—
1937	4.42	10.00	14.56	37.42	14.02	—

SOURCE: Directoria Geral de Estatística, *Resumo de várias estatísticas econòmico-financeiras* (Rio, 1924), pp. 7, 11, 12, 33, 38, 98–99, 142, 156, 158; Instituto Brasileiro de Geografia e Estatística, *VI Recenseamento geral do Brasil, 1950: Estado de Pernambuco*, pp. 122, 191–97, 233, 249; José Jobim, *Brazil in the Making* (New York, 1943), p. 96; *Relatório apresentado ao Dr. Ildefonso Simões Lopes* (Recife, c. 1924), pp. 48, 185; Ministério das Relações Exteriores, *Brazil, 1942* (Rio, 1942), p. 80; M. F. J. de Santa-Anna Nery, *Le Brésil en 1889* . . . (Paris, 1889), p. 451.
[a] Negligible.

to win federal sympathy.[5] The unremitting demands for relief ultimately led to Vargas's creation of the IAA in 1933. But as we have seen, though that step staved off disaster, it also helped to stabilize the Northeast's essentially noncompetitive agricultural system.

Given their state's declining position in the hierarchy of federal power, Pernambucano political brokers dealt with other units of the federation with care. The way proved frequently treacherous. Beyond the constantly shifting set of alliances, states were forced not only to jockey with one another for patronage, but also to prevent insurgents in their own midst from joining forces with rival groups. For all but the two or three most powerful states, the wrong presidential choice brought certain punishment from the victorious candidate.

Under these circumstances, Pernambuco had little choice but to assume a respectful client-like posture toward these states and toward the federal government. Meanwhile, it did what it could to enlarge its national role, aggressively imposing its own leadership on its northeastern neighbors. Its commercial weight created a sphere of influence that extended to Sergipe in the south and into Piauí in the north. But it was in the narrower compass of the satellite bloc that its real economic power made itself felt. Table 6.4 illustrates how thoroughly it dominated the five-state region in the representative years between 1909 and 1918.

Much as the state desired to seize the role of regional champion, however, the competitive federal system obstructed political unity. Economic necessity set one northeastern state against another, intensifying old animosities. Each state, desperately seeking increased sources of revenue in times of emergency, such as after droughts, as well as for normal budgetary needs, fought tenaciously for its own interests. And the weaker states certainly had good reason to question Pernambuco's motives. Consequently, the only truly regional solutions to local problems under the Republic came from Rio de Janeiro, and in almost all cases these occurred after 1930.

One continuing source of regional antagonism concerned Pernambuco's refusal to resign itself to the loss of the Comarca of São Francisco, the 100,000 square kilometers that had been carved out of its territory in 1824 to be ceded first to Minas, and later to Bahia. Through all these years the Pernambucanos had never ceased to demand that the national government repair this injustice, which had reduced their state to a "geographical monstrosity," condemned to administrative discontinuity and

TABLE 6.4

Pernambuco's Predominance Over Its Satellite Bloc

(Percent of five-state total)

Category and year	Pernambuco	Satellite bloc			
		Alagoas	Ceará	Paraíba	Rio Grande do Norte
Total state militia, 1917	43.26%	11.49%	16.73%	19.74%	8.76%
Usina sugar production, 1916–17	80.34	17.42	—	2.00	0.22
Total sugar production, 1917–18	75.32	20.77	—[a]	3.89	—[a]
Capital employed in industry, 1917	46.79	17.18	4.97	1.50	31.04
Total state revenue, 1912	51.94	10.64	17.17	12.72	7.51
Total município budgets, 1909	62.68	8.37	13.03	9.01	6.89
Bank deposits, 1909	59.39	9.52	19.93	6.66	4.47

SOURCE: *Relatório apresentado ao Dr. Ildefonso Simões Lopes* (Recife, c. 1920), pp. 39, 114, 191; Directoria Geral de Estatística, *Annuario estatistico do Brazil*, 1908–1912, 2: 20, 266, 280, 304, 310; Instituto Brasileiro de Geografia e Estatística, *Anuário estatístico do Brasil*, 1938, p. 301.

NOTE: Percentages do not sum to 100 due to rounding.

[a] Negligible.

cut off from its own rural interior.[6] But Bahia stoutly resisted any change, and a federal boundary conference in 1920 failed to resolve the dispute, though Pernambuco did sign minor territorial accords with Paraíba and Ceará. Another dispute, with Alagoas, also remained unsettled, with Alagoas standing by its charges that Pernambuco had invaded and held Alagoan territory.[7]

With northeastern agricultural products competing for the same markets, the disputes over economic territory were even more disruptive. For primarily commercial reasons, Pernambucan officials attempted to extend railroad lines not only farther into their own states, but also into Piauí, Ceará, and Paraíba, even while they complained of economic pressure from other states on their own outlying territory. Sometimes violence flared. In 1930 bands of men incited to riot by merchants in the capital of Paraíba cut the new rails of a Recife-Paraíba route in order to resist Pernambucan inroads into local commerce.[8]

Railroad construction served as a major battleground in the struggle for regional economic advantage. Recife grain brokers argued for an extension of rail links into the Sertão to capitalize on the fact that agricultural producers in Ceará's Cariri Valley were angry at political neglect from Fortaleza, and would gladly switch to trading directly with Recife to take advantage of lower shipping rates and the reduced cost of imported goods.[9] Though western Alagoas (and southwestern Pernambuco) fell into Bahia's economic orbit, both Alagoas and Paraíba relied exclusively on their rail connections with Recife. A proposal in 1890 to construct a line from Imperatriz in Alagoas to the western São Francisco River was opposed bitterly by Recife's Commercial Association on the grounds that the route would drain off commerce from Alagoas and Bahia.[10]

Pernambuco's role in the elaboration of the so-called drought industry, a carefully orchestrated effort to gain national sympathy that was created, mostly by Cearense politicians, after the 1877–79 drought, is instructive in several ways. Imperial officials in Recife generally took little initiative in dealing with drought-related problems, even though western Pernambuco had been threatened by hordes of starving refugees, especially in 1878 and 1879. Drought relief lagged and was hindered by partisan maneuvering over financial responsibility; drought refugees sat interned in temporary camps without assistance while politicians fought to avoid jurisdiction.[11] With the Imperial government loath to offer direct financial relief, provincial officials devised a scheme whereby drought victims would be subsidized to provide cheap labor for the still-incomplete public works that had been initiated in the 1860's under better economic conditions. Accordingly, refugee labor was used to complete the Recife–São Francisco Railway; the Liberal administration in Rio de Janeiro set into motion a plan to build the Baturité and Sobral railroad lines in Ceará; and the Viscount Sinimbú, an Alagoan planter and Minister of Agriculture, used the excuse of the drought to win a concession for a railroad between Recife and Paulo Affonso—over the objections of engineers, who claimed the line was impracticable.[12]

Playing on national sympathies, drought-region politicians won Imperial funds for the construction of an expensive and ultimately ineffective network of reservoirs and dams. The largest project, the Quixadá dam in Ceará, took 22 years to complete and was the only one of the 49 projects initiated before 1889 to survive. Every dam built between 1889 and 1910 either silted up or was abandoned within a decade of its completion.[13]

With the drought cycle recognized as a national problem, the federal government responded in 1909 by creating the Federal Anti-Drought Inspectorate (IFOCS). Over the next two decades it sponsored extensive regional surveys and supervised the construction of dozens of water retention projects, mostly in Ceará, Rio Grande do Norte, and Paraíba. For unknown reasons, Pernambucanos chose to take only minor roles within the drought lobby except in times of acute crisis, when funds for refugee labor could be sought. Then they joined the chorus of northeastern voices against the "cruelty" of such national figures as Campos Sales, who as President ignored all pleas for emergency credits.[14]

One who did not remain indifferent was Epitácio Pessôa, the Northeast's only President. He poured massive amounts of public funds—up to 15 percent of the federal budget in 1921–22—into anti-drought public works in the region. But the Northeast did not enjoy that luxury for long. Artur Bernardes, his successor, abruptly suspended payments in 1923 under his policy of retrenchment, bringing most construction to a halt and throwing thousands out of work. Not coincidentally, banditry increased throughout the Sertão; the same year saw the beginning of the violent career of the elusive Lampião.

Spurred by the drought of 1932, the Vargas administration restored the Pessôa formula of federal public works spending to construct federal, state, and municipal dams (all federally financed), road networks into isolated parts of the backlands, and irrigation canals. The drought was unusually severe; rainfall had been steadily diminishing since 1926, and the advent of the feared seca in 1930 brought panic and led to the looting of warehouses in interior towns and a stream of migrants out of the Sertão. This mass exodus so strained state resources that federal officials were forced to intervene. Refugee camps were hastily built, mostly in Ceará, to house 800,000 people; 8,000 of these refugees were shipped to Pará with the promise of land; the rest were put to work as manual laborers by the IFOCS, which had been inactive since the 1920's.[15]

Government spokesmen claimed that federal grants to the stricken region exceeded all previous totals, though they neglected to take inflation into account. For unstated reasons but certainly in part because the administration considered Pernambuco to have been spared the worst of the drought calamity, the state was omitted from the initial relief budget. An angry Lima Cavalcanti, taking this as a personal affront (and under pressure to fund relief measures for the streams of drought victims who crossed from Piauí and Ceará into Pernambuco), dispatched a near-daily barrage of letters and telegrams to the regional commander, Juarez Távora, to Public Works Minister José Américo de Almeida, and to Vargas himself, demanding additional funds.

José Américo, a politician from neighboring Paraíba, took eight months to acknowledge that Pernambuco needed any assistance at all, and even then he grudged the state a bare 10 percent of the aid given to the region. The battle between Lima Cavalcanti and José Américo took on angry personal proportions, and must have slowed what little relief funds there were. It also led to charges from Lima Cavalcanti's detractors that he was using the drought refugees as hostages, an allegation that may have had a grain of truth to it, since up to 20,000 refugees were interned in 1931 to prevent their moving closer to Recife.[16]

The federal government's unwillingness to speed even the funds that finally were promised, coupled with the threat of Great Western Railway officials not to employ refugees whose wages could not be guaranteed by the state government, moved Lima Cavalcanti to accuse José Américo publicly in 1932 of a personal vendetta against the State of Pernambuco.[17] For the moment, this had its effect, and the promised funds were released. But the campaign alienated Vargas, who, irritated at Lima Cavalcanti's intense lobbying and embarrassed by the signs of disharmony in the Liberal Alliance camp, turned a deaf ear to further entreaties. On the advice of Agamenon Magalhães, Vargas took a new and different approach to the drought, one that was designed to bypass the states altogether and to concentrate instead on strengthening the regional agricultural economy. Northeastern agronomists and journalists had been advocating just such a regional approach for decades, but their proposals had been ignored under the Old Republic since they promised no political mileage to state political machines.[18]

Regional Cooperation

The inability of the individual state governments to police the backlands prompted the first formal efforts at northeastern collaboration. The first anti-banditry pact, signed in 1912, was credited with the capture of the bandit Antônio Silvino in 1914.[19] A few Pernambucan politicians opposed such cooperation; a notable example was Deputy Andrade Bezerra who in 1918 accused the Paraíba government of arming jagunços to attack marketplaces over the border in Pernambuco. But most of the state's leaders endorsed the new spirit of regional collaboration. During the 1920's each and every governor of Pernambuco made it a point to invite neighboring officials to coordinate efforts against bandits.[20] Representatives negotiated arrangements to allow police forces to cross state lines, discussed strategy, and exchanged information. The systematic penetration of the backlands by federal troops after 1930, the improving highway system, better communications, and more effective military technology all helped to reduce banditry and virtually eliminate it by the end of the decade.

Contact among northeastern state interventors increased markedly after Vargas's accession to power. In a manner reminiscent of the Imperial practice of appointing provincial presidents with no ties to their constituencies, the provisional government named military officers to nearly all the interventor positions in the North and Northeast between 1930 and 1932, and most of the others were filled by men from the outside, chosen for their loyalty to the national administration and the professedly apolitical goals of the Revolution.[21] In Pernambuco, however, Vargas permitted an exception to the rule, leaving affairs in the hands of a local man and a civilian, the PD leader Lima Cavalcanti. From the start, Lima Cavalcanti exhorted his fellow interventors to cooperate on a wide range of issues and to devise a common strategy for the national Constituent Assembly, which began in 1933.*

But by the time the assembly convened, national officials had long since grown tired of the political bickering in the state and had set out to mend the situation. Vargas's assignment of Juarez Távora as the "viceroy" of the Northeast was more than just a new regional approach to the administration of that part of the country; it was specifically intended to curb the autonomy of the individual states. As early as 1931 steps were taken in Rio that eventually led to the standardization of public administration, the creation of intraregional regulatory agencies, and the establishment of more direct contact—including military pressure—between the central administration and the states on the periphery.[22]

Publicly, Lima Cavalcanti endorsed the new approach. The Society of the Friends of Alberto Torres, led by Pernambucan intellectuals linked to the tenente October 3 Club, sponsored a congress on the problems of the

---

*See, for example, in the Arquivo Público Estadual de Pernambuco, letter, Lima Cavalcanti to Getúlio Vargas, Sept. 22, 1931; telegram, Lima Cavalcanti to interventors, Espírito Santo to Amazonas, Dec. 31, 1931; and Ofício no. 14, Jan. 21, 1931. In May 1931 Lima Cavalcanti submitted a detailed plan to other northeastern interventors for the coordination of all anti-bandit activities, based on an earlier proposal by Távora. In it he suggested that militia troops be allowed to move freely across state borders, that these forces be organized into small units under the command of regular Army officers and under the strictest discipline, and that the men be paid a regular (daily) salary "so that they will not have to loot, like Lampião, to live." (Arquivo Público Estadual, telegram, Lima Cavalcanti to all northeastern interventors, May 28, 1931.)

Northeast, which met in Rio de Janeiro at the same time as the Constituent Assembly. Another meeting, organized with less fanfare, was the
Congress on the Economic Life of the Sertão, held in the Pernambuco
town of Triunfo. With the increased attention to regional issues came
occasional signs of social awareness. Rio Grande do Norte's Governor José
Augusto Bezerra de Medeiros, for example, argued that banditry could be
ended only by the elimination of poverty and the abuses of coronel rule in
the interior. This contrasted sharply with the attitudes prevalent before
1930, which typically viewed regional hardships solely as the function of a
lack of revenue or of an inadequate administrative apparatus.[23]

Pernambuco in the Federation

In an imaginative essay calling for a study of the Empire written from
the vantage point of the Northeast, José Antônio Gonsalves de Mello
Neto traces the pattern of local ire over preferential treatment for the
South—feelings that in 1817, 1824, and 1848 had contributed to regionalist insurrections. In the nineteenth century Pernambucanos had complained about many of the same issues that irked their descendants during
the Republic: local taxes were spent on the improvement and beautifica-
tion of Rio de Janeiro; the Northeast was not adequately represented in
the cabinet; the central government took more in taxation from Pernambuco than it spent there (an illogical argument, to be sure, since it did not
take into account such national expenses as the cost of government, but
one that nevertheless persisted from decade to decade).[24]

Proposed solutions tended to the political, ranging from such eminently
sensible ideas as regional alliances to the absurd notion, ventured by a
senhor de engenho from Palmares, that the Northeast secede and seek
annexation to the United States.[25] Pernambuco, a 1927 editorial in the
Diário da Manhã proclaimed, "is the natural axis of a powerful political
concentration capable of counterbalancing the disequilibrium of the
South's hegemony," demonstrating that even as the Old Republic neared
its end the wishful goal of regional unity still hung in the air.[26]

In contrast, the conflict over interstate taxation demonstrated that the
structure of the federation itself forced the states to act in their own
interests and doomed the kind of unity regionalists yearned for.[27] Though
the federal Constitution did not permit states to impose tariffs on goods
imported from other states, they were allowed to tax "imported" compet-

ing goods (*semelhantes*), and this loophole was used by Pernambuco and other northern states to protect such local products as cachaça and processed sweets. This protectionist bent on the part of local authorities was reinforced by the fact that many states, especially those in the North governed by landed oligarchies, were unwilling to consider land or income taxes to raise needed revenues.

Not surprisingly, the levying of such "import" taxes by a state precipitated retaliatory action from its trading partners. One of the bitterest of these tax wars, a six-year-long affair waged by Pernambuco and Rio Grande do Sul between 1902 and 1908, saw increasingly vindictive duties imposed on Pernambucano rum and Gaúcho jerked beef. The imbroglio exacerbated the strained relations between Rosa e Silva and Pinheiro Machado, and was settled only after federal arbitration.[28] Pernambuco engaged in similar disputes with Alagoas, Bahia, Ceará, Minas, and Pará. Though in 1903 Paulista deputies succeeded in ramming through legislation banning taxes on all interstate commerce, the Congress was unable to end the problem; and interstate taxes survived in disguised forms for another 30 years and more, until they were finally wiped out under the Estado Novo.[29]

In 1914 the Recife Commercial Association took its case to the federal government, complaining that discriminatory import taxes allowed the State of Pará to charge only 600 reis per liter of alcohol imported from Hamburg, but 900 reis for the same product from Pernambuco. At the same time, the Recife merchants' proposed solution could only have made matters worse; they demanded that their state be granted the right to maintain its own schedule of import taxes, arguing that this was the only way to fight the bullying tactics of stronger states.[30]

Mostly such complaints left the federal government unmoved, and when appeals for relief did win an audience, local critics argued that the concessions made were usually small. Successful lobbying in 1921 by Deputy Andrade Bezerra, who acted as unofficial spokesman for the Commercial Association, resulted in a law extending new lines of credit to state banks; and federal authorities also granted a fare reduction for the Great Western line, to the association's delight.[31] Partial aid in a major area of concern—the need to expand rail links within the region—came not from legislative good fortune but from the success in 1911 of the Great Western in consolidating its network of 12 formerly separate and inde-

pendent lines. It did so at the cost of relinquishing the financial guarantees given by the Brazilian government in the nineteenth century, but the
cost was not all that high, since the guarantees were scarcely honored
anymore. Yet though the new system linked the northeastern coastal
economies to Recife's port, no federal aid for railroad construction into the
interior was granted. Divisiveness among the northeastern congressional
delegations weakened any chance for such largess.

By the 1920's Pernambuco's political isolation was so great that its governors felt it necessary to spend months at a time in the federal capital,
relying on personal lobbying to gain favors and turning over the administration of the state to the next in command.[32] Lima Cavalcanti not only
maintained the practice; he added the tactic of throwing his state on the
mercy of the federal government.[33] But neither careful negotiation nor
obsequiousness produced results. In 1948, when Governor Alexandre
José Barbosa Lima Sobrinho feted visiting President Eurico Gaspar Dutra
at the International Club (in much the same style as his predecessors had
hosted receptions for Campos Sales, Afonso Pena, Epitácio Pessôa, and
Getúlio Vargas), he complained loudly—and backed his complaints with
statistics—about what he termed the federal government's unequal
treatment of his state.[34] Though this speech had little effect, the governor
kept up the battle. Echoing the themes of past administrations, he renewed the attack:

Difficulty, misery, profound and grave economic disequilibrium prevails in Pernambuco. . . . For this reason, I ask the Union for help. . . . Under the federal
system income is distributed generally, without considering the particular needs
of each state and region; . . . thus a state that exports lives better than one that
does not; and the best taxes—income, sales, and import duties—go to the Union.
Pernambuco sends 57 percent of its entire income [to Rio de Janeiro], leaving
only 43 percent for state and municipal uses.[35]

Nor did the accession of northeasterners to high federal positions
guarantee favored treatment. The vice-presidencies of Rosa e Silva and
Estácio Coimbra produced no visible favors, nor did the service of the
Zona da Mata planter and usineiro José Rufino Bezerra Cavalcanti as
Minister of Agriculture from 1915 to 1918 yield any tangible benefits.[36]
The banking credit law that Andrade Bezerra had worked so hard to push
through in 1921 was repealed in 1926, when a Pernambucano, Anibal
Freire, was Minister of Finance. Epitácio Pessôa proved the exception to

the rule as far as aid to the Northeast was concerned, but he was antagonistic to Pernambuco's state administration, which accused him of meddling in its affairs through his cousins, the Pessôa de Queiroz clan.[37]

Evidence of the impact of Pernambuco's declining fortunes under the Republic can be tracked through the years in newspapers and private correspondence. Less than a year after the fall of the Empire, one of the state's few Historical Republicans, Paes Barreto, lamented what he called Pernambuco's "real suffering" under unequal and unjust conditions.[38] An editorial in 1908 complained that São Paulo (which it called "the Brazilian Prussia" in tribute to its powerful police force), took the lion's share of federal largess, leaving the North "condemned to a diet of bread and water."[39] A local demographer pointed out at the Fourth Brazilian Congress on Geography, meeting in Recife in 1915, that only Minas and São Paulo had adequate topographic and land-use maps, handicapping efforts at regional planning. In 1920, perhaps angry at not being allowed to inflate state figures proportionately (that census overestimated the national population by some 3,000,000), state officials charged that the census takers had undercounted Pernambuco's population by 31 percent, omitting 676,500 persons, according to their own calculations based on diocese records.[40] In 1928 the *Jornal do Recife* castigated President Washington Luis, a recent visitor to Pernambuco, for his approval of increased railway rates, linking the President of the Republic to "those who set their dogs on beggars."[41] Five years later Lima Cavalcanti, protesting the exclusion of northeastern representatives from an important constitutional draft commission, reminded Juarez Távora that the region was "only remembered when the federal government needs troops for its defense."[42]

In sum, federation weakened Pernambuco's capacity to defend its interests. Whether the state would have benefited significantly from a different constitutional system cannot be measured; nor is it so certain that the successful creation of a northern bloc would have yielded important benefits.

Pernambuco's leaders accepted national unity in the absence of a realistic alternative, though the nostalgic probably would have preferred the de facto regional independence of the colonial period. The elite faced the prospect of integration warily. But Pernambucanos were as anxious as any other Brazilians to have the modern accoutrements that symbolized progress as long as they left the old values unaffected, and the federal government was looked on by many as the only means by which these things could be introduced into their impoverished region.

Integration, then, will provide the focus for the next chapter, which will examine, in turn, the role of the armed forces and state military organizations, the growing exchange of ideas through the creation of formal associations, and most important, the need for government funds and the allocation of revenue within the federal system.

CHAPTER SEVEN

Toward Integration

NATIONAL INTEGRATION, the forging of links across state lines toward closer ties within the federation, developed steadily after 1889, despite countervailing pressures caused by regional disparities and individual state ambitions. It reflected the shift of loyalties, goals, and expectations to a new center, one in which elite attitudes became "refocused [quoting Ernst Haas] on a new set of central symbols and institutions."[1] Though Rio de Janeiro became the new national center, Recife remained the unifying central symbol for the Northeast, especially after the awakening of cultural regionalism in the 1920's by Freyre and others. But as in Minas, political and economic forces eroded the regional ideal, which was finally shattered in the early 1930's with the humiliation of the Lima Cavalcanti government and the loss of the last trappings of autonomy.

In the end, all of the states of Brazil shared Pernambuco's fate, though not with the same loss of face. São Paulo's military defeat at the hands of federal troops in 1932 cost the Paulistas their political freedom, though they retained their economic independence. Minas's acceptance of client status from Vargas diluted that state's long effort to build an economic base sufficiently strong to guarantee autonomy. Rio Grande do Sul was hobbled when its intervenor, after waging and losing a cat-and-mouse game with Vargas, fled into exile and was replaced by a military officer.

Military Federalism

Integration proceeded on two planes: horizontally, as groups began to reach out in common interest across political boundaries, and vertically, as increasing interdependence began to draw state institutions into a national framework. The militia's role, at the very intersection between federal and state power, illustrates the process of vertical integration.

In the cities the events of the early Republic and the seeming need for more forceful instruments of social control encouraged the growing middle class to favor the creation of a stronger military establishment. Canudos exposed the fact that the federal Army could not deal with local acts of defiance short of full-scale invasion; the rural coronéis who ruled the interior showed themselves to be outside of national law; and the middle class saw a strong military as a potential champion of their own interests.[2] The result was a vigorous campaign for obligatory military service after 1900 and a drive to modernize the armed services. Fueled by an unsuccessful, vaguely monarchist uprising in the Military Academy in 1904 and a rising fear of Argentine military reorganization, this campaign led to the enactment of a conscription law in 1908 and further military reforms in 1915.

Nationalist in character, the military trend was complemented by the development of kindred associations and clubs throughout the country. Most notable in this respect were the civilian shooting clubs, the *linhas de tiro*, which sprang up in the first decade of the century. Established at the state level at first and given congressional endorsement in 1906, the tiros blended civilian patriotism, itself a factor encouraging integration, with military interest in training reserves for use in emergencies. Participation in the tiros exempted youths from other military service, thereby guaranteeing the success of the venture. Army officers provided instruction and individual tiro clubs were coordinated under the Ministry of War.

The first tiro in the Northeast was organized in early 1909, the thirteenth in Brazil, with Recife's mayor, Archimedes de Oliveira, as honorary president.* By 1919 there were 39 tiro clubs in the state, three in the capital and the remainder spread across the Zona da Mata and Agreste. In inaugurating the Goiana Tiro in 1912, the Army's spokesman, a lieutenant-colonel, proudly offered his reasons for the need for such groups: "[In the tiros, we have] a joint civilian-military institution that will allow us to rejoice in the new triumphant military spirit among us, and that will carry us, in the near future, to the same role on the South American continent as the strong and powerful Germans play in Europe."[3]

---

*There had been an attempt to form a linha de tiro before this, in 1887, but the organization never got off the ground and was disbanded.

The tiros occasionally became involved in local political warfare. Recife's Tiro 13, for example, patrolled the streets during the 1911 electoral
crisis, intimidating anti-Hermes partisans; and later, Interventor Lima
Cavalcanti praised 11 of the clubs for the way they had fought alongside
the pro-Vargas forces during the 1930 insurrection. The nationalistic fervor that promoted the growth of the tiros also found expression in a civilian society, the Liga da Defesa Nacional, founded in 1916. The activities
of these military patriotic groups, along with the efforts of the advocates
of a strong military force, contributed to the atmosphere of growing
national awareness and, ironically, also fed the currents of discontent that
erupted in the revolts within the military in 1922 and after.

Military power increased significantly after the First World War at
both the state and the federal level. During the post-1918 "era of armed
federalism" the independent state armed forces symbolized the power of
the state political machines to maintain order, and, for the stronger units
of the federation, to defend their autonomy. For the weaker states, with
few pretenses to autonomy, the right to bear arms meant little more than
an annual financial burden.

During the Empire Pernambuco consistently maintained only a small
number of regulars in its provincial forces, building up its troop strength
as the need arose, during the Paraguayan War, for example, and in
periods of drought. The establishment of the Republic saw an immediate
doubling of the state's troop strength with the addition of a Home Guard,
bringing its total contingent to 2,058 men. The troop level then dropped
off, but rose again during the last years of Barbosa Lima's administration
and reached a second peak in 1910, when Rosa e Silva's PRF readied itself
for the upcoming presidential campaign.

This strengthening of the state's Força Pública was quickly countered
—and more—by the federal military authorities in support of the Salvacionista candidate. By 1911–12 the federal forces in Pernambuco's military region, just 300 men in 1909, numbered 2,500. The state's military
strength likewise rose sharply in 1922, during another confrontation with
the federal military authorities, and again in 1928, when it reached an unprecedented total of 3,226 men, many of them deployed in the Sertão to
combat banditry.

Except for 1911–12 the federal forces in Pernambuco were never as
large as the state's own police force. But the federal command could mus-
ter thousands of reinforcements at a few days' notice, as in 1922, when

troops were brought in by sea from as far away as Rio de Janeiro and São Paulo, supported by a torpedo boat and a destroyer. Other areas were equally vulnerable to federal intervention: the State of Rio de Janeiro was practically occupied militarily during the Bernardes presidency in punishment for its pre-election opposition. Only the big three states, with their powerful militias, had the manpower to stave off the federal forces: the Army did not achieve clear superiority until the late 1930's.

Given a choice between state and federal soldiers, many rural Pernambucanos preferred the latter, who were paid more regularly and often were local youths, owing to the Army's policy of stationing recruits in their home town garrisons. In 1912 Pernambuco's governor, the former War Minister Dantas Barreto, noted ruefully that state troops were fed on a daily per capita allotment of 900 reis, or about 40 cents, one-quarter less than the amount allocated to federal soldiers, who were no models of stamina themselves.[4] Pernambuco's militia was about the same size as or larger than the Força Pública Mineira until about 1920, but by the end of the decade the Mineiros had put more than twice as many men under arms. Even so, the strength of these two states paled before São Paulo's 14,000 men on active duty in 1925 and 1926. The Paulista Força Pública was practically a professional army, with its own military academy, foreign military mission, artillery, and air corps.

Vargas accomplished the phasing out of the state militia in a careful and systematic fashion, using both the carrot and the stick. The weaker states were summarily ordered to place their police forces under federal control by a simple decree. At the same time, he offered all the states strong incentives to integrate their forces into the Army, including equipment, uniforms, and financial relief.[5] Rio Grande do Sul's powerful force, the last to capitulate, was absorbed in October 1937, leaving Vargas free to plot, with his generals, the overthrow of his own constitutional government a month later. The transfer of military power to the Union not only symbolized the passing of state autonomy, but heralded the emergence of integrated political control.

Congresses and Meetings

The horizontal process of national integration was under way well before such institutional changes were made. This trend was manifested in the efforts of members of local occupational and interest groups to meet their counterparts from outside, using as their vehicle the new associations that came into being after the late 1880's. Professionals, educators, students, labor representatives, and religious leaders began to travel from one city to another in a growing wave of congresses and meetings; their gatherings interpreted values and priorities to the public at large and demonstrated what leading Brazilians considered important and how they regarded possibilities for change.

National congresses in Brazil proliferated during the 1890's, a by-product of the rise in international meetings 20 years before. Owing to the federal structure, meeting sites rotated among the major state capitals, with Recife usually alternating with Salvador as the "northern" host.

The flow of information at international meetings spotlighted areas of concern throughout the Atlantic basin. Brazilians were influenced by the latest thinking in penology, medical science, and aviation, to name but a few of the topics covered. The scope and content and even the sequence of congresses held in Brazil must have been deeply influenced by what was happening abroad. On the whole Brazil was a follower nation across the spectrum of issues raised first in the international arena.

Yet as students of dependency have often pointed out, the flow of influence between the center and the periphery is not a one-way street. The term valorization, for instance, a word derived from the Portuguese, came into English usage following the coffee price-support schemes outlined in the 1906 Taubaté Convention. Cultural nationalism fostered the search for roots and a national tradition. Thus though the northeastern folkloric congresses paralleled similar events in the United States and Europe, it would be difficult to say that the Brazilian events were derivative. Granted that the international dimension is important, this subject will be approached from the regional perspective—as it were, from the bottom up.

Such a regional perspective on the "congress phenomenon" reveals a Brazilian twist, unique at least for Latin America with its centralist traditions: many meetings were based explicitly on a federalist format. It is by no means true that meetings stemmed primarily from the national capital. There are examples of congresses whose scope and influence were limited to the Federal District, with its unique city-state constituency of local interests and politicians; and of others that were distinctly limited to a state or even to regions within a state. However, the interplay of state and nation was a marked characteristic of many meetings during the period under study.

In fact, several meetings, expositions, and associations that initially had only a statewide appeal eventually spread to other states within a federal framework.* To be sure, the Federal District saw many of the first professional, cultural, and economic meetings and associations. But Rio was only the most important of several active centers. As we have seen, within four years the Brazilian Academy of Letters, founded in 1897, had a Pernambucan counterpart, and São Paulo and Minas followed suit in 1909 and 1910, respectively.

As time passed, national congresses and associations tended to overshadow state and local groups, even as both—and particularly on the regional level—grew increasingly specialized. By the 1920's Brazilians were beginning to look for national solutions to problems that transcended local boundaries; growing federal initiative, as the role of the national government expanded, complemented this trend. More and more national meetings were held in Rio, the seat of government administration. Education congresses, which had been noted for their innovative independence in the states, shifted to the Federal District, where the Ministry of Education imposed bureaucratic stability at the expense of experimentation. Feminists, active in Minas since the 1920's, participated in a series of congresses in Rio under the nominal patronage of Vargas's wife until he suppressed the movement in the right-wing backlash of the mid-1930's.[6]

Pernambucanos responded positively to the opportunity to meet with their fellows from other states, partly in order to represent their state and partly with the thought of bringing back new ideas from outside. For Pernambuco, the phenomenon of officially organized and sponsored congresses is clearly associated with the second political generation, those members of the elite born between 1869 and 1888. Older politicians appear to have been preoccupied with political and economic questions, whereas the younger group began to become concerned with local social and institutional matters. Thus the few conferences in which Pernambucanos participated—either out of state or at home—before 1910 were mostly related to agriculture, especially sugar. The post-1910 period saw a marked proliferation of congresses and meetings whose subjects ranged

---

*Just as Rio Grande do Sul's Varig Airlines and São Paulo's highway department, both established in the 1920's, soon crossed state borders, the one to become the country's national airline, the other to become a model for a federal department.

TABLE 7.1

Pernambucan Participation in Meetings, Congresses, and Expositions, 1875–1937

First in-state meeting held on subject	Out-of-state meetings attended by Pernambucanos
1875–1900	
Agriculture, 1878	Agriculture, various dates
1900–1910	
Syndicalism and problems of industrial labor, 1903	Syndicalism and socialist ideology, 1902
Medicine, 1909	Geography, 1909
	Student life, 1909
	History, 1910
	Commerce and industry, 1910
1911–1920	
Catholicism, 1913	Workers' organizations, 1913
Public administration, 1915	Road building, 1916
Geography, 1915	Journalism, 1917
Municipal trade, 1918	
Anti-illiteracy, 1918	
Police and anti-banditry, 1920	
1921–1930	
Agricultural labor, 1925	Medicine, 1925
Commercial associations, 1925	Higher education, 1927
Regionalism, 1926	Primary education, 1927
Public health, 1926	Automobiles, 1928
Law and jurisprudence, 1926	Aviation, 1928
Education, 1927	Public credit, 1930
Road building, 1927	Mortuary science, 1930
1931–1937	
Rural journalism, 1931	Problems of the Northeast, 1933
Labor unions and health problems, 1933	Orthopedic surgery, 1934
Medical students, 1933	Rural education, 1934
Backlands' economic problems, 1934	Antiwar organization, 1934
Afro-Brazilian culture, 1934	Cancer research, 1935
Cattle raising, 1934	Drug control, 1936
Antiwar organization, 1934	State treasury matters, 1937
Economic integration, 1935	
Carnival associations, 1936	

SOURCE: Pernambuco, Archivo Público Estadual, newspaper files.

from public administration to professional matters to highway construction (see Table 7.1).

Recife was the host city for almost all the congresses that were held in the state. Not until after 1930 was another site in Pernambuco so favored. Nevertheless, as the table shows, even in that most urban of settings, rural and regional affairs were being given attention by the 1920's. As the table also shows, it was primarily the larger congresses—at the national and international levels—that grappled with the innovations and problems of the modern world. Nevertheless, Pernambucanos participated in those congresses and no doubt brought their messages home. In any event by the 1930's the local meetings clearly reflected a narrower range of specialization and concern.

Horizontal integration was also being achieved through this period at a different level of society: more and more, the employed working classes of the region were linked through unionization or at least concerted action against the generally repressive methods used against strikers throughout the period. Strike activity in Pernambuco took place as early as 1890, when textile workers struck "peacefully" for higher wages.[7] Efforts at labor organization were suppressed in the state through the 1890's, but in 1900 the socialist João Ezequiel succeeded in founding a worker's protective association (Centro Protetor dos Operários em Pernambuco) and edited a socialist newspaper, *Aurora Social*. The organization grew in the same halting manner as other Brazilian socialist groups, but it managed to spur the formation of a variety of workers' associations, mostly in Recife and Maceió. These included relatively strong unions among transportation workers, cigarette rollers, sugar warehouse carriers, and stevedores.[8] An associated union was organized among Maceió's seamstresses in 1913, the first women's union in the Northeast.[9]

Major strikes involved railroad machinists (1902); sugar carriers, trolley conductors, bakery workers, and stevedores (1906); and Great Western workers (a battery of outbreaks, 1908–35). The two most important actions of all occurred in 1919, when a general strike briefly paralyzed Recife—the first of its kind in Brazil—and in the months of July and August in 1922, when a longer and more effective general strike brought out almost every industrial and commercial worker in Recife. The second strike resulted in the temporary cancellation of a 50 percent rise in the sales tax, a measure labeled the Monster Law by strike leaders.* Months later the new governor, Sérgio Loreto, retaliated, brutally crushing union organization and shipping labor leaders to the desolate offshore island prison of Fernando de Noronha. The severest repression was reserved for labor organizers at the Great Western Railway and Pernambuco Tramways, a practice that backfired in the late 1920's, when the opposition

---

*Hermínio Linhares, "As greves operárias," pp. 222–26. The name Lei Monstro was inspired by the John Barrymore film *Dr. Jekyll and Mr. Hyde*, then playing in the city (José Costa Pôrto, *Dantas Barreto*, p. 157).

press began to attack foreign firms with a xenophobic fervor that raised some local sympathy for strikers.

Labor violence played a major role in two Recife-based uprisings that have received relatively little attention: a barracks revolt in 1931, which was finally put down by Col. Jurandyr Mamede, the commander of the newly combined federal-state military brigade; and a Communist Party–inspired uprising in 1935, one of three such outbreaks in the country (the others were in Natal and Rio's Praia Vermelha) and the only one in which soldiers and workers fought side by side.[10] Organized labor fared unevenly under the Vargas regime. On the one hand, repression continued to be widespread during the 1930's, and Pernambuco's interventor placed press coverage of strikes near the top of his list of topics proscribed to newspaper editors.[11] On the other hand, the federal government passed the first major law regulating labor organization nationally, under which several non-Communist unions in Pernambuco were reestablished. Strike activity thereafter was concentrated against the Tramways, the Great Western, and the Lundgren Textile Mills in the northern suburb of Paulista, a bastion of paternalistic employer-employee relations enforced by anti-labor organizing brutality. The Great Western union claimed 4,682 members in 1933, 3,500 in Pernambuco and most of the rest in the states of the satellite bloc.[12]

Fiscal Federalism

By surrendering the right to tax exports to the states under the 1891 Constitution, the Union undermined its own tax-gathering powers and contributed to the rapid rise of state revenues among the wealthier units—at both its own expense and that of the poorer states. São Paulo's and Minas's ratio of state to federal income doubled from 1901 to 1937. Meantime, Pernambuco's only held constant, with a state income equivalent to under 3 percent of federal receipts through the period.[13] Per capita federal income fell by about 25 percent in the first Republican decade alone.[14] States and municípios could now borrow from abroad, though foreign lenders set interest rates commensurate with the financial risks involved. Unequal opportunities for borrowing represented still another example of the burden of the federal system borne by the weaker units.

The inability of the states to become fiscally solvent played a critical role in the integration process, since the have-not states found themselves compelled to beg for federal assistance. The relief measures demanded from the Union invariably lay outside the boundaries of federalism established by the authors of the federation; moreover, when federal aid was granted, it served to limit state independence. Though the big three states all made impressive fiscal gains with the change of regime from Empire to Republic, São Paulo was by far the greatest beneficiary. Its real receipts jumped from 43,000 contos in 1900 to over 200,000 contos in the 1930's. The visual impact of Figure 4 is distorted by the use of a semi-log scale. On a conventionally drawn graph, São Paulo's revenue and expenditure curves literally fly off the top of the page, while Pernambuco's real (1912) revenues and expenditures hug the bottom, barely rising above the line of origin.

Between 1888 and 1930 São Paulo contracted 25 large foreign loans, and its outstanding foreign debt—a measure of its ability to attact capital for internal development—was 26 times larger than Pernambuco's in 1933. São Paulo became so prosperous under the Republic, in fact, that it raised its own funds to subsidize immigration (keeping labor costs down) and to support coffee prices. As for Pernambuco, its income at the end of the period was still well under São Paulo's at the turn of the century, and not much higher than the income of Minas.[15]

Most of the states lived close to fiscal default. Few raised enough revenue to allow for the construction of schools, hospitals, and the other improvements essential to modernization, even during the relatively flush days of the 1920's. In times of retrenchment (between 1898 and 1909; after 1929) state services shrank. Even Minas, the Union's second economic power, found it difficult to finance its needs without incurring unacceptable levels of indebtedness. The plight of the states immobilized internal growth and virtually forced the central government to assume a national economic role.

Pernambuco, with its vast underdeveloped areas and unbalanced economy, was barely able to raise enough revenue to finance its public debt and pay the costs of government. In the years 1920–37 São Paulo spent more annually on primary education than Pernambuco allocated for its entire annual budgets. By 1937, moreover, São Paulo's share of total state receipts had risen to 37.8 percent, compared with 29.3 percent for the 1897–1906 period. Minas's share had also risen substantially, from 10.6 percent to 15.7 percent, whereas Pernambuco's had dropped slightly, from 5.5 percent to 4.9 percent.[16]

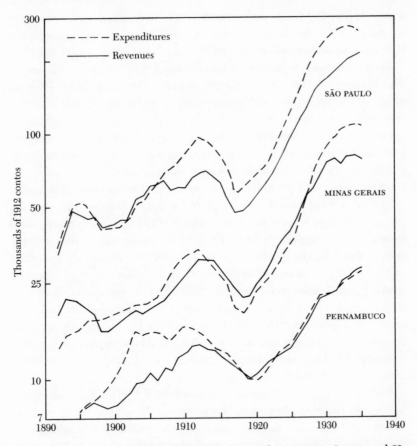

Fig. 4. General revenues and expenditures, Pernambuco, Minas Gerais, and São Paulo, 1892–1935. Five-year moving averages in thousands of 1912 contos. Compiled from Appendix C, series A-3 and B-3; data for São Paulo and Minas are in the companion books. No budgets were passed in Pernambuco in 1892 and 1893, years in which the legislature was forced to close.

The state's budget was balanced only 14 times in the 47 years of the Republic, and never did the annual surplus exceed 2,000 (1912) contos. Fiscal scandals (the loudest of which surfaced during the Loreto administration in the 1920's) further clouded the issue; allegations were rife that large bites of the funds allocated for public expenditures found their way into the pockets of corrupt politicians.[17] Most of Pernambuco's foreign loans carried interest charges of 7 percent, against 4–5 percent paid by the southern states. With carrying charges and other discounts, the

£400,000 loan the município of Recife negotiated with Dunn, Fisher and Company of London in 1910 actually yielded only £340,000, pushing the true interest rate beyond 6 percent.[18]

Before we look into the state's finances any further, a caveat is in order. The Pernambuco Treasury Department unlike the departments of some of the other states, never published summary budgetary information. The revenue data issued were nearly always projections, not the actual amounts collected. In addition, there are large discrepancies among the budgets that exist in more than one version, both in the printed form and in the raw statistics, no doubt because administrations customarily reissued budgetary series with an eye to enhancing their own fiscal image.

Insofar as fiscal records can be pieced together from conflicting data, the greatest deficits were incurred during the Rosa e Silva dynasty, when Pernambuco struggled to deal with the continuing sugar crisis and the costs of financing the transition to usina production. Though these deficits occurred during a period of fiscal orthodoxy at the federal level, the state treasury was strained to the breaking point by the high cost of modernizing Recife, and came up short when sugar industrialists defaulted on usina loans. Only once after 1890 did Pernambuco achieve surpluses in three consecutive years, and this during the 1930's, when the state administration suspended payment on its foreign debt and adopted other accounting devices to cover real losses.

Federal taxes in Pernambuco were collected by the Recife customshouse and by small stations in the interior. Municípios relied on individual agents to make the collections, a practice that led to widespread abuse. Federal taxes and revenue accounted for about half of all the revenues collected in the state; state taxes accounted for most of the rest. The ratio of state to município taxes was 4:1 between 1927 and 1934, for example. But the coffers of the municípios were even barer than these proportions suggest, for Recife not only collected about half of all the município revenue in the state (its budget was 8,656 contos, or about U.S.$ 890,000, in 1929), but also received a substantial portion of the state's funds.

The ratio between Recife's municipal budget and that of the average interior município at this date was roughly 100:1 (with the poorest backlands municípios struggling along at a ratio of 300:1). But even this gross imbalance represented progress from earlier years. In 1890 the annual budgets of the state's poorest municípios were as small as 300 milreis, a tiny percentage of what Recife spent and a fact that as much as anything contributed to the enormous psychological distance that separated the interior from the coast. By the 1930's the growing commercial centers of the Agreste had surpassed the agricultural municípios of the Zona da Mata in revenue and in total budget expenditures. The highest growth rate in the state was posted by Garanhuns, the commercial center of the southwestern Agreste, which by the 1920's had become one of the most important cities in the state.*

Unequal taxation discouraged fiscal integration within the state. The residents and businesses of Recife and its surrounding municípios carried most of the burden. Rural interests in the legislature successfully resisted any imposition of a land tax until 1917, and until 1934 the tax never accounted for 1 percent of the total state revenue. The greatest single share of the state's income came from export levies, accounting for as much as 43.6 percent (1915–16) in the years before 1927 and falling to an average of 20.6 percent thereafter, as taxes on consumers rose. As the owner of one of the country's major ports, Pernambuco at least enjoyed this economic advantage over its neighbors, of course. But its reliance on exports was a two-edged sword, since as an agricultural producer it was wholly dependent on good harvests and favorable market conditions. The revenue gained from export taxes fluctuated widely from year to year, a fact that made budgetary projections particularly difficult.

Exporters, and all other businessmen too, objected constantly and strenuously to the large variety of state and local taxes demanded of them. There were taxes on the execution of contracts, on property transfers, and on urban buildings, and worst of all from their viewpoint, a hated direct tax on industries and professions (which furnished more than 15 percent of state revenues between 1890 and 1905 and from 5 to 10 percent thereafter). By the mid-1920's the state came to rely on a sales tax, a particularly regressive levy in a state lacking any tax on income or accumulated wealth. By 1937 sales taxes contributed 10 percent to the state's income.

Municípios levied regressive taxes as well. Half of the total município receipts came from market licenses and fees for slaughtered cattle. Most

* Its annual rate of increase between 1885–86 and 1934 was 12.8 percent, compared with 6.7 percent for Recife, 7.6 percent for Escada and Goiana in the Mata, and 9.8 percent for Pesqueira in the Sertão. The annual rate of growth of income is based on the formula $Y_t/Y_o = e^{rt}$, where e = natural logarithm, Y_t = income in year t, Y_o = income in year zero [$Y_t = Y_o e^{rt}$; $t = 48$].

local expenditures went for salaries and administrative costs (about 25 percent) and construction (from 10 to 20 percent). Public health and assistance generally took less than 3 percent of a município's revenues.

The state budget increased nearly 27 times over between 1890 and 1937, representing what administrators called a struggle to meet debt obligations, to pay for improvements, and to maintain minimal services. Though as we have seen, most government employees were poorly paid, public salaries frequently came under attack. As early as 1892 state deputy Manoel Borba demanded publicly that the governor's salary be halved, to 12 contos, or $2,933.[19] Officials could have cut the public payroll to reduce expenditures, but since the political system depended on patronage, such action was never seriously considered. Budgetary flexibility became possible only when revenues exceeded expectations—a rare occurrence—or when the debt service fees fell off temporarily.

Table 7.2 shows the state's expenditures in several important sectors over the years 1894–1937. Note that in the entire period education and public works got the highest priority at the start, in 1894–99, reflecting in part Barbosa Lima's strenuous effort to modernize the state. Police expenditures remained relatively high.* Education outlays declined substantially in the succeeding decades, a fact that probably compelled talented elite youths to leave the state, and debt servicing became the largest budget item. Public works spending dropped off even more steeply but made a considerable comeback in the 1920's and early 1930's. Public health expenditures rose from about 1910 onward, reflecting the growing state role and, in the 1920's, the mildly progressive social outlook of the Loreto and Coimbra administrations. Subsidies to agriculture remained surprisingly low for a state so dependent on sugar, cotton, and other agricultural exports, though, as we shall see below, the state made efforts in 1922 and after to educate planters in new, improved agricultural techniques.

The first governor to face the problem of insufficient revenues squarely was José Rufino Bezerra Cavalcanti, whose 1922 budget request for a 50 percent increase in the sales taxes led to the general strike mentioned earlier. The strike forced the administration to reduce the projected tax increase, but by the end of the decade the state's expenditures had dou-

---

*Annual budgetary allocations for this category usually included prisons and related (non-magisterial) costs.

TABLE 7.2

Expenditures in Pernambuco: Percent of Actual Budget by Decade, 1894–1937

Years	Debt service	Education	Força pública and police	Public works	Public health	Agriculture
1894–99	14%	14%	16%	22%	2%	4%
1900–1909	18	8	12	9	2	2
1910–19	21	5	12	9	8	1
1920–29	20	5	16	16	7	1
1930–37	19	10	17	16	7	3

SOURCE: See Appendix C.

NOTE: Where data on specific budget items were not available in a given year, I excluded that year's total expenditures in calculating the percentages of the period. For example, the figure for debt service in the period 1910–19 is based only on the total expenditures for 1910–12 and 1914–18 for lack of a budgetary breakdown on the years 1913 and 1919. Credit operations are not included, nor are all expenditures.

bled in real terms, and most of the new revenues were drawn from the consuming population.

Complaints by state officials that the economic structure of the federation harmed Pernambuco's well-being were a constant theme through the entire period, and need only be cited briefly here. As early as 1890 we find the authorities lamenting their state's "deplorable" economic condition and insisting that it was the "pariah" of Brazil. In 1893 the governor declared that the Pernambucan economy could not bear the weight of the petty taxes the state was forced to impose in the absence of federal relief. The export tax, as he and his successors inevitably pointed out, was unreliable. The Recife Commercial Association in 1906 warned the visiting President-elect that high local taxes were crippling the working population and impeding the circulation of money, thereby creating a fictitiously high salary scale and in turn raising the costs of production and restricting purchasing power.[20]

State officials further complained that the central government blatantly discriminated against Pernambuco in the granting of Bank of Brazil loans. In 1906, at the height of Rosa e Silva's power, the region's leading planter association approached the Bank for a loan of 4,000 contos, only to be offered the sum of 200, which it termed "ridiculous" and refused.[21] In 1910 an opposition newspaper charged that fiscal crisis had left Pernambuco destitute, and with no major improvements in 15 years.[22] Though the Bank did grant Pernambuco some loans in the late 1920's, the state continued to be financially strapped. The Vargas government was not a month old before the new state administration began imploring federal authorities for additional loans, averring that otherwise it would have to default on its other loans and many local banks would fail.[23] In 1934, in spite of a new federal commitment to less-developed regions, the five-state satellite bloc received only 8 percent of the funds the Bank of Brazil lent to states, against a total of 66 percent for the big three states, and against 11 percent for the Federal District alone.[24]

Finally, as touched on earlier, an important, even critical, economic fact of life of the Republic was the ability of the strongest states, most notably São Paulo, to reach beyond the Union for fiscal aid. Coffee valorization, the carefully administered program of price supports for coffee producers, was underwritten by foreign investors. Efforts in the early 1920's to extend the same concept of "permanent defense" to such other agricultural commodities as sugar, rubber, cocoa, cotton, tobacco, and mate failed, though the central government moved closer to direct intervention by creating the IAA and other regional agencies.

State and Federal Economic Intervention

For all the negative effects that federalism had on individual states, it also had a positive side, giving them a new freedom to deal with local problems through legal or fiscal initiative. Pernambuco set aside prevailing orthodoxy in two major areas: subsidies for the industrialization of sugar processing, and tax exemptions for factory construction. In 1906, responding to the coffee boom in the South (and the apparent success of valorization), the state granted an annual subsidy of 30,000 contos to the federation of planter organizations, and established the first agricultural commission in Brazil to gather information on land use, crop yields, and other matters. But the program proved premature. The commission's efforts were ignored, and it was quietly dismantled.[25] A private effort between 1906 and 1908 of usineiros and sugar exporters to create a producer's cartel (colligação) had no better success.

But gradually change began to take hold. Northeasterners traveled more; roads began to dot the hinterland where trains had never penetrated. More persons came to Recife from the smaller urban centers of the region as opportunities for specialized education expanded, and more of the affluent northeasterners traveled abroad. The state created its public health service in 1909, setting the stage for the small burst of innovation in the 1920's by state health officials, most of whom brought their ideas from the South, where they had worked and studied.

The year 1922 saw a renewed effort on the part of the authorities to aid agriculture with the addition of a Cotton Department empowered to study farming conditions and to classify cotton varieties. In 1927 Pernambuco's Secretary of Agriculture organized the first state federation of local credit institutions in Brazil. A conference at that same time brought together representatives from every município in the state to discuss road building. A final effort to coordinate agricultural information—the establishment of a Sugar Institute in 1927 and of a Sugar Cooperative in the following year—produced few measurable results but signaled the state's willingness to accept responsibility in this realm before the initiative passed to the federal government.[26]

The provisional government's regional agencies assumed control of a host of matters formerly left to the states. Vargas's Municipal Inspectorates in the northeastern states attempted to impose uniform bookkeeping practices, required that fiscal records be preserved, and offered technical aid, reserving as well the right to question or deny budget items challenged by their officials.[27] The federal Agricultural Ministry absorbed Pernambuco's Cotton Service in 1933 and established the IAA to regulate sugar production. New federal social legislation created uniform standards and sent payments to the states for pension and other welfare programs from the federal treasury.[28]

In the end no state was able to preserve its economic freedom of action. The turning point came rather quickly after the 1930 Revolution, when the Vargas government was gripped by a nationalistic impatience with states that requested aid while still demanding to be treated as autonomous: it is no wonder that Vargas treated Minas with favor when the Mineiros acquiesced to client status peacefully. The shock of the worldwide depression removed the final pretenses of state financial autonomy. In 1933 the Aranha Plan empowered the federal government to underwrite all internal and external debts for ten years, to the woe of lenders in 1938 when this arrangement was suspended. Pernambuco itself received 30,000 contos in credits to stave off default. In some ways, times had not changed very much. The state's 1934 budget listed the grant as "income," leading Lima Cavalcanti to boast that he had achieved a surplus of 1,300 contos in that year.[29]

The elite accepted the new rules, if not with equanimity, then at least with a tacit awareness that its own role probably would not be altered.

The new national perspective appealed to some, especially those who, if they found life too confining, could take advantage of their interregional and national ties to establish themselves outside of the Northeast. Even such men as João Cleofas, a major state political figure in the 1920's and 1930's and both a planter and usineiro, diversified their business interests, buying into refineries in the state of Rio de Janeiro, one of the Northeast's prime economic competitors. The tendency to preserve social mores, and the very vastness of the country itself, softened the impact of change. The new roads that linked the prosperous South with the northeastern backlands bypassed Recife and drained population from the region. This fact accentuated the still far from complete integration between the interior and the coast, and helped preserve the older ways. For the time being, the life-styles of most of the inhabitants of Pernambuco and the satellite bloc remained unaltered, despite the encroachment of the federal government.

Conclusion

IN HIS WORK *The Revolt of the Catalans*, J. H. Elliott reminds us that Catalan authors extolled the beauty of their region but ignored banditry and other manifestations of underlying social malaise.[1] Elliott's observation holds equally true for many writers in post-1889 Brazil—for example, Rui Barbosa, who often likened Salvador to Athens and simply overlooked his city's poverty and endemic disease.[2] Pernambucan writers, however, have tended to go to one of two extremes, describing their state either in terms of lavish praise or in terms of gloomy despair, each a rather fashionable convention that served to exempt the author from criticism. It is not so surprising, then, that some local scholars consider Oliveira Lima's pessimistic *Pernambuco: seu desenvolvimento histórico* (1895) to be the state's greatest historical study.[3]

This is not to say that Pernambucanos were unable to identify the causes of malaise or offer remedial courses of action. But two themes emerge out of the historical fabric of the Republican era: first, the state's major problems not only remained unresolved but in some cases worsened; and second, serious efforts to speak to reality and generate structural change invariably provoked resistance even to the point of violence.

Participants had to play according to the rules of the system. Members of the elite could switch political allegiances indiscriminately or assail their opponents with malice, and still remain socially welcome. But the rules were finely drawn, and those who broke them paid for it. For example, when the federal senator (and former governor) Manoel Borba published a book leveling specific charges of corruption against Governor

Sérgio Loreto, the "conservative classes" were scandalized and Borba's career was ruined.[4] Similarly, though Lima Cavalcanti attacked his fellow usineiro Estácio Coimbra almost daily in his opposition *Diário da Manhã* during the late 1920's, Coimbra continued to stop over for lunch at his enemy's father's usina when he traveled home to Barreiros. Upon becoming interventor in 1930, Lima Cavalcanti ordered the confiscation of the exiled former governor's property and took punitive measures against Coimbra's home município. Even this was tolerated. It was only when Lima Cavalcanti opened his administration to social reformers identified with the Left that he was considered to have overstepped the bounds of propriety, and then he met the same fate as Borba.

Most political rhetoric was harmless, since it fell within the boundaries of the "official ideology," acceptance of which remained the basic requirement for entrance into the political elite.[5] An unwritten condition stood at the center of that ideology: modernization and change were desirable only if they neither challenged the established order nor threatened to alter the social status quo.

A "political museum," Pernambuco made a relatively smooth transition from Empire to Republic, with a Republican Party that was weak and leaderless and the Republican program vulnerable to preemption by Monarchists who flocked to the new ideology to save their political skins. In politics as well as in society it was axiomatic that the old ruling class conceded power and legitimacy to new groups only after securing guarantees that their rights and prerogatives would be preserved, if not increased.[6]

Attempts at change that threatened the system were dealt with accordingly. The dearth of potential challengers during Pernambuco's Republican history is instructive. There were few working-class immigrants, and no cohesive social group in which to sow the seeds of socialism and anarcho-syndicalism, ideologies that took hold in the South. The state lacked a concentrated industrial proletariat, since the usinas were scattered throughout the Zona da Mata; and university students tended to be conservative—not even abolitionism had flourished at the Recife Law School in the 1880's. The leading opposition factions were run by men cut from exactly the same cloth as their incumbent rivals. Coronelismo was a pragmatic accommodation (if not what the historian Victor Nunes Leal terms a compromise) to the distance between the coast and the hinterland, representing, as it were, the superimposition of a structure of legitimacy on the lawless and violent forms of rule in the backlands.[7] Anachronistic or not, coronel hegemony survived in altered form well beyond the period under study.

Though the promulgation of the Republic only mildly affected the control and exercise of power, the federal system undercut Pernambuco's national influence and forced the state's spokesmen to fight for its political survival. The federal government's blunt imposition of Barbosa Lima as interventor in 1892 signaled Pernambuco's vulnerability, and not even the prestige of Rosa e Silva during the heyday of the PRF could stave off the even greater humiliation of federal intervention in 1911.

The members of the state's political and social elite were unable to adjust to the far-reaching changes that accompanied the deterioration of the Northeast's economic position as the region lost its foreign markets and became increasingly uncompetitive with agricultural producers in the Center-South. Planters resisted group action despite chronic economic difficulties; instead they came to rely on appeals for outside aid. To be sure, the situation may have been hopeless. But it is still a fact that on the whole the cane growers failed to support their own associations, and the usineiros seemed to be content to default on some of their debts and to repay others in bonds whose market value was 25 percent of their nominal worth.[8]

Politically, the persistence of internal divisiveness sped Pernambuco's banishment to the periphery of the federation and played into the hands of the state's rivals. Dantas Barreto, who had vowed to throw out the old planter-bacharel oligarchy, solved none of the state's problems; the former War Minister was unable even to influence his successor, who drove him into the political camp of his old archenemy, Rosa e Silva. The collapse of the Old Republic in 1930 brought a widening of base of the political elite; but by then the state's role had shrunk to insignificance. Moreover, the state soon became even more politically divided, with the emergence by 1933 of a right-wing coterie dedicated to the destruction of the "communistic" Lima Cavalcanti administration. At the very time São Paulo's antagonistic political factions joined together out of mutual interest at the Constituent Assembly, Pernambuco's delegation split into three blocs, creating an uncontrollable delegation and further diluting the state's influence.

The most striking consequence of the post-1889 system for Pernambuco was its defenselessness against federal intervention. In response, it affected deference to the states whose politicians influenced federal actions, while seeking to work its will among the neighboring states in the name of leadership of the mostly fictional northern bloc. Both postures failed. The satellite bloc states resolutely resisted Pernambuco's economic power plays; indeed even Recife's economic domination of its hinterland faded as truck routes began to draw off trade to new centers like Campina Grande in Paraíba and directly to the South. Pernambuco's neighbors likewise resisted political pressure from Recife, though they occasionally cooperated on matters of mutual benefit. From the Pernambucanos' point of view, it was their ill-fortune that the two northeasterners who attained highest national power during the Republic—Epitácio Pessôa and José Américo de Almeida—were both Paraíbanos and for that reason openly hostile to Pernambuco's demands.

In principle, Pernambuco and other second-rank states could have swung some weight by acting in concert. But the federal system militated against alliances among the weaker states, setting them against one another in the competition for favors. Pernambuco and Bahia might have cooperated—they shared similar problems—but instead they consistently fought in the legislative arena. The bitter and useless argument over Pernambuco's claims to the São Francisco territory continued unabated and inflamed their long-standing mutual distrust. Leaders of both states soon chose to stake out separate spheres of influence, allowing Bahia to draw the State of Sergipe into its orbit, as well as the middle reaches of the São Francisco region—including the Pernambucan municípios of Petrolina, Boa Vista, and Cabrobó—a result of the railroad line between Salvador and Joaseiro and the absence of similar transportation connections to Recife.

Not a single prescription for change outlined by Governor Barbosa Lima in the early 1890's was followed in the decades after his stormy administration. His list of problem areas was remarkably thorough: the isolation of the interior; education (Pernambuco, he wrote, spent more on prisons and barracks than on schools); the fraud and coercion inherent in the coronel system; inadequate facilities for sanitation, water supply, urban housing, and public health; insufficient sources of município revenue; transportation difficulties; and the deleterious effect of federal economic policy on northeastern interests.[9]

Two decades later, Pedro Souto Maior identified the same needs, urging local officials to follow the example of the United States in seeking immigration ("to enrich the country and raise the level of civilization") and subsidizing railroads. Souto Maior pointed to another local deficiency: Recife's stultifying domination of life in the state, which he contrasted with the rise of dynamic medium-sized cities in the leading states of the Center-South.[10] His warnings passed unnoticed. By the First World War, moreover, Recife had lost much of its former attraction as a magnet for the sons of the region's elite. Upwardly mobile youths now merely made Recife a temporary home on their way to the South or bypassed the city (and its law school) entirely. Expatriate colonies of Pernambucanos flourished in Rio de Janeiro and São Paulo.*

In many ways one could describe Pernambuco's history as a history *malgré soi*, because so many internal developments essentially came about simply in response to external events and pressures. But since the federation gave each Brazilian state a unique responsibility to fend for itself, the policies that were adopted stand as evidence at least of the governing elite's own predilection for change. Below are what I conceive to be the main themes in Pernambuco's Republican experience.

Attempts at change and innovation usually provoked resistance. Barbosa Lima, who did more than any other governor to strengthen the economy by subsidizing industrialization, was considered an outsider and ostracized. His efforts to attract foreign technicians and educators to the state were opposed despite a tradition of such recruitment in Pernambuco dating back to the mid-nineteenth century. His drive to promote agricultural and technical education was thoroughly unappreciated, and his model training school, the Escola Industrial Frei Caneca, was closed by his successor. As Souza Barros reminds us, "doutor de máquinas ainda cheirava mal"—the title "doctor of machines still left a bad odor."[11]

Advances in education and public health under Estácio Coimbra met even more violent opposition. The state's Secretary of Education, recruited from São Paulo where he had earned an unimpeachable reputation, was hounded from his post and driven from the state.[12] After 1930 the Vargas administration, seeking to win the support of the Catholic Church and its allies on the political Right, tolerated and indeed helped create a new and ugly atmosphere opposed to progressive innovation. In Pernambuco this took the form of scathing attacks on several of the inter-

*In the 1920's three Pernambucanos—Henrique Lage, Ernesto Pereira Carneiro, and Guilherme da Silveira—played a major role in the industrial development of the Federal District.

ventor's cabinet members and aides, some of whom were linked to the well-publicized proposal for a study of the working conditions of usina workers in the Zona da Mata. The state administration in the closing years of the decade resorted to repressive tactics of the worst sort and stood as one of the most intransigent in all of Brazil.

As Peter Eisenberg and Jaime Reis have shown, the state's sugar planters rejected all forms of modernization that threatened social change. Like Bahia, Pernambuco imported modern technology in the closing decades of the Empire, but the planters for the most part chose not to take advantage of it. Cheap labor was readily available, thus reducing the attractiveness of labor-saving methods and equipment. Many planters preferred low-yield, disease-resistant cane to higher-yield (and less-resistant) varieties, most ignored other sorts of technological innovations that promised increased output, and virtually all of them opposed efforts to improve the living conditions of rural workers.[13]

Owing to the sugar aristocracy's resistance to change, steps taken to modernize the economy produced uneven and incomplete results. The usina system improved the efficiency of sugar processing but dealt neither with the inefficiency of cane production nor with the poor system of regional transportation. The establishment of the federal IAA staved off financial collapse in the Northeast, but it also discouraged crop diversification and accelerated the trend toward land concentration. As late as 1959 Pernambuco ranked last among the Brazilian states in the utilization of farmland, with almost 40 percent of its territory unproductive and only 3 percent of its agricultural land under permanent cultivation.[14] Meanwhile, the increased efficiency on the processing side acted to lower wages in an already depressed labor market.

Pernambuco was not aided to any meaningful degree under the federation. None of the political machines in the state, not even Rosa e Silva's PRF at its peak, ever came close to achieving the sort of influence and control exerted by the Paulista and Mineiro machines, perhaps reflecting the less-disciplined, lower level of political organization in the Northeast. From Henrique Pereira Lucena (1890) to Agamenon Magalhães (1937) nine state administrations antagonistic to their immediate predecessors controlled the governorship.[15] The state's constantly divided legislative delegation failed to obtain federal aid except in times of extreme crisis. Rosa e Silva, the most prominent national figure produced by Pernambuco, showed nothing but disdain for his own state and rarely visited it even at the height of his power. Between 1890 and 1930 Pernambuco placed only a handful of its representatives in high federal posts. Only Magalhães played any major role in the federal administration during the 1930's, and he was used by Vargas to neutralize the political appeals from the leader of his own state for greater federal assistance.

Life for most of the state's inhabitants was brutal. High fertility, high mortality, malnutrition, and violence are not necessarily endemic to impoverished areas, but may be seen as consequences of social policy. Contemporaries have testified to the squalor of life in Recife, half of whose residents in 1923 lived in mocambos.[16] In 1937 the rate of infant mortality in Recife was higher than the rate for French and Belgian cities in the period 1650–1755.[17] The cities and towns of the interior had a façade of cosmopolitanism, but this masked a lifelessness that drove thousands from the region.[18] On the eve of the Second World War 65 percent of the municípios in Pernambuco had no agronomist, 88 percent no engineer, and 94 percent no veterinarian; 87 percent of the Mata inhabitants surveyed at that time habitually wore no shoes.[19]

The affluent viewed the poor as criminals. Martins Júnior, the Republican spokesman, advocated that the impact of abolition be softened by "strong work laws, the repression of vagabondage, [and] military colonies."[20] Employers took advantage of periods of economic calamity to cut wages; women and children were employed for virtually nothing.[21] Violence pervaded northeastern life, from the regular police raids on the beggars crowding Recife's bridges, to the cruel punishment of the prisoners taken during the Quebra-Quilos revolt,* to the alcoholic *festas* (festivals) in the sugar zone, to the outbursts of street rioting in the state capital during Carnival, especially during the years between 1915 and 1921. All of this, plus of course the almost routine depredations of both the bandits and the political thugs of the interior. Travelers reported a more silent kind of violence at weekly rural feiras, where mothers offered their virgin adolescent daughters for ten reis.[22]

In some ways Pernambuco had less in common with the prosperous states of the Center-South than with such fragmented, developing societies as southern Italy. Like that region, the Northeast lay isolated within the larger national community, upon which it was dependent.[23] Both are predominantly agricultural regions that saw the growth of some

---

*They were staked out in the broiling sun with a strip of wet rawhide bound tightly around their necks, doomed to a slow and painful death by strangulation.

factories, but of a type that, in David Apter's words, left the economy "commercialized but not industrialized."[24] In the Mezzogiorno, as in the sugar-producing Northeast, the process of national integration has hampered economic growth. Agriculture in that region has been hindered by inefficient farming methods and by the same sorts of tenancy and wage-labor patterns that characterized the Mata; and one could justly apply Sidney Tarrow's description of trade and commerce in southern Italy as "more typical of the anarchic, personalized bazaar economies of traditional societies" to at least the interior of Pernambuco and the Northeast. The same is true of his representation of commercial enterprises as a "bare escape from unemployment."[25]

There are still other points of similarity between the two regions. The Mezzogiorno, like the Northeast, has traditionally lost population to mass out-migration and high mortality; has a large portion of economically active persons dependent on public employment; and has a lower class that lacks a clearly defined occupational role structure, a result of the expanded commercialization of the economy without a commensurate development of new economic roles usually associated with industrialization. Finally, like the Brazilian Northeast, the Italian South has lagged well behind the rest of the country in agricultural and technical education. With unproductive landholding retaining its social prestige, society has tended to favor esoteric rather than practical fields of study.[26]

Still, as we have seen, because of the homogeneity of Brazilian society, Pernambuco did in fact have much in common with the other states of Brazil, the strong and powerful ones no less than those in its own economic straits. No clear relationship existed between social differentiation and political change. And the composition of political elites, as I have shown in Chapter 5, did not differ in major ways from state to state. As in São Paulo, the political opposition in Pernambuco was largely made up of members of the traditional elite who were excluded from power. There, as elsewhere, evidence that the landed aristocracy retained its traditional prerogatives is seen in the reluctance of the state legislature to introduce meaningful land taxes despite chronic fiscal deficits.

Yet even the power of landowning groups in the Northeast was not sufficient to force state governments in the region to reduce export duties in order to make their products more competitive. The very need for fiscal survival dictated that export taxes be kept high. On balance, it would be unfair to accuse the Pernambucanos of having no one to blame

for their problems but themselves. The state-subsidized usinas represented a bold attempt to revitalize the economy, even if the state's
finances ultimately proved too anemic to provide the needed complemen-
tary structural changes. Pernambuco leaders struggled for years to obtain
better railroad and port facilities, lower shipping rates, and a greater
share of federal tax revenue. Under the Old Republic, few requests for
assistance from the weaker states were heeded.

Across Brazil, the Republican-era elites never lost confidence in their
ability to use change for their own ends. Politics was based on the unholy
alliance between rural bosses and the state machines, leaving those who
hoped to bring about reform by working within the system little realistic
chance for success. Added to this in the Northeast was the fact that the
region's economic base remained largely unchanged from 1889 to 1937,
and its relative political and economic strength declined during that
period. All of this tended to prolong elite rule.

By the third political generation the state political elite had become
modified to the extent that fewer of its members were likely to have been
drawn from the landed aristocracy of the region; more men fit into the
bureaucratic-technocratic mold. Yet this shift recalled a similar broadening of the elite at the outset of the period, when the elite opened its doors
to recruit and absorb young men (the bacharel graduates of the law school)
to deal with changing legal and economic conditions; for in this instance,
as in the earlier ones, the doors to the elite were merely opened a crack,
only as much as was necessary to cope with the assorted new duties of
government.

The major divisions in the society remained vertical; and its only major
conflicts continued to be fought out within the elite itself. The parochial
system of state government yielded to a somewhat more sophisticated
and centralized form of national government, as Vargas recast the federal
system along patron-client lines, closed the Congress, and squelched
state autonomy. But the elite continued to adapt. Coronéis shed their
traditional images and retired to the legitimacy of federal patronage sinecures, though after 1945 they again sought local political offices. The
loyalties of the Vargas-era bureaucrats shifted to the national administration, acceding, as it were, to the state's virtual total dependence on the
central government. When the new measures—the regional agencies, the
coordinated efforts to combat the effects of drought—basically failed to
live up to their promise, the poverty-stricken states of the Northeast were

driven psychologically further from the center, now even stripped of the illusion of being able to chart their own course.

The new political atmosphere that accompanied the 1930 Revolution and the impulse given to national integration by the Vargas administration wounded regionalist pride, though, as in the case of the Society of the Friends of Alberto Torres in the mid-1930's, it served to encourage regional interaction. Centralization accomplished little for Pernambuco as long as the social and economic issues vital to its interests remained low on the list of national priorities; integration may have harmed the Northeast insofar as it drained off talent.

Ironically, the trend to fuller national integration served to isolate the region still further from the national center. Neither Vargas nor "viceroy" Juarez Távora made any effort to protect Lima Cavalcanti from his enemies. Nor did they attempt to stem the backlash against cultural and social experimentation that occurred with stronger force in the Northeast than anywhere else in Brazil. Symbolically, the tacitly centralist and dictatorial Estado Novo marked the passing of the old era. But nothing changed very much in practice after 1937. The "new" state offered no new solutions to the old political and social problems of the Northeast.

Appendixes

A Note on Elites

THE POLITICAL ELITE examined in Chapter 5 is a group defined as hold-
ers of important positions in state parties and governments, plus the state's
representatives in important federal posts, during the years from the birth
of the Republic to the Estado Novo. Thus, statistically speaking, the elite
is a population rather than a sample. Since some persons held office for as
little as one day, a 90-day minimum tenure was required for inclusion
during the period November 15, 1889, to November 10, 1937. All persons
are included who could be identified by name and dates of tenure, whether
or not any other information was discovered. In fact, however, virtually
complete biographies were obtained for more than 90 percent of the elites
of the three states—Minas Gerais, Pernambuco, and São Paulo.

The authors agreed on the inclusion of 17 to 18 state government posts
and 17 at the federal level. In the states the list consisted of the governor
and his important elected and appointed assistants in the executive, and
top-ranking legislative and judicial figures. Federal posts were defined
analogously, but were included only when held by representatives of the
state under study.

Specifically, state elite members consisted of the governor; the lieutenant
governor; the secretaries of justice, finance, agriculture, transportation, education and health, security, and the governorship; the state chief of police;
the president of the state bank; the prefect of the state capital; leading administrators peculiar to each state (viz., presidents of the Coffee Institutes
in São Paulo and Minas; director of the state press in Minas; director of the
port authority and inspector of municípios in Pernambuco); the presidents
of the state chamber and senate; the majority leader in the chamber; and
the president of the state supreme court.

Federal officials included the president of the Republic; the vice-president; the ministers of justice, finance, agriculture, transportation, education,
labor, and foreign affairs; the president of the Bank of Brazil; the prefect of
the Federal District; the president of the National Coffee Department; the
president of the federal chamber of deputies; the vice-president of the

senate;* the majority leader of the chamber; the leader of the state delegation in the chamber; and members of the federal supreme court.

Thus the elites were defined uniformly except for the "leading [state]
administrators" specified above. To have eliminated such key positions as
the presidencies of the Coffee Institutes in São Paulo and Minas because
the post did not exist in Pernambuco seemed unduly procrustean, since the
central purpose of the definition of elites was to obtain comparable *wholes*
from each state. The size of the elite populations ranged from 214 in Minas
Gerais, to 263 in São Paulo, to 276 in Pernambuco.

Three nongovernmental positions are also included in the elites—the
executive committee of the Republican Party (the "establishment" party in
the Old Republic), and those of the most important non-Republican party
before 1930, and from 1931 to 1937. (The roles of the Republicans and
their opponents were reversed after 1930, or new establishment parties
brought in many leaders of pre-1930 opposition groups.) It seemed essential to include this nongovernmental sector of the elite because of its
leading role in the larger political process. Separate computer runs of party
executive committee members against nonmembers tended to confirm our
qualitative judgment on this point: committee members held more elite-
defining positions than nonmembers, and they were more prominent in the
economy and society. Thus, in the manner of Frank Bonilla's definition of
the Venezuelan political elite, in *The Failure of Elites* (Cambridge, Mass.,
1970), p. 16, party executive committees were included to better approxi-
mate the effective power structure.

The elite was defined to exclude military and naval officials, since these
groups were members of virtually self-regulating corporations and had
tenuous ties with the three state machines. In the cases of the ministries of
war and navy, in only one administration (Pessoa, 1919–22) were civilians
appointed to the posts; they were excluded from our elites, though officers
holding the specified "civilian" posts were not. Regional military commanders, with the possible exception of those in Rio Grande do Sul, had no
enduring ties with state political machines, and these career officers were
rotated around the country. Commanders of the state military police forces
were subordinated to the civilian political leadership, and in none of the
three states did they play significant roles in political decision-making.

In each case our institutional definition omitted a few individuals who
might have been included had the elite been defined on a "reputational"
basis. Yet the exclusion of two or three persons in a group of 753 seemed
an acceptable sacrifice to maintain a cohesive definition across the states:
those left out would have changed the profile of the group only a percentage point, and many data were too "soft" to justify claims of precision
at a fraction of a point.

Approximately 100 variables were recorded on the elite's characteristics.
They were grouped under the headings of political ideology, roles in major
political events at both national and state levels, social and cultural activities, foreign ties, interstate ties, age, education, occupation, *municípios*

* The vice-president of the Republic was ipso facto president of the senate.

and zones of political activity, and family ties. (For coding schemes, the reader may obtain code books from the authors.) Biographical data were strongest on educational and official positions held; they were weakest on economic assets.

Though the computer program was designed to show progression through the elite posts during the period studied, it does not cover whole career patterns, and thus we have not produced a political recruitment study analogous to Frederick W. Frey's *The Turkish Political Elite* (Cambridge, Mass., 1965). Frey's elite is much more simply defined than ours; it includes all members of the Turkish National Assembly serving between 1920 and 1957, i.e. occupants of one post rather than 37 (p. 7).

Data were obtained from a variety of sources: official obituaries in state gazettes, obituaries and centenary-of-birth notices in newspaper morgues, almanacs, membership lists of voluntary associations, biographies, interviews of elite members and their descendents, questionnaires to these groups, professional school graduation lists, publications of political parties, biographical dictionaries and encyclopedias, and commemorative albums.

An initial problem was to construct lists of officeholders and dates of tenure, since in the majority of cases none existed. For the executive committees of the Republican Parties in Minas and São Paulo, it was discovered that elections for state and national offices would always bring forth an "electoral bulletin" signed by the current members of the respective committee. Historical reconstruction of the committees therefore began with a search for the dates of elections in the annual reports of the secretary of justice. This was followed by an examination of the *Correio Paulistano* and the *Minas Gerais* on the day preceding the contests to discover the signers of the bulletins. (A similar procedure was used in Pernambuco, but with less success, because of the lower degrees of party cohesion in that state.) The compilation of lists of officeholders and dates of tenure should provide basic chronologies for the historian of institutions, and a complete listing for the state is found in Appendix B.

Conventions Used in Classifying Elite Characteristics

1. Members of the elite had to be Brazilian nationals.

2. If a member held the same post more than once, he was coded for each separate tenure of that office.

3. In the absence of data for a given characteristic in cases where data were virtually complete, it was assumed the elite member lacked the attribute, and the item was coded negatively. Only in those cases where the overwhelming majority of data were missing was "missing data" coded.

4. The "not applicable" code was entered whenever a member was too young to have participated in a given event, had already died, or had withdrawn from political activity.

5. All events and experiences that were coded positively occurred during the stated chronological limits, except those specifically referring to pre-1889 events and items pertaining to education, foreign parentage, and residence abroad, all of which included pre-1889 experience as well.

6. If a member represented a state in a federal post other than the one

for which he was coded, that portion of his career outside the state under study was not coded. (E.g. Rivadávia Correia in his youth was a member of the São Paulo elite, but later represented Rio Grande do Sul as a federal minister.)

7. Multiple professions were coded, viz., all those professions and occupations ascertainable in the 1889–1937 period. Specific conventions: an exporter was also classified as a merchant; a comissário was not classified as a banker, since the latter term implies a director of a larger operation (though there was considerable overlap); newspaper publishers, building contractors, and railroad builders were all coded as industrialists, and all magistrates were also classified as lawyers.

8. All state supreme court justices were coded as having their political base in the appropriate state capital. Since most were professional magistrates, they were so classified because they had no home constituency and depended on directives from the state government to which they were attached.

9. Presidents of the Bank of Brazil included only that group who held office between 1906 and 1937. The bank was completely reorganized in 1906 with a more fully national mission. Before the reorganization it had no agencies outside the Federal District, and by 1927 there were 70.

The Brazilian Elite—Political Offices Held

STATE

Secretary of Justice, or General Secretary
Secretary of Finance
Secretary of Agriculture
Secretary of Education and Health (Interior)
Secretary of Transportation (*Viação*)
Secretary of Security (*Segurança*)
Secretary of Governorship or Interventorship
Governor or Interventor
Lieutenant Governor
Prefect, State Capital
Police Chief of State
Top State Administrator (SP [São Paulo] def.: pres., Coffee Institute. MG [Minas Gerais] def.: director, State Press, and pres., Mineiro Coffee Institute. PE [Pernambuco] def.: dir., Port Authority and Inspector General of municipalities)
President, State-owned bank
President, State Senate
President, State Chamber, or President, Constituent Assembly
Majority Leader, State Chamber
President, State Supreme Court
Leader of largest non-PR party or coalition, through 1930 (SP def.: member, executive committee, Partido Democrático. [MG: not applicable.] PE def.: member, Martins Jr. and José Mariano factions; member, pre-1910 anti–Rosa e Silva group; member, anti-Dantas group, 1911–18; member, Partido Democrático, 1920's)

Leader of largest non-PR party or coalition, 1931–37 (SP def.: member, executive committee, PD [1931–34]; member, executive committee, Partido Constitucionalista, 1934–37. MG def.: member, executive committee, Partido Progressista. PE def.: member, dissident Partido Social Democrático bloc [anti-Lima Cavalcanti faction])

Member, executive committee, Partido Republicano (MG def.: PR, 1889–90; Partido Republicano Constitucional, 1893–97, defined as leaders signing voting slates; Partido Republicano Mineiro, 1897–1937)

FEDERAL

Minister of Justice
Minister of Finance
Minister of Agriculture
Minister of Foreign Affairs
Minister of Education
Minister of Labor
Minister of Transportation
President of the Republic
Vice-President of the Republic
Prefect, Federal District
President, Conselho Nacional do Café, or its successor, Departamento Nacional do Café
President, Bank of Brazil (1906–37)
Vice-President, Federal Senate
President, Chamber of Deputies, or President, Constituent Assembly
Majority Leader, Chamber of Deputies
Leader, state delegation (*bancada*), Chamber of Deputies
Minister, Supreme Court (*Supremo Tribunal Federal*)

*The six-page table that follows shows variables and
values for Pernambuco, Minas Gerais, and São Paulo*

Variables and Values in the Three Elite Studies
(Adjusted frequencies in percentages)

Categories and variables	Pernambuco		Minas Gerais		São Paulo		Composite	
	Value	Number	Value	Number	Value	Number	Value	Number
POLITICAL EVENTS								
1a. Monarchist who adhered to the Republic by public affirmation, Nov. 15, 1889–Dec. 31, 1891	73.8%	80	48.2%	83	49.5%	105	56.3%	268
1b. Monarchist who adhered to the Republic, 1892–1900	3.8	80	2.4	83	0	105	1.9	268
1c. Historical Republican: a self-proclaimed Republican before abolition (May 13, 1888)	21.3	80	41.0	83	49.5	105	38.4	268
1d. Eleventh-hour Republican: publicly declared self a Republican between May 13, 1888, and Nov. 14, 1889	1.3	80	8.4	83	1.0	105	3.4	268
2. Abolitionist before Jan. 1, 1887, calling for complete termination of slavery within one decade or less	16.8	95	8.6	116	19.8	111	14.9	322
3. Deodoro backer: supported Deodoro's attempted coup between Nov. 3 and 24, 1891	5.2	97	5.9	118	12.3	122	8.0	337
4. Break on valorization: break with the state establishment's position at any time	0	114	0	131	1.0	206	0.4	451
5. Break with state establishment's position over presidential succession in 1909–10	23.7	135	10.7	149	7.9	164	13.6	448
6. Break with state establishment's position over presidential succession in 1921–22	6.8	117	4.6	151	0.6	178	3.6	446
7. Break with state establishment's position over presidential succession in 1929–30	22.1	113	5.9	136	3.2	125	9.9	374
8. Tenente: Tenente or political associate of tenentes after Oct. 24, 1930	18.9	111	2.9	138	5.8	171	8.3	420
NONPOLITICAL LEADERSHIP								
9. Magistrate: Juiz de direito or higher	25.9	205	16.8	214	19.4	242	20.6	661
10. Cultural leader: member, state academy of letters, or national academy of letters	8.2	196	4.7	214	5.8	241	6.1	651
11. Labor leader: officer, labor union (local), or higher unit or organization	1.0	196	0	214	0	243	0.3	653

	%	N	%	N	%	N	%	N
12. Social club member: any one or more of the following: SP def.: Sociedade Hípica, Clube Comercial, Jockey Clube, Clube Atlético Paulista, Automóvel Clube. MG def.: Automóvel Clube, Jockey Clube. PE def.: Clube Internacional, Jockey Clube Sport, Centro Pernambucano do Rio	15.3	196	11.2	214	27.4	241	18.4	651
13. Agricultural society officer: SP def.: Sociedade Rural Brasileira, or any of its constituent entities before consolidation—Centro Agrícola, Sociedade Paulista da Agricultura, Liga Agrícola Brasileira, or Associação de Lavradores de Café. MG def.: Sociedade Mineira de Agricultura. PE def.: Sociedade Auxiliadora de Agricultura de Pernambuco	6.6	196	1.9	214	6.7	239	5.1	649
14. Officer, state Commercial Association	4.1	196	0.5	214	3.7	242	2.8	652
15. Officer, Ordem dos Advogados or Instituto dos Advogados	0.5	196	5.1	214	4.1	242	3.4	652

FOREIGN TIES

	%	N	%	N	%	N	%	N
16. Lawyer for foreign company operating in Brazil. Def. of foreign: at least 51 percent of stock owned by foreign nationals	4.3	187	2.3	213	0.8	240	2.3	640
17. Importer: manager or director of, or investor in, importing firm	1.1	188	0	214	2.9	239	1.4	641
18. Exporter, manager or director of, or investor in, exporting firm	7.4	189	0.5	214	6.7	239	4.8	642
19. Manager or director of, or investor in, foreign firm operating in Brazil; foreign defined under 16	2.7	188	2.4	211	9.2	239	5.0	638
20. At least one foreign-born parent	4.3	188	2.8	213	4.6	239	3.9	640
21. Foreign-born wife	1.1	188	0	214	2.1	238	1.1	640
22. At least one year of foreign study at any level	6.9	189	5.1	214	13.4	239	8.7	642
23. Residence abroad for at least six months	20.3	187	7.5	214	31.9	238	20.3	639
24. Consul for foreign government	2.1	188	0	214	0.4	239	0.8	641
25. Decorated by foreign government	1.6	188	0.9	214	8.8	239	4.1	641

NOTE: This is not a list of all variables tested; in some cases data were too incomplete to be recorded here. Values omit cases where no data were found and those for which the item was not applicable. Number refers to the number of valid cases from which the percentages were derived.

Variables and Values in the Three Elite Studies (Continued)

Categories and variables	Pernambuco		Minas Gerais		São Paulo		Composite	
	Value	Number	Value	Number	Value	Number	Value	Number
26. Procurer of immigrants: director or manager of, or investor in, private or government immigration-promoting enterprise	0.5%	188	0.9%	214	4.2%	239	2.0%	641
27. Naturalized Brazilian	1.1	188	0.5	214	0.4	239	0.6	641
28. Foreign title: holder of foreign or papal title of nobility	2.1	188	0.5	214	0.8	239	1.1	641
INTERSTATE TIES								
29. Political or administrative officeholder in another state: *Juiz de direito*, state deputy or federal deputy, or above	6.9	195	6.1	214	7.1	238	9.7	647
30. Professional career in another state, then returns: minimum time, one year	12.9	194	3.3	214	7.1	240	7.6	648
31. Professional career in Federal District	17.5	194	14.5	214	1.3	240	10.5	648
32. Professional career in Federal District, then returns	7.2	194	2.3	214	5.8	240	5.1	648
33. Employee in any official interstate agency: e.g. an interstate coffee convention	4.6	195	0.5	214	0.4	239	1.7	648
34. Out-of-state birth	14.5	193	13.1	214	18.6	236	15.6	643
35. Political or administrative officeholder in another province or in the Município Neutro before Nov. 15, 1889: Def. officeholder is *Juiz de direito*, provincial deputy, general deputy, or above (i.e. imperial equivalents of posts cited in 29)	21.2	193	4.2	214	12.5	112	12.3	519
36. Colégio in another state or Federal District: minimum time, one academic year	8.3	193	13.6	211	19.7	234	14.3	638
EDUCATION								
37. Law degree, in state	71.8	196	14.1	213	62.5	240	49.8	649
38. Law degree, other state or Federal District	3.6	193	42.3	213	5.0	241	16.8	647
39. Law degree split: at least one year at law school in a state (or Federal District) other than the one where he graduated	1.6	193	5.1	214	2.9	242	3.2	649

40. Medical degree, in state	0.5	193	0	213	0.4	241	0.3	647
41. Medical degree, other state or Federal District	7.3	193	10.4	212	5.0	240	7.4	645
42. Medical degree, split: analogous to 39	0	193	0.9	214	0	242	0.3	649
43. Engineering degree, in state	3.1	193	8.4	214	4.5	242	5.4	649
44. Engineering degree, other state or Federal District	2.6	193	2.3	213	2.1	242	2.3	648
45. Military degree: graduation from Agulhas Negras, Escola Militar in Rio, Colégio Militar in Pôrto Alegre, or its imperial equivalent in Ceará	4.1	193	0.9	214	2.1	241	2.3	648
46. Pharmacy degree	0.5	193	3.7	214	1.2	242	1.8	649
47. Other university degree	4.1	193	0.9	214	10.4	241	5.4	648
48. Secondary school graduate, but no higher degree	4.7	193	7.1	210	5.8	241	5.9	644
49. Up to secondary school, but no diploma	1.0	193	1.9	209	1.7	241	1.6	643
OCCUPATION								
50. Lawyer	55.1	214	67.9	212	69.3	241	64.3	667
51. Physician	7.1	197	12.1	214	7.1	241	8.7	652
52. Journalist	35.0	197	23.8	214	26.6	241	28.2	652
53. Fazendeiro: owner of estate producing agricultural or pastoral goods primarily for cash sale	18.8	197	16.7	210	37.7	239	25.1	646
54. Merchant	13.3	196	5.6	213	16.6	241	12.0	650
55. Industrialist: owner of, or investor in, manufacturing or processing operation (e.g. usineiro)	12.6	199	17.8	214	27.8	241	19.9	654
56. Banker: manager, director, or legal counsel of, or investor in, bank	9.1	198	15.0	214	18.3	241	14.4	653
57. Educator: secondary- or university-level teacher	27.3	199	32.2	213	21.2	241	26.6	653
58. Engineer	9.4	202	12.7	213	9.9	242	10.7	657
59. Cleric	2.5	198	0.5	214	0	253	0.9	665
60. Military officer	4.6	197	0.5	214	2.5	242	2.5	653
61. Magistrate: Juiz de direito or above	19.8	197	17.3	214	19.1	241	18.7	652
62. Rural land dealer	1.0	197	0	214	2.9	241	1.4	652
63. Comissário: Short-term lender to fazendeiros	0	197	0	214	3.8	240	1.4	651
64. Manager, director, or legal counsel of, or investor in, railroad company operating in Brazil	0	197	5.6	214	9.5	241	5.4	652
65. Mine owner or investor in mining	1.0	197	3.3	213	0	241	1.4	651
66. Other profession or occupation	2.0	197	6.5	214	4.6	241	4.4	652

Variables and Values in the Three Elite Studies (Continued)

Categories and variables	Pernambuco Value	Pernambuco Number	Minas Gerais Value	Minas Gerais Number	São Paulo Value	São Paulo Number	Composite Value	Composite Number
FAMILY TIES								
67. Related to at least one other member of same state elite, through first cousin—consanguineal or affinitive	34.3%	198	46.3%	177	42.5%	240	41.0%	615
68. Member of, or related to, imperial elite, through first cousin, con. or aff., or direct descendant through grandson. Def. of imperial elite: senators, or title-holders of *barão* or above	27.4	197	16.2	185	19.7	239	21.1	621
69. Related to at least one member of any other analogously defined state elite (not just those of PE, SP, or MG), through first cousin—con. or aff.	12.0	192	4.3	185	0.8	241	5.3	618
70. In federal congress: served at least once (appointed or elected) for 90 days or more, in chamber or senate	55.7	192	51.2	209	31.7	252	45.0	653
71. In state legislature: served at least once (appointed or elected) for 90 days or more, in chamber or senate	30.9	194	47.4	209	48.6	255	43.0	658
OTHER VARIABLES: COMPOSITES OR ITEMS DERIVED FROM "POLITICAL OFFICES HELD"								
Historical Republican: composite of 1c–1d	22.5	80	49.4	83	50.5	105	41.8	268
Adherent to the Republic: composite of 1a–1b	77.6	80	50.6	83	49.5	105	58.2	268
Age at first elite-defining position:								
Minimum	19	186	23	181	25	230	—	597
Maximum	78	186	80	181	85	230	—	597
Mean	43.0	186	43.3	181	46.0	230	44.2	597
Median	42.3	186	41.9	181	45.1	230	43.3	597
Age at first elite-defining position, grouped in 10-year intervals:								
29 or less	16.7	186	5.0	181	3.5	230	8.0	597
30–39	22.0	186	36.5	181	23.9	230	27.1	597
40–49	29.6	186	32.0	181	39.6	230	34.2	597
50–59	18.3	186	20.4	181	21.3	230	20.1	597
60 or over	13.4	186	6.1	181	11.7	230	10.6	597

Political generation:

First: born before 1869	50.8	193	50.3	181	46.1	230	48.8	604
Second: born between 1869 and 1888	29.5	193	31.5	181	33.9	230	31.8	604
Third: born in 1889 or later	19.7	193	18.2	181	20.0	230	19.4	604
Held first office after 1930 Revolution	14.9	268	21.5	214	37.3	263	24.7	745
Out-of-state job: composite of 29–33	43.6	195	22.4	214	16.8	238	26.7	647
Out-of-state link (education, experience, family tie): composite of 29–34, 36, 38–39, 41–42, 44–45, 69	64.9	185	72.1	183	39.3	229	57.3	597
Foreign tie: composite of 16–28	33.3	186	15.7	210	48.1	237	33.0	633
Bacharel: composite of 37–42	81.3	194	73.8	210	76.2	239	76.9	641
Lacking university degree: composite of 48–49	5.7	193	9.2	206	7.5	241	7.5	640
Businessman: composite of 54–56, 63–65	24.4	197	34.9	212	41.3	240	34.1	649
Member of agricultural export complex: composite of 13, 18, 53, 63	26.2	187	17.1	210	40.3	233	28.4	630
Relative of Republican or imperial elite: composite of 67–69	45.3	192	52.9	170	49.6	236	49.2	598
Member of PR executive committee	14.9	276	32.2	214	28.5	263	24.6	753
Opposition leader: composite of all members of non-PR executive committees	10.5	276	8.4	214	20.5	263	13.4	753
Party leader: composite of all members of PR and non-PR executive committees	25.4	276	38.8	214	48.3	263	37.2	753
Governor	6.2	276	7.9	214	8.0	263	7.3	753
Legislative experience: composite of 70–71	65.6	276	68.4	209	57.1	252	63.2	737

The Elite and Their Positions

TENURE DATES for the state positions were uncertain in too many cases to make a list with the terms of office worthwhile. I have therefore preferred to indicate only the year in which the members of the elite assumed their posts. Though I could have supplied the full terms of office for the federal posts, I have chosen for consistency to list only the starting year.

During most of the period the lieutenant governorship was not a separate post. After 1894 the position was held by the presidents of the state Senate and the state Chamber of Deputies in alternate years. Similarly, though the position of majority leader of the Chamber was occasionally a separate one, the president of the Chamber usually served in that post, too. Finally, a word about the title general secretary. Especially during the early years of the Republic the general secretary, normally a minister without portfolio, often carried out the responsibilities conventionally assigned to some cabinet member or department head (Secretaries of Justice, Treasury, etc.). In such cases I have listed the officeholder by the duties he performed. The general secretary list, then, is limited to those whose functions clearly fell within the boundaries of executive secretary to the Governor.

Governor or Interventor

José Simeão de Oliveira, 1889
José Vincente Meira de Vasconcelos, 1890
Henrique Pereira Lucena, 1890
Alexandre José Barbosa Lima, 1892
Joaquim Correia de Araujo, 1896
Antônio Gonçalves Ferreira, 1900
Sigismundo Gonçalves, 1904
Herculino Bandeira, 1908
Emídio Dantas Barreto, 1911
Manoel Borba, 1915
José Rufino Bezerra Cavalcanti, 1919
Sérgio Loreto, 1922
Estácio Coimbra, 1926
Carlos de Lima Cavalcanti, 1930
Agamenon Magalhães, 1937

Lieutenant Governor (as separate office)

Manoel da Trindade Peretti, 1890
A. E. Correia de Barros, 1891

Secretary of Justice

Júlio de Melo, 1894
Claudino Rogoberto dos Santos, 1894
Antônio Pedro Silva, 1898
José Osório Cerqueira, 1901
Elpídio de Abreu Lima Figueiredo, 1905
Anibal Freire, 1908
Antônio Vicente Andrade Bezerra, 1911
Afonso Viriato de Medeiros, 1911
Hercílio Lupércio de Souza, 1913
Afonso Viriato de Medeiros, 1917

Esmaragdo de Freitas, 1920
Carlos Xavier Paes Barreto, 1922
Anibal Fernandes, 1923
Francisco Martins Ribeiro, 1925
Antônio Carneiro Leão, 1930
Jurandyr Mamede, 1931
Luis Delgado, 1932
Adolfo Celso Uchôa Cavalcanti, 1932
Nelson Coutinho, 1933

Secretary of the Treasury

Afonso de Albuquerque e Melo, 1891
Ribeiro da Costa Diniz Júnior, 1893
João Augusto Ferreira Lima, 1893
Pedro José de Oliveira Pernambuco, 1894
Felipe Figueiredo Faria Sobrinho, 1898
João Ferreira de Andrade Guimarães, 1902
Elpídio de Abreu e Lima Figueiredo, 1907
Anibal Freire, 1909
José Osório de Cerqueira, 1910
Hercílio Lupercio de Souza, 1912
Antônio Vicente de Andrade Bezerra, 1916
Francisco Pinto de Abreu, 1921
José de Goes Cavalcanti, 1924
Pereira Caldas, 1924
João Peretti, 1926
Joaquim Bandeira, 1927
Afonso das Neves Batista, 1930
Edgard Teixeira Leite, 1931
Francisco Barreto Campelo, 1932
Heitor Silva Maia, 1932
Nelson Coutinho, 1933
Sílvio Granville, 1935
Manoel Lubambo, 1937

Secretary of Education and Public Health,
1922–

José Campelo, 1922
Costa Ribeiro, 1922
Amaury de Medeiros, 1923
Anibal Fernandes, 1925
José Ribeiro Escobar, 1929
Luis Delgado, 1931
Adolfo Celso Uchôa Cavalcanti, 1932
Nelson Coutinho, 1935
Nilo Pereira, 1937

Secretary of Agriculture, 1924–

Samuel Hardman Cavalcanti e Albuquerque, 1924
Luis Correia de Queiros Barros, 1930
Jader de Andrade, 1930
Apolônio Sales, 1931

Paulo Barredo Carneiro, 1932
Nelson Coutinho, 1934
Lauro Montenegro, 1936

Secretary of Transportation Industry and
Public Works, 1925–

Odilón de Souza Leão, 1925
Jader de Andrade, 1929
Nestor Moreira Reis, 1931
Gercino Pontes, 1937

Secretary of Security, 1932–

Sérgio Magalhães, 1932
Etelvino Lins de Albuquerque, 1937

General Secretary (cabinet level)

Henrique M. de Holanda Cavalcanti (Baron
of Suassuna), 1889
João Augusto Ferreira Lima, 1893; 1895
Elpídio de Abreu e Lima Figueiredo, 1908
Anibal Freire, 1909
José Osório de Cerqueira, 1910
Hercílio Lupércio de Souza, 1912
Thomé Gibson, 1916
Antônio Vicente de Andrade Bezerra, 1916
A. Vieira de Moraes, 1917
Antônio Vicente de Andrade Bezerra, 1917
Gercino Pontes, 1920
Francisco Pinto de Abreu, 1921
Samuel Hardman Cavalcanti de Albuquerque, 1924
Gilberto Freyre, 1928
Milton Costa Pinto, 1930
Thomas Lobo, 1932
Alde Sampaio, 1932
Júlio Barbosa, 1932
Ulisses Pernambucano, 1934

Mayor of Recife

João Ribeiro de Brito, 1890
José Mariano Carneiro da Cunha, 1892
Alfredo Pinto, 1894
Afonso Gonçalves Ferreira Costa, 1895
Esmeraldino Bandeira, 1898
José Coelho Cintra, 1898
Francisco Costa Maia, 1899
Luis Cavalcanti de Almeida, 1902
Manoel dos Santos Moreira, 1903
Eduardo Martins de Barros, 1905
Cornélio Padilha, 1906
Eduardo Martins de Barros, 1907
Archimedes de Oliveira, 1909
Eudoro Correia, 1913

Manoel Antônio de Moraes Rego, 1917
Eduardo de Lima Castro, 1920
Antônio de Goes Cavalcanti, 1923
Joaquim de Souza Guerra, 1927
Francisco da Costa Maia, 1929
Lauro Borba, 1931
Antônio de Goes Cavalcanti, 1931
João Pereira Borges, 1933

Chief of Police

José Isidoro Martins Júnior, 1889
Júlio de Melo, 1892
Alfredo Vieira de Melo, 1892
Francisco de Gouveia Cunha Barreto, 1895
Benjamin Bandeira, 1896
Francisco Cabral Silveira, 1896
Lafaiete Rezende, 1906
Leopoldo Lins, 1909
Ulisses Vianna, 1910
Ulisses Alves da Costa, 1910
Francisco de Andrade Lima, 1911
Elpídio de Abreu Lima Figueiredo, 1911
Ulisses Alves da Costa, 1912
Artur Henrique Albuquerque Melo, 1916
José Novais, 1919
Jonathan Castro, 1922
Carlos Xavier Paes Barreto, 1923
Artur Silva Rêgo, 1924
Eurico Souza Leão, 1926
Joaquim Guerra, 1928
Adolfo Simões Barbosa, 1929
Joaquim Nobre de Lacerda, 1929
Adolfo da Cruz Ribeiro, 1930
Pedro Callado, 1930
Aluísio Baltar, 1931
Atenor Machado, 1931

Superintendent, Port of Recife, 1918–

Abílio de Campos, 1918
Jean Charles Philbert, 1919
José Teixeira Coimbra, 1922
José Maria de Figueiredo Júnior, 1922
Francisco Farias, 1923
Antônio Ferreira Júnior, 1927
Antônio de Goes Cavalcanti, 1930
Humberto Ferreira, 1931
Odilón Lima de Souza Leão, 1934
José Teixeira de Melo, 1935

*Inspector-General of Municipalities,
1931–33*

Jorge de Melo, 1931
Nelson Melo, 1932
Humberto Moura, 1933

President, State Bank

José Maria Andrade, 1898
Erasmo Vieira de Macedo, 1910
Tavares da Cunha Melo, 1920
Gaspar Peres, 1921
Manoel Castro Leal, c.1922
Alvaro Lins, c.1922
João Pessoa de Queiroz, c.1925
José Pessoa de Queiroz, c.1926
Aristóteles Solano Carneiro da Cunha,
    c.1931

President, State Senate (also Lieutenant
    Governor in alternate years after 1894)

José Soriano de Souza, 1891
Albino Gonçalves Meira de Vasconcelos,
    1892
Francisco Teixeira de Sá, 1895
Ermínio Coutinho, 1895
Henrique M. de Holanda Cavalcanti (Baron
    of Suassuna), 1897
Sigismundo Gonçalves, 1898
Antônio Pedro da Silva Marques, 1899
Sigismundo Gonçalves, 1904
Pedro José de Almeida Pernambuco, 1906
Fábio da Silveira Barros, 1912
José Pereira de Araujo, 1915
José Henrique Carneiro da Cunha, 1915
José Pereira de Araujo, 1917
Eurico Chaves, 1919
Severino de Queiroz Pinheiro, 1921
Júlio Bello, 1923
Mario Domingos da Silva, 1924
Florentino Santos, 1924
Júlio de Melo, 1928

*President, State Chamber of Deputies or
    Constituent Assembly* (Lieutenant
    Governor in alternate years; also usu-
    ally Majority Leader)

José Maria de Albuquerque Melo, 1891
Moreira Alves, 1893
João Coimbra, 1895
Elpídio de Abreu e Lima Figueiredo, 1895
José Marcelino Rosa e Silva, 1896
José Mariano Carneiro da Cunha, 1897
José Marcelino Rosa e Silva, 1898
Elpídio de Abreu e Lima Figueiredo, 1900
Justino da Mota Silveira, 1900
João Coimbra, 1904
Estácio Coimbra, 1907
Manoel Alexandrino da Rocha, 1912
José de Barros de Andrade Lima, 1913
José Henrique Carneiro da Cunha, 1918

Octávio Tavares Bastos, 1921
Mário Domingos da Silva, 1922
Júlio Bello, 1925
Antônio Vicente Andrade Bezerra, 1933
Félix Pimentel Barreto, 1935
Nestor Melo e Silva, 1935
Antônio Vicente Andrade Bezerra, 1935

Majority Leader (as separate office)

Artur Muniz, 1900
José de Fonseca Castro, 1907
João Coimbra, 1908
Manoel Borba, 1912
Arnaldo Bastos, 1915
Solidano Leite, 1917
Antônio da Silva Souto Filho, 1927

President, State Supreme Court

Francisco Luiz Correia de Andrade, 1893
Gaspar Guimarães, 1897
Manoel Fonseca Galvão, 1898
Carlos Vaz, 1908
Francisco Correia de Araujo, 1910
Argemino da Cunha Galvão, 1916
Abdias de Oliveira, 1924
Antônio da Silva Guimarães, 1925
Belarmino Gondim, 1926
Artur da Silva Rêgo, 1927
Argemino da Cunha Galvão, 1928
Belarmino Gondim, 1929
Argemino da Cunha Galvão, 1931
Felisberto dos Santos Pereira, 1931

Opposition Leader

Antônio José da Costa Ribeiro, 1891
Ayres Bello, 1893
Anibal Falcão, 1893
Esperidão Monteiro, 1893
José Gonçalves Maia, 1894
José Mariano Carneiro da Cunha, 1894
Lourenço Sá e Albuquerque, 1895
João Ribeiro de Brito, 1896
Manoel Gomes de Matos, 1898
Juvencio Mariz, 1905
Manoel Neto Campelo, 1908
Henrique Millet, 1909
Julio Maranhão, 1910
Frederico Lundgren, 1911
Francisco Pessoa de Queiroz, 1911
Emídio Dantas Barreto, 1916
Joaquim Arruda Falcão, 1926
Arnaldo Bastos, 1927
Carlos de Lima Cavalcanti, 1928
Caio de Lima Cavalcanti, 1928

José Costa Pôrto, 1929
Ernesto Pereira Carneiro, 1929
João Alberto Lins de Barros, 1934
Gilberto Osório Andrade, 1937

Executive Committee, Republican Party

Belarmino Carneiro, 1890
Gaspar Drummond, 1890
João Vieira de Araujo, 1890
Luiz de Andrade, 1894
Manoel da Trindade Peretti, 1894
Barros de Lacerda, 1894
Leopoldo Lins, 1895
José Medeiros e Albuquerque, 1895
Miguel Pernambuco, 1896
Francisco de Assis Rosa e Silva, 1896
Malaquias Antônio Gonçalves, 1897
Joaquim de Almeida Pernambuco, 1897
João Ferreira de Aguiar, 1898
José Marcelino Rosa e Silva, 1900
Joaquim Correia de Araujo, 1900
Celso Henriques de Souza, 1904
Antônio Joaquim Amorim Júnior, 1905
Elísio de Araujo, 1906
Archimedes de Oliveira, 1906
Francisco de Assis Rosa e Silva Júnior, 1908
Herculino Bandeira, 1913
José de Castro Fonseca, 1913
Estácio Coimbra, 1913
Anibal Freire, 1913
Domingos de Souza Leão Gonçalves, 1913
Júlio de Melo, 1913
Gervásio Fioravante Pires Ferreira, 1915
Agapito Jorge dos Santos, 1915
Antônio Gonçalves Ferreira, 1918
João Elípio de Castro Fonseca, 1918
Luis Veiga Pessoa, 1918
Luis Correia de Brito, 1921
Manoel Silva Pinto, 1922
Bianor de Medeiros, 1923
Antônio Austregésilo, 1924
Alfredo de Moraes Coutinho, 1926
Samuel Hardman Cavalcanti e Albuquer-
que, 1926
Sérgio Loreto Filho, 1926
Davino Pontes, 1926
Antônio da Silva Souto Filho, 1928

FEDERAL POSTS

Vice-President

Francisco de Assis Rosa e Silva, 1898
Estácio Coimbra, 1923

Minister of Justice (formerly Interior)

João Barbalho Uchôa Cavalcanti, 1891
José Higino Duarte Pereira, 1892
Esmeraldino Bandeira, 1896
Clovis Bevilaqua, 1904
Alfredo Vieira de Melo, 1920
Agemenon Magalhães, 1934

Minister of the Treasury

Henrique Pereira Lucena, 1891

Minister of Agriculture

Henrique Pereira Lucena, 1891
Joaquim Pessoa Guerra, 1904
José Rufino Bezerra Cavalcanti, 1915
Estácio Coimbra, 1922

Minister of Labor, 1930–

Agemenon Magalhães, 1935

Justice of Supreme Court

Luis Correia de Queiros Barros, 1890
João Antônio de Araujo Freitas Henriques,
    1891
Francisco Faria Lemos, 1892
Esperidão de Barros Pimentel, 1892
José Higino Pereira Duarte, 1893
Eduardo Pindaiba de Matos, 1894
Hermínio Francisco de Espírito Santo, 1894
Esmeraldino Bandeira, 1894
Luis Antônio Franco, 1894

André Cavalcanti de Albuquerque, 1897
João Barbalho Uchôa Cavalcanti, 1897
Alfredo Vieira de Melo, 1922
José Soriano de Souza Filho, 1927
Frederico Barros Barreto, 1936

President, Chamber of Deputies

Francisco de Assis Rosa e Silva, 1894
Sebastião de Rêgo Barros, 1922

*Leader, State Delegation, Chamber of
    Deputies*

João Siqueira Cavalcanti, 1896
Francisco Fonseca Lima, 1900
Baltazar Pereira, 1912
Adolfo Simões Barbosa, 1912
Eurico Chaves, 1919
Anibal Freire, 1922
Augusto Cavalcanti de Albuquerque, 1933
Oligário Mariano Carneiro da Cunha, 1933
Alfredo Arruda Câmara, 1934
Alexandre José Barbosa Lima Sobrinho,
    1935

President, Bank of Brazil, 1906–37

João Alfredo Correia de Oliveira, 1913

Mayor, Federal District

Manoel Cicerino Peregrino Silva, 1918
Pedro Ernesto Batista, 1930
Olímpio de Melo, 1936

Select Budgetary Data, 1890-1937

I HAVE CONSTRUCTED the following series to complement similar series for the two companion volumes. However, in gathering the data for Pernambuco I encountered special problems. Since the state's Treasury Department never provided a printed budget, I was forced to rely on a variety of printed and archival sources, which often presented conflicting sets of figures. In such cases, one's only recourse is to settle on an average or arbitrarily choose one set of figures on the basis of intuition. Furthermore, for most of the period before 1900 the only available figures were those in the projected budgets; there are no records of the actual amounts taken in and spent during those years (and there were no budgets passed at all in the years 1891–93). In the circumstances, the reader is cautioned to look with considerable skepticism at the healthy fiscal balances in Pernambuco through this period: it is a historical fact that the successive state administrations had great difficulties avoiding significant deficits during these years, despite the balanced budgets, and even surpluses, that are shown in the "Balance surplus" column.

A brief word on a few of the conventions I have used in the table. (Some notes on the methods used to construct certain series and on other data problems follow the table.) Until 1925 the State of Pernambuco's fiscal year began on July 1. The budgets through that period are treated as covering the later year; July 1, 1895–June 30, 1896, that is, is entered as 1896. The state switched to a calendar-year accounting system in 1925. Blank cells mean that no data were available (and in the case of related columns in the row, "not applicable"). It is worth noting that in many of the years in which no budgets were passed or for which complete figures were not available, federal intervention or political instability was the cause; this is notably true of the early 1890's, 1911–13, and 1919.

Year	Revenues (thousands of current contos) A-1	Expenditures (thousands of current contos) B-1	Revenues (thousands of 1912 contos) A-2	Expenditures (thousands of 1912 contos) B-2	Revenues, 5-yr. moving averages of A-2 A-3	Expenditures, 5-yr. moving averages of B-2 B-3
1890	3.0[a]	3.7[a]	6.8	8.3		
1891[c]						
1892[c]						
1893[c]		4.4[d]		5.1		
1894	5.7[a]	5.5[d]	6.8	6.5		
1895	5.7[a]	5.5[d]	7.2	6.9		7.3
1896	9.4	10.0[a]	9.2	9.8	7.8	7.7
1897	10.4[a]	10.0[a]	8.3	8.3	8.0	8.1
1898	9.3[a]	9.3[a]	7.3	7.3	7.9	8.8
1899	9.8[a]	10.2[a]	7.8	8.2	7.6	9.5
1900	7.3	11.0	6.7	10.2	7.8	10.3
1901	7.0	12.2	7.9	13.7	8.3	11.6
1902	7.8	9.9	9.5	12.0	8.7	13.8
1903	8.1	11.5	9.6	13.7	9.6	15.6
1904	8.9	17.1	10.0	19.3	9.7	15.0
1905	8.8	15.1	11.1	19.5	10.7	15.5
1906	8.0	10.2	8.2	10.5	9.9	15.4
1907	11.2	13.5	12.2	14.7	11.1	14.8
1908	9.9	12.4	10.5	13.2	10.9	14.7
1909	10.6	14.6	11.8	16.3	12.3	16.1
1910	11.1	15.5	13.4	18.7	12.8	16.2
1911	12.8	16.1	13.8	17.4	13.5	16.1
1912	14.5	15.2	14.5	15.2	13.7	15.8
1913	13.8	12.8	14.1	13.0	13.3	14.6
1914	11.6	13.6	12.5	14.7	13.0	13.4
1915	14.8	16.6	11.2	12.6	12.3	13.0
1916	17.4	16.1	12.5	11.3	11.6	12.6
1917	19.0	22.2	11.3	13.2	11.1	11.3
1918	21.1	21.7	10.5	10.9	10.5	10.3
1919	26.1	22.0	9.9	8.3	10.0	10.0
1920	24.3	21.0	8.4	7.3	10.4	10.0
1921	23.9	24.2	10.1	10.2	11.2	10.5
1922	29.4	29.8	13.0	13.2	11.7	11.5
1923	41.0	39.0	14.4	13.7	12.4	12.6
1924	42.4	44.2	12.8	13.3	12.8	13.3
1925	39.2	43.7	11.5	12.8	13.7	14.0
1926	38.3	41.7	12.3	13.4	14.7	15.2
1927	54.0	52.4	17.5	17.0	17.0	17.8
1928	56.8	57.5	19.4	19.6	19.4	19.8
1929	68.8	73.0	24.5	26.0	21.3	21.6
1930	56.3	55.9	23.2	23.0	21.8	22.2
1931	51.2	52.8	21.9	22.6	22.1	22.5
1932	46.6	46.9	19.8	20.0	24.3	24.1
1933	48.8	48.3	20.9	20.7	25.6	25.3
1934	89.4	85.8	35.6	34.2	27.1	26.3
1935	79.4	76.7	30.0	28.9	28.0	27.7
1936	88.3	84.9	29.0	27.9		
1937	80.4	88.2	24.6	27.0		

Budget surplus (thousands of current contos) A-2 − B-2	Price index, 1912 = 100 C-1	One conto in U.S. dollars L-1	Public debt (thousands of current contos) D-1	Public debt (thousands of 1912 contos) D-2	Foreign debt (thousands of current contos) DF-1	Year
−1.5	44.4		8.0^b	19.5		1890
	56.7					1891
	81.3	244.4				1892
	86.8	230.3				1893
+0.3	84.0	207.0				1894
+0.3	79.5	198.5				1895
−0.6	102.0	177.6				1896
0.0	121.0	143.9				1897
0.0	127.0	136.4				1898
−0.4	125.0	146.1				1899
−3.5	108.0	186.2				1900
−5.8	89.0	223.0				1901
−2.5	82.2	234.9				1902
−4.1	83.9	239.9				1903
−9.3	88.8	251.8				1904
−8.4	79.5	309.6				1905
−2.3	97.0	317.5			15.1^e	1906
−2.5	92.0	301.3			14.6	1907
−2.7	94.0	301.8			15.3	1908
−4.5	89.5	303.5	37.2	41.6	15.1	1909
−5.3	82.9	302.7	61.5	74.1	38.7	1910
−3.6	92.6	321.0			43.7	1911
−0.7	100.0	331.8			35.5	1912
+1.1	97.9	321.3	58.7	58.6	35.0	1913
−2.2	92.4	318.0			34.5	1914
−1.4	132.0	292.7	59.1	44.8	37.0	1915
+0.9	139.0	230.6			43.5	1916
−1.9	168.0	247.5			45.1	1917
−0.4	200.0	245.7			41.4	1918
+1.6	264.0	267.4			40.4	1919
+1.1	289.0	225.1			35.6	1920
−0.1	237.0	131.2	55.0	23.2	33.1	1921
−0.2	226.0	129.5	109.2	48.3	87.3	1922
+0.7	285.0	102.3	80.4	28.2	60.7	1923
−0.5	332.0	109.4	109.1	32.9	80.0	1924
−1.3	341.0	122.0	105.9	31.1	69.9	1925
−1.1	312.0	144.4	92.7	29.7	58.8	1926
−0.5	308.0	118.4	145.7	47.3	119.2	1927
−0.2	293.0	119.7	145.4	49.6	117.0	1928
−1.5	281.0	111.1	146.1	52.0	116.4	1929
+0.2	243.0	107.1	156.7	64.5	125.9	1930
−0.7	234.0	70.3	230.2	98.4	172.9	1931
−0.2	235.0	71.2	209.3	89.1	149.6	1932
+0.2	233.0	79.6	207.0	88.8	149.0	1933
+1.4	251.0	84.3	221.5^f	88.2^f	150.3	1934
+1.1	265.0	82.9	218.5^f	82.5^f		1935
+1.1	304.0	85.7	215.5^f	70.9^f		1936
−2.4	327.0	86.4	212.5^f	65.0^f		1937

Year	Debt service (*thousands of current contos*) DS-1	Debt service as % of budget DS-2	Education (*thousands of current contos*) E-1	Education as % of budget E-2	Força pública (*thousands of current contos*) F-1	Força pública as % of budget F-2
1894[a]	0.7	13	0.7	13	1.6	29
1895	0.7[d]	13[d]	0.7	13	0.6	11
1896	1.1	11	1.2	12	1.5	15
1897	1.1	11	1.9	19	1.5	15
1898	1.1	12	1.3	12	1.1	12
1899	2.4	24	1.3	13	1.2	12
1900	2.7	25	1.3	12	1.4	13
1901	2.5	21	1.1	9	1.7	14
1902	1.2	12	1.3	13	1.6	16
1903						
1904	1.9	11	1.0	6	1.4	8
1905	3.2	21	0.9	6	1.4	9
1906						
1907	2.3	17	0.8	6	1.7	13
1908	2.3	19	0.8	6	2.0[d]	16
1909	3.0	21	0.8	5	1.3	9
1910	3.4	22	0.8	5	1.9	12
1911	2.8	17	0.7	4	1.9	12
1912	3.0	20	0.9	6	2.1	14
1913						
1914	3.2	24	0.5[d]	4	2.1	15
1915	3.1	19	1.1	7	2.8	17
1916	4.8	30	1.0	6	2.8	17
1917	5.2	23	0.8	4	2.1	9
1918	3.4	16	1.1	5	2.9	13
1919						
1920	7.1	34	1.1	5	4.2	20
1921	4.6	19	1.1	5	3.4	14
1922	12.4	42	1.2	4	3.6	12
1923	6.3	16	2.0	5	5.6	14
1924	7.8	18	2.3	5	6.0	14
1925	7.3	17	2.6	6	6.4	15
1926	4.2	10	2.6	6	8.8	21
1927	5.7	11	3.3	6	9.4	18
1928	9.2	16	3.1	5	11.0	19
1929	10.6	15	3.8	5	10.6	15
1930	10.1	18	5.3	9	10.7	19
1931	10.7[h]	20[h]	6.5	12	10.6	20
1932	13.4	29	7.1	15	10.3	22
1933	12.0	25	5.0	10	8.5	18
1934	10.9	13	7.9	9	9.2	11
1935	15.6	20	8.0[d]	10	9.1	12
1936	14.2	17	8.3	10	12.8	15
1937	8.0	9	6.7	8	13.4	15

NOTE: See overleaf for further information on column heads.

[a] Projected figures; applies to all items in the row that use A- or B-column data.

[b] Data for 1889.
[c] No budget passed.
[d] My estimate.

Public works (thousands of current contos) I-1	Public works as % of budget I-2	Agriculture (thousands of current contos) M-1	Agriculture as % of budget M-2	Education, per capita expenditures (milreis) E-3	Public health, per capita expenditures (milreis) N-3	Year
0.7	13			0.6	<0.1	1894
1.8	33	0.1	2	0.6	<0.1	1895
2.8	28	0.4	4	1.0	0.2	1896
2.3	23	0.5	5	1.6	0.1	1897
1.8	19	0.4	4	1.1	<0.1	1898
1.8	18	0.4	4	1.1	<0.1	1899
1.7	16	0.4	4	1.1	<0.1	1900
1.7	14	0.4	3	0.9	<0.1	1901
1.0^c	10	0.4	4	0.9	<0.1	1902
				1.0	<0.1	1903
0.7	4	0.3	2		<0.1	1904
0.7	5	0.0	0	0.7	<0.1	1905
					<0.1	1906
0.9	7			0.6	<0.1	1907
0.9	7			0.6	<0.1	1908
0.9	6	0.1	1	0.6	0.5	1909
0.7	5			0.4		1910
1.0	6	0.2	1	0.1	0.5	1911
1.5	10	0.1	1		0.5	1912
		0.2^c	2	0.3	0.7	1913
1.5	11	0.2	1	0.6	0.7	1914
1.6	10	0.3	2	0.5	0.6	1915
1.5	9	0.2	1	0.5	0.6	1916
1.5	7			0.7		1917
2.3	11			0.7		1918
						1919
3.7	18	0.2	1	0.5	0.6	1920
3.9	16	<0.1	<1	0.5	0.6	1921
3.1	10	<0.1	<1	0.5	0.3	1922
3.6	9	<0.1	<1	0.9	0.3	1923
3.8	9	<0.1	<1	1.0	0.7	1924
7.3	17	<0.1	<1	1.0	1.2	1925
10.6	25	0.5	1	1.2	1.1	1926
7.2	14	0.6	1	1.5	1.2	1927
11.0	19	0.7	1	1.3	1.8	1928
14.6	20	0.7	1	1.6	1.8	1929
13.6	24	1.6	3	2.1	2.1	1930
12.8	24	1.6	3	2.6	1.8	1931
6.0^c	13	1.5	2	2.8	1.5	1932
7.8	16	1.3	3	2.0	1.6	1933
9.1	11	1.0^c	1	3.1	1.4	1934
14.2	19	3.0^c	4	3.2	1.8	1935
7.7	9	3.0^c	4	3.3	1.8	1936
7.7^c	9	3.0^c	3	2.6	2.2	1937

^{e} State's first foreign loan in the Republican period.

^{f} Includes Bank of Brazil loan.

^{g} 1890–93 omitted: no data for 1890; no budget passed 1891–93.

^{h} Interest and amortization on foreign loans defaulted.

Notes to Table Column Heads

B-1. General expenditures. Except where otherwise noted, these are actual expenditures. Data here are especially conflicting among different available sources.

C-1. Price index, 1890–1937. This index is a splice of a foodstuffs price index through 1929 and a general cost-of-living index from 1921 to 1939. Both were constructed for the city of Rio de Janeiro, for an upper-middle-class family. The price index is based on the prices of nine food staples, using a weight derived for the year 1919 (E. Lobo et al., "Evolução dos preços e do padrão de vida no Rio de Janeiro, 1820–1930—resultados preliminares," *Revista Brasileira de Economia*, 25, no. 4 [1971]: 235–65). The cost-of-living index was developed by the Instituto Brasileiro de Geografia e Estatística, based on prices of food, clothing, rents, personal services, and general household goods; it is available in the *Anuário estatístico do Brasil, 1939–1940*, p. 1384. The cost-of-living index is clearly superior for our purposes, but it only covers the years 1912–39. The two have been spliced during the 1920's, a period when they behaved quite similarly. In 1921 the price index was given a weight of .9 and the IBGE index .1; in 1922 the former was weighted .8 and the latter .2; in 1929 the former was weighted .1 and the latter .9.

L-1. Value of the Brazilian conto in U.S. dollars, 1892–1940. For the period 1892–1918, the figures are from the *Retrospecto commercial do Jornal do Commercio*, calculated from the mean of the highest and lowest quotation for the U.S. dollar in Rio. From 1919 on, the rates are from the New York exchange as cited in the U.S. Department of Commerce's *Statistical Abstract of the United States*, various years.

D-1. Public debt. Included are internal bonded indebtedness, external loans, and the fluctuating debt made up of local short-term obligations.

DF-1. State foreign debt. All foreign loans were in pounds sterling, francs, or dollars; the foreign debt balance has been converted to contos at current exchange rates on an annual basis.

DS-1. Debt service. The data in this series, as in B-1, are based on varying sources, some of which conflict with one another.

E-1. Education. Some data are suspect, since state governments juggled figures to show respectable outlays in this realm. (Opposition sources charged that allocated funds were often never expended or were diverted for other uses.) Expenditures for the Recife Law School, a federally funded institution, are not included.

Notes

Complete authors' names, titles, and publication data for works cited in short form in the Notes are given in the Bibliography, pp. 211–26. The following abbreviations are used in the Notes:

AC   Archives of the Associação Comercial Beneficente
     de Pernambuco, Recife
AP   Arquivo Público Estadual de Pernambuco, Recife
FO   Foreign Office Archives, Public Record Office, London
PE   Pernambuco

Chapter One

1. M. Melo, *Pernambuco*, p. 18.

2. As far as the Northeast is concerned, some writers, especially geographers, include Sergipe and Bahia in their definition; others, speaking of the "northern states" or a "northern bloc," include Pará and even Amazonas and Goiás. In this study, with its focus on Pernambuco, I follow the narrower definition. For the geographers' view, see Webb. It is true that during the Amazon rubber boom in the early 20th century Ceará was drawn to the Pará-Amazonas orbit, trading extensively with Belém and Manáos, but over the larger span of time the state was drawn to Pernambuco's political and economic axis, and can properly be defined as part of its satellite bloc.

3. Tricart, pp. 5–8.

4. Dutra, "Duarte Coelho," pp. 430–31, including letters, Duarte to Jesuits of Coimbra, Pernambuco, June 4, 1552, and to King, Olinda, Nov. 25, 1550; Eisenberg, *Sugar Industry*, pp. 124–25. The cited Dutra work is an excellent source on Pernambuco's early history. See also Almeida Prado; Sette and Correia de Andrade, pp. 41–46; M. Melo, "Chorographia," pp. 66–77; Barbosa Vianna, esp. p. 14; and M. Melo, *Tipos*, p. 4. For a general historical overview, see Silva Bruno, pp. 25–74.

5. Brazil, *Annuario estatistico*, 1927, pp. 24–25. See also O. R. Dantas, p. xxvii; and Eisenberg, *Sugar Industry*, p. 209.

6. "Yearly Floods," p. 5; "A miséria normal," *Veja e Leia*, 100 (Aug. 5, 1970): 28.

7. See Brandão. Pernambuco's authorities repeatedly called for aid from the national government, but without success. See, for example, PE, *Mensagems . . .* Barbosa Lima (1893, 1895, 1896), p. 42.

8. M. Melo, *Pernambuco*, p. 37.

9. Eisenberg, *Sugar Industry*, p. 124. Eisenberg estimates that the Zona da Mata covers 5,792 square miles (15,000 square km).

10. Diegues Jr., *Regiões*, p. 191.

11. Tejo, *Brejos*, pp. 89–90. See also Webb, pp. 25–55.

12. Tejo, *Brejos*, pp. 90–100.

13. See Correia de Andrade, *Terra*, pp. 144–71.

14. Castro, *Death*, p. 37. See also Webb, p. 35.

15. Cardim, p. 292; Euclides da Cunha, pp. 25–26; Castro, *Death*, pp. 51–56.

16. Eudes Pinto, p. 33; Vasconcelos Sobrinho, p. 189.

17. Johnson, p. 46. See also pp. 43–45.

18. Brazil, *Recenseamento*, 1940, pp. 69–70; Brazil, *Anuário estatístico*, 1939–40, p. 1302.

19. Eisenberg, *Sugar Industry*, p. 148.

20. See, in addition to Degler, Graham, "Brazilian Slavery"; and Viotti da Costa. The traditional view is posited by Gilberto Freyre in *The Mansions and the Shanties*.

21. Eisenberg, *Sugar Industry*, pp. 182–83. The rise in the proportion of free workers is not hard to explain. According to the British consul in Recife in 1872, the life expectancy of slaves was much lower than that of non-slaves (Leff, "Long-Term Viability," p. 107).

22. Sette and Correia de Andrade, p. 26. See also Freyre, *Nordeste*; Ferraz and Andrade Lima Jr., *Morfologia*; Ferraz and Andrade Lima Jr., *Perfil*; and Johnson, p. 23.

23. This claim is most clearly expressed in Magalhães, *Nordeste*, pp. 54–86. See also Freyre, *Nordeste*, p. 77; and Levine, "First Afro-Brazilian Congress," pp. 185–94.

24. Gorton, p. 12. In 1950, 43% of the population of the Northeast was classified as white, 13% as black, and 44% as mulatto.

25. O. R. Dantas, p. xxvii.

26. Oliveira Lima, p. 316.

27. See, for example, Jorge Amado; Freyre, *Nordeste*, p. 150; and J. M. Bello, *Memórias*, p. 14.

28. Castro, *Death*, p. 17.

29. Diegues Jr., *Regiões*, pp. 183–84; Della Cava, *Miracle*, pp. 169–70.

30. Souza Barros, *Década*, pp. 47–48.

31. See esp. Louis Chevalier's impressive study *Laboring Classes and Dangerous Classes*.

32. See Cowell, pp. 46–47. See also Graham and Hollanda, p. 115 (Table 3); and Skidmore, pp. 129–30.

33. Cowell, pp. 57–58.

34. M. Melo, *Migrações*, pp. 81–89, cited in *ibid.*, p. 55.

35. Chevalier, p. 50.

36. Castro, *Death*, p. 77.

37. See Freitas, *Trabalhos*, p. 2; and Brazil, *Anuário estatístico*, 1939–40, pp. 89, 655–56.

38. PE, *Annuario estatístico*, 1927, p. 120.

39. *Annaes do 1º Congresso Médico*, pp. 32–35. See essay by Artur Orlando da Silva, "O trabalho como phenómeno econômico e physiológico," esp. pp. 107–11. Another participant argued that workers' housing should be built with proper sanitation facilities because a worker's health was his only capital and was ruined by poor housing (Olympio Leite Chermont, "Casas para proletários," pp. 559–603).

40. See Recife, *Recenseamento*, pp. 79, 83.

41. Chaves, pp. 47–48.

42. See *Annaes do 1º Congresso Médico*, p. 107.

43. Rodolpho Theophilo, cited in Castro, *Death*, p. 52. Epidemic references taken from *Almanach de Pernambuco*, 1900, p. xxvii; 1910, pp. iii, v, xi–xii; AP, *Mensagem do exm. sr. Desembargador Sigismundo Gonçalves*, p. 4; Montenegro, p. 239; Cámara, p. 45; Galvão, pp. 60–61, 345–46; M. Melo, "Sinopse," pp. 86, 99, 105, 109, 113, 116, 118, 119, 125; Freitas, *Medicina*, pp. 26, 51–52; *Annaes do 1º Congresso Médico*; and Anibal Fernandes, p. 53. Hindsight reveals that had Imperial officials acted quickly and followed emergency contingency plans, drought victims could have been aided in their home areas, reducing the high death toll taken by the epidemics in the overcrowded port cities. See Cuniff, "Great Drought."

44. J. Almeida, *Parahyba*, p. 115.

45. Lemos Filho, pp. 133–36.

46. Souto Maior, pp. 244–45. See also Maranhão, p. 146; and Magalhães, *Relatório*, p. 93.

47. Great Western RR, 1911 report, p. 17, Gavin Black collection, Recife.

48. O. Barbosa, p. 108.

49. On the early economic and demographic history of the city, see Paul Singer, pp. 274–76.

50. The urban freguesias were São Frei Gonçalves, Santo Antônio, Boa Vista, Graças, and São José; the suburban ones were Afogados, Várzea, and Poço de Panela.

51. Of the dwellings listed in the 1923 census, 19,079 were classified as residences, and 19,947 as mocambos (PE, *Recenseamento do Recife*, pp. 3–5). See also Bezerra, p. 46; Paul Singer, p. 344; and PE, *Observações*.

52. Olinda, in reality part of Recife, ranked sixth in density. See Melo, *Migrações*, p. 32; and M. Silva, "Tentativa," pp. 288–89. In order, the eight most densely populated cities were Recife, Niteroi, Rio, Belo Horizonte, São Paulo, Olinda, Pôrto Alegre, and Fortaleza.

53. See Cowell, p. 47; and Brazil, *Sexo*, pp. 421–22.

54. Silva Bruno, p. 206.

55. PE, *Annuario estatístico*, 1930, pp. 278–80.

56. *Ibid.*, pp. 88–89, 98, 107, 112, 158, 175, 323–24.

Chapter Two

1. Celso Furtado, *The Economic Growth of Brazil* (Berkeley, Calif., 1963), pp. 68, 78–81; Leff, "Economic Development," pp. 244–46.

2. Galloway, "Last Years," pp. 600–601.

3. Eisenberg, "From Slave to Free Labor," cited in Klein, p. 583.

4. Jaime Reis, paper read at Columbia University seminar on Brazil, Nov. 11, 1971. Reis, citing *Brasil Agrícola* (1882), notes that after the Free Womb Law of 1871 planters often treated the children born to slave mothers worse than regular slaves, since if the children died they would not have to be compensated on manumission at age 21, as the law required.

5. José Antônio Saraiva, *Relatório* (Recife, 1859), p. 6, cited in Cuniff, "Great Drought," p. 26. Cuniff treats agricultural labor in extensive detail, focusing mostly on the backlands.

6. L. F. Tollenare, *Notas Dominicais*, cited in Correia de Andrade, *Terra*, p. 79.

7. Denslow, letter to *Hispanic American Historical Review*, 52, no. 3 (Aug. 1972): 538–40; Galloway, "Last Years," pp. 601–2; Dé Carli, *O açúcar*, p. 33.

8. Dé Carli, *Processo histórico*, p. 23.

9. See Sund, p. 12. Census data are available for 1920 and 1940, though they are classified differently in the two censuses. See Brazil, *Recenseamento*, 1920, pp. 172–77; and *Recenseamento*, 1940, Table 1.

10. Azevedo, p. 115.

11. Dé Carli, *Aspectos de economía açucareira*, pp. 293–94, cited in Azevedo, p. 177.

12. Denslow, "Sugar Production," p. 51; Henry Koster, *Travels in Brazil*, cited *ibid.*

13. Denslow, "Sugar Production," pp. 63–64; R. Graham, *Britain*, pp. 152–54; Eisenberg, *Sugar Industry*, pp. 101–6; Paul Singer, p. 207.

14. Denslow, "Sugar Production," pp. 66–68.

15. Paul Singer, pp. 308–9. Jaime Reis effectively tempers the myth of the planter's benevolence toward his work force ("Bangüe," pp. 30–35).

16. Paul Singer, pp. 311–14; Dé Carli, *O açúcar*, p. 35.

17. Paul Singer, p. 314.

18. Early draft versions of the quotas gave Pernambuco a higher share, over 40%. See Dé Carli, *História contemporánea*, p. 28; and Paul Singer, p. 325. Post-1940 figures in *Balanço geral*, Table 2.

19. See Dé Carli, *Aspectos de economía açucareira*, pp. 60–72; and Dé Carli, *História contemporánea*, pp. 78–94.

20. Paul Singer, p. 283.

21. John C. Branner, *Cotton in the Empire of Brazil*, cited in Denslow, "Sugar Production," p. 38.

22. Denslow, "Sugar Production," pp. 101–2.

23. *Ibid.*, p. 101.

24. *Ibid.*, pp. 103–5. See Stein, *Brazilian Cotton Manufacture*, pp. 23–24, 35.

25. Banco do Nordeste, pp. 10–14, an account derived closely from Peres and Cavalcanti, pp. 63ff.

26. Denslow, "Sugar Production," pp. 103–5.

27. *Ibid.*, pp. 105–6.

28. PE, *Annuario estatistico*, 1927, p. 318. See also G. Peres, "Accidentes," pp. 109–10.

29. PE, *Annuario estatistico*, 1927, pp. 408–13, and 1942, pp. 274–81.

30. *Ibid.*, 1934, pp. 367–69, 982–83.

31. FO, 1889 Annual Series, no. 606, p. 3.

32. The factors, in this role, were called *commissários*. See Eisenberg, *Sugar Industry*, pp. 63-64, 77.

33. *Ibid.*, pp. 73-74.

34. See *Trabalhos do Congresso Agrícola*, 1878; Brazil, *Congressos*, pp. 16-40; and Eisenberg, *Sugar Industry*, pp. 75-76.

35. British consul Arthur L. G. Williams, "Report for the Year 1894 on the Trade of the Consular District of Pernambuco," cited by Eisenberg, *Sugar Industry*, p. 81. The Banco do Crédito Real offered mortgages at 8%. See the bank's "Relatórios," 1889-1913, Recife. See also Pereira da Costa, "Notícia," pp. 95-112.

36. Denslow, "Sugar Production," p. 6; PE, *Annuario estatistico*, 1930, p. 216. These followed on a 1905 loan in the value of £1,000,000 from Bemberg & Cie. and H. Legru, Paris. See Brazil, *Finanças do Brasil: Síntese*, pp. 397-98.

37. Eisenberg, *Sugar Industry*, p. 83.

38. See, for example, AC, annual "Relatórios," 1900-1925.

39. *Ibid.*, 1903, pp. 30-34.

40. Azevedo, p. 115.

41. PE, *Estado*, p. 108.

42. Lloyd et al., pp. 924-26. See also Wileman, pp. 754-57.

43. See Estévão Pinto, *Associação*, esp. pp. 283-88.

44. Brazil, *Resumo*, pp. 152-53. Pernambuco's land tax accounted for only .3% of the state's revenue in 1922, compared with .8% for São Paulo, 7.6% for Minas, 12.3% for Santa Catarina, and 14.1% for Pará.

45. See Love, *Rio Grande do Sul*, p. 125.

46. Great Western RR, reports of May 29, 1916, pp. 3-4, 8, 13, 18, and June 25, 1918, pp. 4-15, Gavin Black collection, Recife; AC, "Relatório," Jan. 8, 1919, p. 57, and "Relatório," 1918, pp. 34-35; PE, *Mensagem . . . Bezerra Cavalcanti*, p. 6.

47. Great Western RR, report of Dec. 31, 1919, p. 17, Gavin Black collection, Recife. A similar report was offered after an unsuccessful general strike in 1901 (report of Dec. 31, 1901).

48. *O Pernambuco* (Recife), Jan. 16, 1909, p. 1. See also the issue of Jan. 17, 1909, p. 1; and *O Leão do Norte* (Recife), Aug. 24, 1912, p. 2.

49. "A Great Western: Inglezes e brasileiros," *O Leão do Norte* (Recife), May 14, 1913, p. 1.

50. FO, 371/7091/3671, clipping from the London *Times*, March 1, 1923, p. 23, cols. 6, 7. See also Buley, p. 107.

51. FO, 371/14207/3746, 1929 annual report, p. 13.

52. See, for example, Aliança Nacional Libertadora, "O proletariado e as massas populares de Pernambuco," leaflet, Nov. 10, 1935 (courtesy of Roberto Sissón); and *O Syndicalista* (Jaboatão), 1, no. 1 (June 1935): 1.

53. M. Melo, "Chorographia," p. 106; U.S. consular report, Recife, Dec. 27, 1930, p. 11b; National Archives, Washington, D.C.; "A navigação de cabotagem," *Diário da Manhã* (Recife), Dec. 30, 1927, p. 1.

54. *Boletim da União dos Syndicatos Agrícolas de Pernambuco* (Recife), 4, no. 4 (Jan. 1910): 52-53; Marc, p. 245.

55. Brazil, *Anuário estatístico*, 1939-40, pp. 274-76, 281-82.

56. Gondim, p. 10; *Memorial . . . Affonso Penna*, pp. 9, 21.

57. According to the English, the charge of corruption and inefficiency ex-

tended, in fact, to all Brazilian ports and customhouses. In an acid 1907 annual report (FO, 371/200, pp. 25–26), the British correspondent accused the customhouses of "gross mismanagement" and compared Brazil unfavorably with Ecuador, Venezuela, Paraguay, and Argentina, "to which Brazil pretends to be superior."

58. See PE, *Mensagem . . . Bezerra Cavalcanti*, p. 11; "Quem esta com a palavra?," *Diário da Manhã* (Recife), July 12, 1927, p. 3; *Album do Pôrto do Recife*, esp. pp. 45–54, 70–72.

59. See J. Reis, "Bangüe," pp. 16–17.

60. "Concentrada na zona a população pernambucana," *Correio da Manhã*, ca. 1950, n.p. (clipping file, Estado de São Paulo).

61. See PE, *Annuario estatistico*, 1927, pp. 425–35; and PE, *Estado*, pp. 106–7.

62. For a general theoretical discussion of economic organization and geography, see Edward Whiting Fox, *History in Perspective: The Other France* (New York, 1971), esp. pp. 25–26.

63. Letter, Manoel Lubambo to José Vasconcellos, Olha d'Agua dos Bredos, Pernambuco, Nov. 8, 1925. Courtesy of Dulce Lubambo Calogias, Recife.

64. Leff, "Economic Development," pp. 252–60.

Chapter Three

1. Freyre, *Mansions*, p. 46.

2. J. M. Bello, *Memórias*, pp. 10–11.

3. Souza Barros, *Década*, p. 49.

4. Diegues Jr., *Regiões*, p. 116.

5. Nabuco, p. 263, quoted in Ringawa, p. 9.

6. *Almanach de Pernambuco*, 1884, pp. 43–44. Pernambuco's nobility included one count, four viscounts, and numerous barons, and totaled 45 in 1883.

7. Souza Barros, *Década*, p. 45.

8. Cavalcanti de Albuquerque Mello, pp. 26–27.

9. *Ibid.*, p. 24.

10. *Ibid.*, pp. 35–42 *passim*; Freyre, *Perfil*, p. 199.

11. Cavalcanti de Albuquerque Mello, p. 146.

12. *Ibid.*, p. 140; J. M. Bello, *Memórias*, p. 14. For a stereotype of the Brazilian family, see Schmitter, p. 55.

13. See J. M. Bello, *Memórias*, pp. 20–59.

14. Dep. Ruy Bello, in *A Cidade* (Recife), May 7, 1935, p. 3.

15. A 1937 sociological study based on interviews with 1,639 engenho workers listed 33% as *brancos* (whites), 15% as *pretos*, and 52% as *pardos*, with the latter subdivided into *mulatos, cabras, cafusos,* and *brancoides* (P. Dias, pp. 12–13).

16. Brazil, *Recenseamento*, 1940, pp. 1, 38, 58–59.

17. Castro, *Death*, p. 26.

18. Cowell, p. 49. The allegations that vagrants are murdered are still heard in Recife, though there is no evidence that this is true. Courtesy of Luis da Câmara Cascudo, Natal, interview April 1965.

19. See, for example, Tobias Barreto on the poor, cited in Chacon, *Escola*, p. 32.

20. DiTella, p. 81.

21. P. Dias, pp. 14–23.

22. Tejo, *Brejos*. These are isolated sentences drawn from pp. 135–61.

23. M. Mota, *Paisagem*, pp. 49–51; Pereira da Costa, *Comarcas*, pp. 22–23; Brazil, *Recenseamento*, 1920, pp. 140–41.

24. Almeida and Siqueira, esp. pp. 9–10. See Wirth, Chap. 3.

25. Lamartine, pp. 25–65 *passim*.

26. Brazil, *Annuario estatistico*, 1908–12, 1: 449. Priests combated what they called pagan influences among the poor, especially the Carnival-like Festa do Rosário of the region's blacks and caboclos (Lamartine, pp. 65–70). The coast's high religiosity is discussed in M. Melo, *Pau d'Alho*, p. 41.

27. A. Gonçalves Fernandes, *Região*, pp. 33–34, 67–71.

28. These included Queimados (3.1%), Moxotó (3.3%), and Glória de Goitá (3.5%). See Brazil, *Recenseamento*, 1940, pp. 255–61.

29. Rabello, *O nordeste*. See also Freyre, *Região*.

30. See Brazil, *Recenseamento*, 1940, pp. 6, 24–25, 208.

31. Paul Singer, pp. 342–43. The 1920 census for Recife, for example, lists 16,541 persons in the personal services category, or 12.9% of the population, and 53,480 persons, or 41.8%, as unemployed. According to the 1940 census, by then only 22,844 persons, or 11.6% of the population, were unemployed, and there were 104,661 persons, or 53.2%, in "personal services." The 1920 census is presumably the more accurate of the two.

32. Agamenon Magalhães, preface to PE, *Observações*, p. 304.

33. Cited in Freyre, *Região*, pp. 150–51. See also pp. 134–35.

34. José Verissimo, quoted in *ibid.*, pp. 159–60.

35. See Gilberto Amado, p. 35; Cámara, p. 138; *Almanak do Recife*, 1910, p. xxvii; and *O Pernambuco* (Recife), March 12, 1909, p. 1.

36. See Reina, Chap. 1, esp. pp. 35–37.

37. See *A Lanceta* (Recife), Feb. 3 and Feb. 6, 1912, pp. 6, 3, respectively.

38. PE, *Observações*, p. 18.

39. A. Diaz, p. 270.

40. See J. M. Bello, *Memórias*, p. 22; A. Diaz, p. 272; and Wright, p. 316.

41. PE, *Observações*, p. 21.

42. José Pernambuco, *passim* and esp. Chap. 1.

43. Gorringe, pp. 158–59.

44. For a foreigner's view of the city in 1902, see Waterton, pp. 65, 71.

45. M. Melo, "Sinopse," pp. 85–114; Rocha, *Roteiros*, p. 12; Barbosa Vianna, p. 25.

46. Souto Maior, n.p.

47. See Galvão, pp. 65–66.

48. See Freyre, *Guia*, p. 167.

49. Carvalho, "Jornaes," p. 41.

50. See Peres, *Pernambuco*, appendix; M. Melo, *Imprensa*, p. 12; and PE, *Annuario estatistico*, 1930, p. v. See also O. R. Dantas, p. 102; and Brazil, *Estatistica da imprensa*, p. 123.

51. For this treatment of education I have drawn on the archives and libraries of the Recife Law School, the Ginásio Pernambucano, and the Instituto Arqueológico of Recife.

52. *Leão do Norte* (Recife), Jan. 18, 1913, p. 1; PE, *Mensagem . . . Bezerra Cavalcanti*, p. 19. According to the second source, Rio Grande do Sul spent 20% on education, Minas and São Paulo both spent 15%, and Pernambuco spent 5%. See also Brazil, *Estatística da Instrução*, p. ccviii; and *Diário oficial*, Feb. 21,

1922, cited by C. R. Cameron, U.S. Consul, Pernambuco, "Report on Educational Courses in Foreign Schools," part 5, p. 4, RG84, National Archives, Washington, D.C.

53. See, for example J. M. Bello, *Memórias*, p. 20; and Cámara.

54. Cameron, "Report," cited in note 52, above.

55. PE, *Annuario estatistico*, 1927, p. 161. See also pp. 147–60.

56. PE, *Mensagem . . . Bezerra Cavalcanti*, p. 21. See also AP, *Mensagem . . . Coimbra*, p. 9; and *Montenegro*, pp. 81–292.

57. Barbosa Vianna, pp. 90–91; AP, *Mensagem . . . Correa de Araujo*, p. 29; Havighurst and Moreira, p. 85.

58. Freyre, quoted in Sette and Correia de Andrade, pp. 68–69.

59. See the criticism by A. J. de Melo Moraes in 1872, cited in Freyre, *Região*, p. 176. See also Morse, pp. 95, 240; and *Diário de Pernambuco* (Recife), March 23, 1909, p. 1.

60. See, for example, Paim, *A filosofia*; and Chacon, *Escola*.

61. Chacon, *Escola*, p. 27. See also "Ainda o bacharelismo," p. 4. An example of bacharel oratory is Marcos Vinícius Vilaça, *Presença na faculdade*. The bacharel is satirized in Lima Barreto's novel *Numa e nympha: Romance da vida contemporánea*.

62. "Ainda o bacharelismo," p. 4. Students paid a variety of fees, ranging from examination fees (U.S.$10 for matriculated students, $40 for non-matriculated students) to certificates of examination results ($5) to diploma fees ($30) to the doctor's examination fee ($60). These, plus tuition, clearly excluded the nonaffluent. See Cameron, "Report," cited in note 52, above, p. 186.

63. See N. Pereira, "Expulsão."

64. See Della Cava, "Catholicism."

65. See Arquidiocese de Olinda e Recife, *Album*. In Palmares in 1902 a judge founded the Liga Contra o Protestantismo, and in 1913 a Pernambuco chapter of the Rio-based Liga Anti-Clerical opened briefly. See *O Correio* (Palmares), Nov. 9, 1903, p. 3; and *A República* (Recife), Aug. 1, 1913, p. 5.

66. Arquivo da Congregação Mariana, 1: 124–30, 181. Separate retreats were held for young men and women. See also Antônio Fernandes, esp. pp. 30–31; and Lubambo, *Contra Nassau*.

67. See, for example, J. M. Bello, *Memórias*, p. 44; *O Leão do Norte* (Recife), Aug. 24, 1912, p. 2; and Roett, p. 95.

68. Calogeras, pp. 60–61.

69. Works by Escola figures include Tobias Barreto's *Recordação de Kant* (Recife, 1887) and Sílvio Romero's *História da literatura brasileira* (Recife, 1888).

70. "O pintor Tiago diz . . . ," *Jornal do Comércio*, March 22, 1970, p. 3.

71. See Freyre, "Manifesto," esp. p. 29.

72. *O Jornal* (Recife), Feb. 14, 1926, p. 2; Freyre, "Manifesto," p. 22.

73. See Freyre, "Estado," pp. 9–17. Courtesy of Gilberto Freyre.

74. Freyre, "Os médicos e as reformas sociais em Pernambuco," in *Estudos pernambucanos*, p. 55.

75. See *Estudos afro-brasileiros*; Freyre et al., *Novos estudos*; and Levine, "First Afro-Brazilian Congress."

76. Paachans, "O bolshevismo e o afro-brasilismo."

77. Gov. Coimbra, in his annual message, promised to raise expenditures to 13%, but the funds were never appropriated. See AP, *Mensagem . . . Coimbra*, pp. 5–9.

78. Mário Cunha, p. 203; Escobar, esp. pp. 27–39; *O ensino de didáctica*, pp. 3–26.

79. *Diário da Manhã* (Recife), April 10 and April 14, 1929, p. 1 of both.

80. From the statement of Nilo Pereira, in *Folha da Manhã* (Recife), Dec. 15, 1937, p. 1.

81. During his convalescence after a heart attack, mysterious automobiles constantly blew their horns in front of his family's home. For Pernambucano's biography, see Lacaz, p. 84; Freyre, *Nordeste*, pp. 154–56; and *Estudos pernambucanos*, esp. pp. 13–56.

82. For an anthropologist's similar conclusions about a small Mineiro town, Minas Velhas, see Harris, esp. p. 277.

Chapter Four

1. H. Christian Borstel, U.S. Consul, Pernambuco, to William F. Wharton, Asst. Secretary of State, Nov. 16, Nov. 21, Dec. 12, 1889, Consular Despatches, vol. 14, roll 14, National Archives, Washington, D.C.

2. Letter, Jan. 2, 1889, cited in Costa Pôrto, *Barbosa Lima*, p. 14.

3. *Ibid.*, p. 22.

4. Costa Pôrto offers the fullest treatment of the story; see his *Rosa e Silva*, p. 20, and *Barbosa Lima*, pp. 48–49.

5. Fafe, p. 41.

6. Barbosa Lima's campaign of repression is well documented in the Artur Orlando papers. See also Costa Pôrto, *Barbosa Lima*, pp. 109–10; and Coelho Cintra, in *O Pernambuco* (Recife), June 14, 1894, p. 11.

7. *Almanach de Pernambuco*, 1895, entries for Nov. 28 and Nov. 29, 1894.

8. See Freire, *Rosa e Silva*, pp. 17–18; and Costa Pôrto, *Rosa e Silva*, pp. 8, 150.

9. Gilberto Amado, pp. 255, 372. The other material in the text on Rosa e Silva is drawn from Austregésilo, pp. 121–40; Azedo, p. 146; PE, *Annaes*, 1898, March 11; Barroca, pp. 9–60; and *Diário de Pernambuco*, July 2, 1929, p. 3 (Rosa e Silva's obituary).

10. Pimenta, pp. 127, 180. Attempts to overthrow the results of fair competitions did not always succeed. See *O Pernambuco* (Recife), May 9, 1910, p. 1; AP, telegram, Lima Cavalcanti to Ministry of Education and Public Health, March 11, 1931; AP, letter, Abdias de Oliveira to Estácio Coimbra, Olinda, Sept. 22, 1911.

11. Borba, pp. 460–63.

12. See, for example, in AC, Companhia Industrial Pernambucana, "Relatório," 1892; Fábrica de Tecidos e Camaragibe, "Relatórios," 1892–1921; Companhia de Beberibe, "Relatório," 1892, p. 158; and Banco de Crédito Real, "Relatório," 1912.

13. *O Pernambuco* (Recife), Feb. 11, 1909, p. 2.

14. Decree no. 153, Aug. 3, 1893, in Brazil, *Collecção*, p. 28; PE, *Annuario estatistico*, 1930, pp. 151–57.

15. See J. M. Bello, *History*, pp. 214–23.

16. On Juarez Távora's role, see his published memoirs, *Uma vida e muitas lutas*, vol. 1 (Rio, 1973).

17. AP, telegram, Estácio Coimbra, Recife, to Minister of War, Sept. 13, 1930 (Ofício no. 210).

18. See Alvaro Lins, "O desprestígio da intelligencia," *O Estado* (Recife), Feb. 23, 1934, p. 3.

19. Manifesto, União Libertadora, quoted in *O Estado* (Recife), Sept. 25, 1934, p. 1. On Lima Cavalcanti's feud with José Américo, see AP, telegrams, Lima Cavalcanti, Recife, to Pedro Ernesto Batista, Rio, Jan. 12, 1932; to Prefeito, Bodocó, Aug. 17, 1932; to José Américo, Rio, Sept. 9, 11, and 13, 1932; and to Getúlio Vargas, Rio, Sept. 16, 1932.

20. Telegram, Getúlio Vargas, Rio, to Lima Cavalcanti, Recife, Nov. 19, 1934, Arquivo Nacional, Rio de Janeiro, lata 15.

21. See Levine, *Vargas Regime*, esp. Chap. 5.

22. The Foreign Ministry was asked to investigate whether Lima Cavalcanti had consorted with undesirables in Europe. See Brazil, Foreign Ministry Archive, Telegrafias e Cópias, Berlin, 1931–37, 397/4/10, telegram, Moniz Aragão, Rio, to Brazilian Embassy, Berlin, May 13, 1937. Courtesy of José Honório Rodrigues.

23. "Hatchet man" courtesy Juarez Távora (interview), Rio, Aug. 1970; "O mongol," in *O Estado* (Recife), March 16, 1934, p. 1. See also N. Pereira, *Agamenon Magalhães*.

24. See Ferraz de Sá, esp. pp. 81–83.

25. See Tarrow, pp. 7–8.

26. See Brazil, *Annuario estatistico*, 1908–12, 1: 66.

27. Saffioti, pp. 274–76.

28. See, for example, *Jornal Pequeno* (Recife), Nov. 7, 1911, p. 1.

29. On coronelismo, see Pang, "Politics," esp. pp. iii–iv, 2–8. See also Della Cava, *Miracle*; Bitú; and P. Cavalcanti, *Equívocos*, pp. 16–17.

30. The man was Triunfo's Correia da Cruz. See Lins de Albuquerque, p. 156.

31. Pang, "Politics." On Chico Heráclio, see "Só restam dois coronéis," *Veja e Leia*, Oct. 22, 1969, p. 27.

32. Almeida and Siqueira, p. 16; Pang, "Politics," pp. 3–4. On the view from the município, see AP, *Cidade do Limoeiro*, July 1910 and Jan. 1911. See also Lins de Albuquerque, pp. 155–56.

33. Pang, "Politics," p. 28.

34. Twelve years later, in 1922, 5,067 voters cast ballots in Recife, out of a total of 21,500 in the state (*Jornal do Commercio*, June 6, 1922, p. 2). In the same issue (p. 5), the official statistics indicated totally different results.

35. See *A Revolução* (Recife), June 16, 1912, p. 2, citing *Jornal do Recife*, Nov. 8, 1911. See also *Jornal Pequeno* (Recife), Nov. 7, 1911, p. 1.

36. See Pang, "Politics," pp. 138–213. In 1931 Vargas's provisional government put all município affairs in the Northeast under tenente control. See AP, *Minutas-Ofícios*, Sept.–Dec. 1931, telegrams sent Oct. 15, 1931.

37. I include under the rubric "political violence" not only armed clashes and riots, but also significantly increased banditry and police repression and urban protests. See Peter H. Smith, "History," in Byars and Love, pp. 17–19.

38. *Ibid.*, p. 19.

39. Antônio Pedro de Figuereido (1848), cited in P. Cavalcanti, *Equívocos*, p. 17; Oliveira Lima, p. 245.

40. Gilberto Freyre, introduction to Cavalcanti de Albuquerque Mello, p. 29.

41. Mário Melo, "O movimento patriótico do Triunfo," manuscript, Instituto Arqueológico, Recife.

42. Artur Orlando papers, Recife: letters to Orlando from Olegária Carneiro da Cunha, June 14, 1894; from J. d'Alvear (pseud. José Maria de Albuquerque

Mello), May 20, 1894; and from José Mariano Carneiro da Cunha, April 17, 1894, implicating Barbosa Lima in the conspiracy. Courtesy of Vamireh Chacon.

43. J. G. Maia, *Horas*; Fafe; Costa Pôrto, *Barbosa Lima*, pp. 92–144; Brazil, *Intervenção*, 3: 51–88.

44. See "Escândalo sôbre escândalo!," *A Justiça* (Caxangá), Aug. 1910, pp. 14–15; *O Pernambuco* (Recife), Nov. 15, 1911, p. 1; Galvão, pp. 99–100; Oscar Melo, pp. 8–81. The Mesquita papers in São Paulo reveal widespread ballot-box fraud on both sides at the national level in 1910. Courtesy of Paul Manor.

46. J. Menezes, *Libello*, pp. 5–21.

47. Cited in Gayoso, p. 84.

48. L. Mota, *No tempo*, p. 193; Vilaça and Albuquerque, pp. 40–41; Oscar Melo, pp. 83–92. "Veado" also refers to presumed homosexuality.

49. See *Revista Criminal*, Sept. 1929, p. 16; Caldas, p. 105; P. E. Callado, pp. 37–40; PE, *Exposição*, pp. 137–45; *O Estado* (Recife), Nov. 30, 1933, p. 3.

50. In this sense, the northeastern cangaceiro does not fit E. J. Hobsbawm's definition of the social bandit as the product of an "endemic peasant protest against oppression and poverty" (*Primitive Rebels*, p. 5).

51. Speech by Manoel Cândido, representative from Buíque, at First Congress on the Sertão Economy (1935), in Torres, p. 31; M. Mota, *Paisagem*, p. 35; Barroso, *Almas*, pp. 61–62.

52. Hobsbawm, *Bandits*, pp. 77–78, citing L. Mota, *No tempo*.

53. AP, Minutas-Telegrammas do Interventor, telegrams, Lima Cavalcanti, Recife, to interventors of Ceará, Rio Grande do Norte, Paraíba, Alagoas, Sergipe, and Bahia, May 28, 1931.

54. Singlemann, p. 61; Hobsbawm, *Bandits*, pp. 53, 68. See also Macedo; AP, "Mensagem . . . 7 Set. 1926 . . . Sérgio Loreto," pp. 115–16; G. Fernandes, *Mobilidade*, p. 45; Lemos Filho, pp. 119–201.

55. João Pessôa, governor of Paraíba, interviewed in *Diário da Manhã* (Recife), Jan. 16, 1930, p. 1.

56. Singlemann, p. 64.

57. FO, 371/13467/3724/A3440/69/6, B. Alston, British Embassy, Rio, "Contrast of British and Brazilian Electoral Campaigns," April 23, 1929.

58. For a comparison with the Italian Mezzogiorno region of Italy, see Tarrow, p. 7. E. V. Walter develops this same theme in *Terror and Resistance*.

59. *Diário de Pernambuco*, Nov. 28, 1910.

60. Stone, p. 23.

61. *Ibid.*, p. 23–24. A similar situation existed in 16th- and 17th-century England.

62. See Facó; Maria Isaura Pereira de Queiroz, *O messianismo no Brasil e no mundo* (São Paulo, 1965); and Della Cava, *Miracle*.

Chapter Five

1. Cavalcanti de Albuquerque Mello, pp. 16–17. The Cavalcanti family alone controlled four of the most important judgeships in the Zona da Mata as well as the position of provincial administrator of tax revenue.

2. Political elite members of this group, defined as those directly related to Imperial senators or titleholders of baron or higher rank, constituted 30% of the sample up to 1911. After that, the figure dropped to 19% among members of the elite in the 20 and above age group.

3. See Soares, p. 35.

4. In the following list, showing the 60-man network I traced among the state's political elite, kinship (through first cousin) is indicated by a dash (—) and business links by three dots (...).

Luis Correia de Brito, Artur Orlando, Joaquim Correia de Araujo, Malaquias Antônio Gonçalves...Francisco de Assis Rosa e Silva—José Marcelino Rosa e Silva—Francisco de Assis Rosa e Silva Júnior—Anibal Freire; Artur Orlando—Antônio Vicente de Andrade Bezerra—José Rufino Bezerra Cavalcanti—José Bezerra Cavalcanti—Edgard Teixeira Leite;...Manoel Carneiro Leão—Luis Cedro Carneiro da Cunha—Aristoteles Solano Carneiro da Cunha...João Cleofas; Francisco Solano Carneiro da Cunha...Carlos de Lima Cavalcanti—Artur Siqueira Cavalcanti—João Siqueira Cavalcanti—Pedro Ernesto Batista—Caio de Lima Cavalcanti; José Marcelino Rosa e Silva...Bianor de Medeiros;...Gilberto Amado—Thomé Gibson...Bianor de Medeiros—Amaury de Medeiros—Sérgio Loreto...Manoel Silva Pinto;—Sérgio Loreto Filho; João Francisco Arruda Falcão—Joaquim Arruda Falcão—Anibal Falcão; Francisco Solano Carneiro da Cunha—José Henrique Carneiro da Cunha; José Mariano Carneiro da Cunha—Olegário Mariano Carneiro da Cunha—André Cavalcanti de Albuquerque—Democrito Cavalcanti—Lourenço Cavalcanti de Albuquerque—José Maria Cavalcanti de Albuquerque—Samuel Hardman Cavalcanti e Albuquerque—Augusto Cavalcanti de Albuquerque—Miguel Pernambuco—Joaquim de Albuquerque Pernambucano—Pedro José de Albuquerque Pernambucano...Francisco Pessôa de Queiroz—Epitácio Pessôa—Henrique de Lucena—João Pessôa de Queiroz; Miguel Pernambuco— ? Ulisses Pernambucano—Antônio Marques; Afonso Albuquerque e Melo—Ayres Albuquerque Gama—Júlio de Melo—Alfredo Albuquerque Gama; José Maria Bello—Estácio Coimbra—João Coimbra—Júlio de Albuquerque Bello.

5. Compiled from N. Maia, *Apontimentos*, pp. 43–54.

6. Over the three generations the percentage of the elite who attended secondary school out of state varied only from 10% to 7% to 5%, a small drop but of no statistical significance. The percentage of those earning professional degrees out of state varied from 3% to 7% to 6%, also not statistically significant.

7. See Zeldin, pp. 113–29, esp. p. 113.

8. PE, *Annaes*, 1898, p. 51.

9. In addition, at least some of the military officers who held political office worked as civil engineers at some time during their careers. See Sodré; Azedo, p. 146; and AP, *Cidade do Limoeiro*, Aug. 30, 1911, p. 1.

10. For a geographer's view of the role of the Agreste and Sertão, see Webb, esp. Chaps. 4, 6, 7.

11. Out-of-state birth: 17%, 13%, 14% (statistically not significant: .7959). Compare out-of-state careers, Table 5.4, above.

12. Statistically significant results for the post-1930 elite are obtained for "bacharel" (.015), "cleric" (.0268), "zone" (.0268), "military" (.0446), and "other university degrees" (.0197).

13. See M. Melo, *Imprensa*, pp. 11–16.

14. For a comparison with French elites, see Zeldin, pp. 15–16.

15. *Almanach de Pernambuco*, 1911, pp. 6–10; *A Revolução* (Recife), June 13, 1912, p. 1.

16. R. Bello, *Barreiros*, pp. 134–35; Brazil, *Recenseamento*, 1920, p. 32; Austregésilo, pp. 143–47.

17. J. M. Bello, *Memórias*, p. 35.

18. Bello's history of the Republic has been translated as *A History of Modern Brazil, 1889–1964*. Data courtesy of Ruy Bello.

19. P. E. Callado, pp. 28–35.

Chapter Six

1. See Fausto, p. 219.

2. For a comparison with Rio Grande do Sul, see Love, pp. 137–38.

3. PE, *Annuario estatistico*, 1929, p. xlix; Brazil, *Anuário estatístico*, 1938, p. 231.

4. Paul Singer, pp. 321–22.

5. On coffee and valorization, see Fausto, pp. 193–248.

6. The protest literature is voluminous. See Brandão; Barbosa Lima Sobrinho, "O dever da constituinte diante de Pernambuco," *O Estado* (Recife), April 6, 1934, p. 3; Souza Barros, *Velhos*, esp. pp. 1–12; and Barbosa Lima Sobrinho, *Pernambuco*.

7. J. G. Maia, *Questões*, p. 47, citing the *Diário oficial* of Alagoas, May 22, 1920.

8. See Thomas Lins Caldas Filho, letter, *Diário de Pernambuco*, Feb. 2, 1918, p. 5; M. Melo, *Imprensa*, p. 19 (referring to plans aired in 1908); and *Memorial . . . Affonso Penna*, p. 19. *O Pernambuco* (Recife), Sept. 15, 1909, p. 1, offers a more pessimistic prognosis. See also Great Western RR, "Proceeding at the Ordinary General Meeting," April 29, 1903, p. 5, Gavin Black collection, Recife.

9. Della Cava, *Miracle*, p. 163.

10. *O Paiz* (Rio), June 19, 1890, cited in AC, "Relatório," 1890, p. 59; PE, *Mensagems . . . Barbosa Lima* (1893, 1895, 1896), p. 134. See also José Maria Bello, address to Partido Republicano de Pernambuco, March 15, 1930, in *Diário de Estado* (Recife), March 15, 1930, pp. 426–27. Bello, speaking of the commitment by Washington Luis and Júlio Prestes to transportation improvements, neglected to point out that as President, Washington Luis had initiated little outside of the Center-South.

11. See Cuniff, "Birth," esp. p. 8.

12. Benévolo, p. 24. Cuniff notes that the president (the Imperial equivalent of governor) of Ceará was a large landowner whose properties lay in the path of the Sobral railroad, and that he was also linked to interests who stood to benefit from the Baturité line.

13. Friese, p. 374.

14. Theophilo, p. 19; O. Barbosa, p. 123–28; Robock, p. 77.

15. See AP, telegrams, Lima Cavalcanti, Recife, to José Américo, Rio, Oct. 8 and Oct. 15, 1931. On Epitácio Pessôa's innovative anti-drought measures, see Hirschman, Chap. 1.

16. See AP, telegrams, Lima Cavalcanti, Recife, to various prefeitos, May 5, 1931.

17. AP, telegrams, Lima Cavalcanti, Recife, to José Américo, Bahia, May 24, 1932; and to Getúlio Vargas, Rio, Sept. 16, 1932.

18. See Souto Maior, pp. 241–43. See also Barbosa Lima Sobrinho, *Interesses*, pp. 7–26 *passim*; and Bouças, p. 26.

19. Gov. Castro Pinto of Paraíba is given credit for having called the meeting initially (Lemos Filho, p. 197).

20. See AP, "Relatório de 1923 Dr. Sérgio Loreto," p. 11; Machado, p. 216; "O

maior problema do nordeste," *Diário da Manhã* (Recife), Oct. 18, 1927, p. 1; and Andrade Bezerra, July 12, 1918, in *Annaes do Congresso Nacional*, 1918, 4: 457–59.

21. Compiled from tables in Peixoto, pp. 402–13.

22. Report, Juarez Távora to Getúlio Vargas, 1932, pp. 18–19, Arquivo Nacional, Rio. Military pressure was applied most directly between 1935 and 1937. See Levine, *Vargas Regime*, Chap. 6.

23. José Augusto Bezerra de Medeiros, in *O Estado* (Recife), Dec. 12, 1933, p. 1. An exception to the lack of social awareness before 1930 is found in Agamenon Magalhães' law school thesis, "O nordeste brasileiro" (written in 1921 and published later, in 1936, under the same title). Though in this work Magalhães is inadvertently racist in the manner of Euclides da Cunha, he argued that the Northeast's salvation would come if the government would modify the habitat of the sertanejo and integrate his world with the urban world of the coast (pp. 85–86, published work). The plea for federal aid is repeated in Otto Guerra, pp. 6–7.

24. Mello Neto, "Por uma história." Moreover, much of the tax revenue came from the federally administered port.

25. Herculano Cavalcante Sá e Albuquerque, in *Diário de Pernambuco* (Recife), July 10, 1878, cited in *ibid.*, p. 58.

26. "O abandono do nordeste," *Diário da Manhã* (Recife), May 20, 1927, p. 3.

27. See Brazil, *Impostos inter-estaduais*, 3: esp. 117–18. 336, 411.

28. Love, *Rio Grande do Sul*, pp. 113–14.

29. See AC, "Relatórios," 1902, 1903, 1908, 1914, 1925. See also *O Pernambuco* (Recife), Nov. 30, 1908, p. 1; and Brazil, *Impostos*, as cited in note 27, above. For a detailed examination of the interstate taxation issue, see Francisco Valladares, "Questões debatidas sôbre competencia tributaria: Impostos inter-estadoaes," in Brazil, *Livro do centenário*, 2: 281–307.

30. AC, "Relatório," 1914, pp. 23–27. See also the "Relatório" for 1906, pp. 19–21; and *A República* (Recife), April 8, 1912, p. 1.

31. Estévão Pinto, *Associação*, p. 71.

32. AP, *Mensagem . . . Coimbra*, pp. 3–4; and "Mensagem, 1929," p. 3.

33. See, for example, AP, telegram, Lima Cavalcanti to president, Centro Académico, Escola de Minas, Ouro Preto, June 11, 1931.

34. See Barbosa Lima Sobrinho, "Saudação ao Presidente Eurico Dutra," July 3, 1948, in *Discursos*, pp. 45–54.

35. Barbosa Lima Sobrinho, "Resposta ao Ministro Clementino Mariani," *ibid.*, p. 56. The 57%, however, included federal port collections.

36. AC, "Relatório," 1926, p. 7; Souza Barros, *Década*, pp. 51–52. This harked back to the days of the Empire when the Viscount Sinimbú, an Alagoan planter, refused as Agriculture Minister to invite northeastern representatives to the 1878 Agricultural Congress (Eisenberg, *Sugar Industry*, p. 95).

37. See AP, Minutas-Telegrammas do Interventor files for 1930–35. See also Amaury Pedrosa, "Dias de outubros," *Diário de Pernambuco* (Recife), May 13, 1974, p. 4.

38. Paes Barretto, "O norte e o sul," address given Sept. 12, 1890, reprinted in his *A abolição*, p. 168.

39. "O Brasil e somente o sul?," *O Pernambuco* (Recife), Dec. 8, 1908, p. 1. São Paulo, of course, also contributed the lion's share of federal taxes.

40. Carvalho, "Cartografia," p. 9; Campello, pp. 139–40. In all probability the

1920 census estimates allowed too many inhabitants for Pernambuco, not too few.

41. "O norte, enteado de uma república madrasta," *Jornal do Recife*, Oct. 7, 1928, p. 1.

42. AP, telegram, Lima Cavalcanti to Juarez Távora, Nov. 7, 1932.

Chapter Seven

1. Haas, p. xxxv.

2. McCann, esp. pp. 1-4.

3. *A República* (Recife), Jan. 9, 1912, p. 1. See also *Relatório do Ministério da Guerra* (Rio, 1919); *Diário de Pernambuco* (Recife), Oct. 15, 1930, p. 3; and Lemos Filho, p. 249.

4. AP, *Mensagem . . . Dantas Barreto* (1912), p. 4.

5. See FO 371/16549/3807, memorandum, Troutbeck, Rio, to Foreign Secretary, London, Oct. 6, 1933.

6. Wirth, p. 201.

7. *Almanach de Pernambuco*, 1900, p. xxvii (events for 1890).

8. Rocha, "Sindicalismo," pp. 8-9; *Aurora Social* (Recife), May 1, 1901, p. 1, and April 23, 1902, p. 1. Ezequiel was one of the two labor leaders briefly co-opted by Dantas Barreto in 1912.

9. *A República* (Recife), March 29, 1913, p. 1.

10. On the 1931 rising, see P. E. Callado. On 1935, see Levine, *Vargas Regime*, Chap. 5; and Vergolino, p. 215.

11. AP, letter, Lima Cavalcanti to newspaper editors, March 19, 1931.

12. Decree Law 19,770 of March 19, 1931. See Rocha, "Sindicalismo," pp. 8-9.

13. Computed from federal and state revenue tables in Brazil, *Anúario estatístico*, 1939-40 and 1942.

14. Data from Brazil, *Anuário estatístico*, 1939-40, p. 1410; price index (see Appendix C, above). The Union also ceded to the states the right to tax property transfers, urban real estate, and licenses.

15. Love, *São Paulo*, Chap. 8.

16. Brazil, *Anuário estatístico*, 1939-40, p. 1416.

17. On the Loreto financial scandals, see Borba; and Lima Cavalcanti, *Pernambuco saqueado*, pp. 8-11.

18. See Valetim F. Bouças, *Finanças do Brasil*, vol. 9, n.p. Courtesy of Joseph L. Love. Rates for southern states did rise to 7-8 percent after World War I, but rates rose higher elsewhere.

19. PE, *Annaes*, 1893 (2d session), pp. 289-90. Cabinet members received seven contos a year (Costa Pôrto, *Dantas Barreto*, p. 157).

20. *Memorial . . . Affonso Penna*, p. 27.

21. *Almanach de Pernambuco*, 1912, p. xii (events of 1906).

22. *O Pernambuco* (Recife), June 26, 1910, p. 1.

23. AP, telegrams, Lima Cavalcanti to president, Bank of Brazil, Dec. 18 and Dec. 1930 (also Jan. 7, 1931); and to Ministry of Finance, Dec. 27, 1930.

24. Compiled from Banco do Brasil, "Relatório," 1937, pp. 67-69. The bank's loans to private interests in each state followed a similar pattern.

25. Mello Barreto.

26. *Relatório apresentado ao . . . Jader de Andrade*, pp. 23, 27; A. Peres and Cavalcanti, pp. 23-25.

27. PE, *Exposição*, pp. 225–27.

28. *Folha da Manhã* (Recife), Nov. 25, 1937, p. 1. See also Venâncio Filho, esp. pp. 93–98.

29. "Discriminação da receita orçada e arrecadada," in PE, *Annuario estatistico*, 1934, pp. 176–83. See the observation by the U.S. consul, Pernambuco, "Revision 1932," *Political Report*, p. 1, File 800, National Archives, Washington, D.C.

Conclusion

1. Elliott, *Revolt*, p. 225.

2. Freyre, *Engenheiro*, 1: 70.

3. Among other things, Oliveira Lima laments Pernambuco's "almost complete lack of European elements" in its population (*Pernambuco*, p. 316). For another example of fashionable pessimism, see Vasconcelos Sobrinho.

4. Lemos Filho, p. 203.

5. See Stone, pp. 21–22.

6. Pang, "Politics," p. 343. In 1889 there were only 33 Republican clubs in the North compared with 204 in the South. Pernambuco had just six all told, against 48 in São Paulo and 58 in Minas. The phrase "political museum" is Charles Anderson's (*Politics and Economic Change in Latin America*, as cited by Schmitter, p. 369).

7. Leal, p. 8.

8. Eisenberg, *Sugar Industry*, p. 116.

9. PE, *Mensagems . . . Barbosa Lima* (1893, 1895, 1896), pp. 18–24.

10. Souto Maior, pp. 227–40.

11. Souza Barros, *Década*, p. 188.

12. See José Ribeiro Escobar's correspondence in the Carneiro Leão collection (Biblioteca Nacional, Rio) and his *O ensino de didática*.

13. Eisenberg, *Sugar Industry*; Eul-Soo Pang, "Bahia's Planter Elites and Their Attempt to Modernize Agriculture, 1842–1889," unpublished manuscript, Racine, Wis., 1975.

14. Eudes Pinto, p. 3.

15. Henrique Pereira de Lucena; Alexandre José Barbosa Lima (1892–96); Joaquim Correia de Araujo (1896–1900); Emídio Dantas Barreto (1911–15); Manoel Borba (1915–19); Sérgio Loreto (1922–26); Estácio Coimbra (1926–30); Carlos de Lima Cavalcanti (1930–37); Agamenon Magalhães.

16. PE, *Recenseamento do Recife*.

17. Laslett, p. 125.

18. See Graciliano Ramos's recollections about his childhood in Buíque in *Infância*, pp. 50–57.

19. P. Dias, p. 22.

20. Eisenberg, *Sugar Industry*, p. 170. See also Berlinck, pp. 91–126.

21. Tejo, *Brejos*, p. 109.

22. *Ibid.*, pp. 35, 53; Barroso, *Almas de lama*, p. 55; Lemos Filho, p. 273. See Roderick Barman, "The Brazilian Peasantry Reexamined: The Implications of the Quebra-Quilos Revolt," *Hispanic American Historical Review*, 57 (Aug. 1977).

23. This comparison draws on Sidney G. Tarrow's provocative analysis of the Mezzogiorno, *Peasant Communism in Southern Italy*.

24. Apter, Chap. 2, cited in *ibid.*, p. 13.

25. *Ibid.*, p. 36. See also pp. 14–34.

26. *Ibid.*, pp. 57, 63. The bacharéis, of course, filled the vacuum. Richard N. Adams suggests that the lawyer's powers are derivative and not productive (*Crucifixion*, pp. 407–8).

Bibliography

Archival Sources, Diplomatic Correspondence, Private Papers and Collections

Arquivo Artur Orlando, Recife.
Arquivo Epitácio Pessôa, Rio.
Arquivo Público Estadual de Pernambuco, Recife. Minutes-Ofícios expedidos pela Inspectoria das Municipalidades, 1931–32.
——. Minutas-Telegrammas do Interventor, 1930–35.
——. Relatórios dos Presidentes da Província, 1885–89.
——. Relatórios e Mensagens dos Governadores do Estado, 1891–1930.
——. Secretaria da Fazenda, 1890–1938.
Arquivo da Presidência da República, "Interventor de Pernambuco," 1930–37, Arquivo Nacional, Rio.
Associação Comercial Beneficente de Pernambuco, Recife. Unpublished manuscripts and minutes; Relatórios, 1880–1937.
Carneiro Leão Collection, Biblioteca Nacional, Rio.
O Estado de São Paulo, Clipping file, São Paulo.
Gavin Black Collection, Recife. Documents on the Great Western of Brazil Railway.
Ginásio Pernambuco, Recife.
Great Britain, Foreign Office, London. Diplomatic and consular reports, 1888–1938.
——. Report on the Railway Systems of Brazil, 1904. Public Record Office.
——. Foreign Office papers, 1906–38.
Instituto Arqueológico, Recife.
United States, National Archives, Washington, D.C. Consular reports, Pernambuco, File 800.
——, Department of State, Washington, D.C. Political reports, 1921–39.

Other Sources

Abranches, Dunshee de. Governos e congressos dos Estados Unidos do Brazil, 1889 a 1917. v.1. São Paulo, 1918.

"Academia Pernambucana de Letras . . . para 70 anos," *Jornal do Brasil*, Jan. 24–25, 1971.

Adam, Heribert. Modernizing Racial Domination: South Africa's Political Dynamics. Berkeley, Calif., 1971.

Adams, Richard Newbold. Crucifixion by Power: Essays on Guatemalan National Social Structure, 1944–66. Austin, Tex. 1970.

"Ainda o bacharelismo," *Diário de Pernambuco*, Feb. 7, 1970.

Album do Pôrto do Recife, ano II, no. 2 (Dec. 1958).

Almanach de Pernambuco. Recife, 1880–1931. (Various spellings.)

Almanak do Recife. Recife, 1882–1910.

Almeida, Batista de, and Cícero Siqueira. O centenário da independência em Canhotinho, 1922. Recife, 1922.

Almeida, José Américo. A Parahyba e seus problemas, 2d ed. Pôrto Alegre, 1937.

———. "Têm a vida muitos mistérios," *Jornal do Brasil* (Rio) July 26–27, 1970 (1º caderno).

Almeida Prado, J. F. de. Pernambuco e as capitanias do norte do Brasil, 1560–1630. 2 v. São Paulo, 1939.

Alves, Durval. A Universidade Federal do Ceará e sua dimensão no nordeste em mudança. Fortaleza, 1967.

Amado, Gilberto. Minha formação no Recife. Rio, 1955.

Amado, Jorge. Gabriela, cravo e canela. Rio, 1958.

Annaes do Congresso Nacional, apuração da eleição do Presidente e Vice-Presidente da República, realizada de 1º de março de 1910. 2 v. Rio, 1910.

Annaes do 1º congresso Médico de Pernambuco, abril a maio de 1909. Recife, 1910.

Apter, David. The Politics of Modernization. Chicago, 1965.

Armstrong, John A. The European Administrative Elite. Princeton, N.J., 1973.

Arquidiocese de Olinda e Recife. Album Jubilar: 29-x-1911–29-x-1936. Recife, 1936.

Arquivo da Congregação Mariana da Mocidade Académica. 3 v. Recife, 1938–40.

Arraes, Raymundo de Monte. Decadência e redenção do nordeste (a política dos grandes estados). Rio, 1962.

Arruda Câmara, Deputado. Os últimos dias de Pompêa (o govêrno do Sr. Carlos de Lima). Rio, 1937.

Austregésilo, Antônio. Afeto e inteligência (perféis de amigos). Rio, 1944.

Azedo, Raul. "Aspectos da reação cívica de 1911," *Revista do Instituto de Arqueologia, Historia e Geografia de Pernambuco*, 31 (1931): 102–49.

Azevedo, Fernando de. Canavais e engenhos na vida política do Brasil. 2d ed. São Paulo, 1958.

Balanço geral, 31 de maio de 1974, Niteroi. Cooperativa Fluminense dos Productores de Açúcar e Alcool, Ltda. Niteroi, 1974.

Banco do Brasil. "Relatórios," 1931–37. Rio.

Banco do Crédito Real. "Relatórios," 1889–1913. Recife.

Banco do Nordeste, S/A. Estrutura da indústria pernambucana. Fortaleza, 1963.

Bandeira, Esmeraldino, O prefeito municipal do Recife a seus concidadaos (refutação de uma calumnia). Recife, 1899.

———. "Reminiscências da Faculdade de Direito do Recife," *A Epoca* (Rio), 20, no. 127 (Oct.-Nov. 1925): 12–26.

Barbosa, Orris. Secca de 32 (impressões sôbre a crise nordestina). Rio, 1935.

Barbosa Lima Sobrinho, Alexandre José. A ação do Instituto do Açúcar e do Alcool. Rio, 1946.

———. Discursos. Recife, 1950.

———. Interesses e problemas do sertão pernambucano. Rio, 1937.

———. Pernambuco e o São Francisco. Recife, 1929.

Barbosa Vianna, A. J. O Recife, capital do Estado de Pernambuco. Recife, 1900.

Barreto, Carlos Xavier Paes. "Origem de algumas famílias nordestinas," Revista Genealógica Brasileira, 7 (2° semestre, 1946): 427–34.

Barreto, Guimaraës. O sentido nacional dos problemas do nordeste brasileiro. Rio, 1959.

Barreto, Leda. Julião-nordeste, revolução. Rio, 1963.

Barreto, Lima. Numa e nympha: Romance da vida contemporanea. Rio, 1959.

Barretto, Castro. População, riqueza e segurança. Rio, 1961.

Barretto, Costa. Povoamento e população: Política populacional brasileira. 2d ed., 2 v. Rio, 1959.

[Barroca, R. Fernando do Teophaceu.] Notas biographicas do Vice-Presidente da República Dr. Francisco de Assis Rosa e Silva. Recife, 1900. Published under the pseudonym "Um Pernambucano."

Barroso, Gustavo. Almas de lama e de aço (Lampião e outros cangaceiros). São Paulo, 1930.

———. Reflexões de um bode. 2d ed. Rio [?] 1935.

Basbaum, Leôncio. História sincera da República de 1889 a 1930. 2d ed. São Paulo, 1962.

Bastide, Roger. Brasil, terra de contrastes. São Paulo, 1959.

Bastos, Tavares. A província: Estudo sobre a decentralisação no Brasil. Rio, 1870.

Beiguelman, Paula. "O processo político no Império de 1840 a 1869," Revista Brasileira de Estudos Políticos, 22 (Jan. 1967): 211–23.

Bello, José Maria. A History of Modern Brazil, 1889–1964. 2d ed. Stanford, Calif., 1968.

———. Memórias. Rio, 1958.

Bello, Júlio. Memórias de um senhor do engenho. 2d ed. Rio, 1948.

Bello, Ruy de Ayres. Barreiros, história de uma cidade. Recife, 1967.

Beltrão, Antônio Carlos de Arruda. O Estado de Pernambuco na Exposição Nacional de 1908: Catálogo dos expositores. Rio, 1909.

Benévolo, Ademar. Introdução à história ferroviário do Brasil. Recife, 1953.

Benton, Peggie. One Man Against the Drylands: Struggle and Achievement in Brazil. London, 1972.

Berlinck, Manoel T. "Concepções populares de marginalidade," in Migrações, v.1, cited below.

Bevilaqua, Clovis. História da Faculdade de Direito do Recife. 2 v. Rio, 1927.

Bezerra, Daniel Uchoa Cavalcanti. Alagados, mucambos e mocambeiros. Recife, 1965.

Bitú, Waldir. Um coronel do sertão. Recife, 1956.

Boletim da União dos Syndicatos Agrícolas de Pernambuco, 1906–12.

Borba, Manoel. Sérgio Loreto e seu governo em Pernambuco (história de 1° quatriennio calamitoso, 1922–1926). Rio, 1926.

Borges, Pompeu Acioly. Analise crítica do relatório do Dr. H. W. Singer sobre o nordeste: Estudo apresentado ao Banco de Desenvolvimento Econômico. Recife, 1954.

Botelho, Daniel da Rocha. Uma aposentadoria em seis mezes (o sertanejo e o Brasil). Rio, 1938.

Bottomore, T. B. Elites and Society. London, 1966.

Bouças, Valentim, F. "Vitalidade e grandeza de Pernambuco e do nordeste," *O Observador Econômico e Financeiro* (Rio), 22, no. 248 (Oct. 1956): 23–31.

Brandão, Ulisses de Carvalho Soares. Pernambuco versus Bahia: Protesto e contra-protesto. Recife, 1927.

Brasileiro, Ana Maria. O município como sistema político. Rio, 1973.

Brazil. Alexandre José Barbosa Lima. Discursos Parlamentares, tomo II: Dez. 1900–ago. 1927. Câmara dos Deputados. Brasília, 1966.

———. Anuário estatístico do Brasil, 1908–60. (Also Annuario; the later years issued by Instituto Brasileiro de Geografia e Estatística.) Directoria Geral de Estatística. Rio.

———. Anuário, 1960 e 1961. Ministério das Relações Exteriores. Rio, 1962.

———. Brasil, 1940–41; 1942. Ministério das Relações Exteriores. Rio, 1941, 1942.

———. O Brasil em números. Instituto Brasileiro de Geografia e Estatística. Rio, 1961.

———. Brazil, 1938. Instituto Brasileiro de Geografia e Estatística. Rio, 1939.

———. Brazil: Statistics, Resources, Possibilities. Ministério das Relações Exteriores. Rio, 1937.

Collecção das leis da República dos Estados Unidos do Brazil de 1893. Partes I e II. Rio, 1894.

———. Congressos açucareiros no Brasil. Instituto do Açúcar e do Alcool. Rio, 1949.

———. Dados biográficas dos Ministros, 1891–1961. Ministério da Viação e Obras Públicas. Rio, 1962.

———. Diário do Congresso, 1894–1930. Rio.

———. Diário oficial, 1889–1937. Rio.

———. Divisão administrativo em 1911 da República dos Estados Unidos do Brasil. Directoria Geral de Estatística. Rio, 1913.

———. Estatística eleitoral da República dos Estados Unidos do Brasil. Directoria Geral de Estatística. Rio, 1914.

———. Estatística das estradas de ferro da união e das fiscalizadas pela união relativa ao anno de 1914. Ministério da Viação e Obras Públicas. Rio, 1919.

———. Estatística da imprensa periódica no Brasil (1929–30). Directoria Geral de Estatística. Rio, 1931.

———. Estatística da instrução, primeira parte: Estatística escolar. v. 1. Directoria Geral de Estatística. Rio, 1916.

———. Finanças do Brasil: Síntese dos volumes I, II, III, VIII, IX, X. v. 19. Ministério da Fazenda. Rio, 1955.

———. Finanças dos estados do Brasil. v. 1. 2d ed. Ministério da Fazenda. Rio, 1934.

———. Finanças: Quadros synopticos da receita e despesa do Brasil (periódo de 1882 a 1913). Directoria Geral de Estatística. Rio, 1914.

———. Grandes regiões: Meio norte e nordeste. v. 2. Conselho Nacional de Geografia. Rio, 1962.

———. Impostos inter-estaduaes, 1900–1911. v. 33. Documentos Parlamentares. Paris, 1914.

―――. Indústria assucareira no Brazil. Directoria Geral de Estatística. Rio, 1919.

―――. Indústria assucareira: Usinas e engenhos centraes. Directoria Geral de Estatística. Rio, 1910.

―――. Intervenção nos estados. v. 2, 3. Documentos Parlamentares. Paris, 1913.

―――. Livro do centenário da Câmara dos Deputados (1826–1926). Rio, 1926.

―――. Notícia histórica e aviliação dos bens do Lloyd Brasileiro. Ministério da Viação e Obras Públicas. Rio, 1922.

―――. Portos do Brasil. Ministério da Viação e Obras Públicas. Rio, 1912.

―――. Projecto, emendas e pareceres. 3 v. Assembleia Nacional Constituinte. Rio, 1933–34. (Privately bound by E. Teixeira Leite.)

―――. Recenseamento do Brasil realizado em 1 de setembro de 1920. Directoria Geral de Estatística. Rio, 1922–29.

―――. Recenseamento geral do Brasil (1º de setembro de 1940). Série regional, Parte IX, tomo 1: Censo demografico, população e habitação. Instituto Brasileiro de Geografia e Estatística. Rio, 1950.

Relatório apresentado ao Dr. José Rufino Bezerra Cavalcanti, Ministro da Agricultura, Indústria e Commércio, pelo Dr. José Luiz S. de Bulhões Carvalho, Director Geral de Estatística. Directoria Geral de Estatística. Rio, 1916, 1921.

―――. Resumo de várias estatísticas econômico-financeiras. Directoria Geral de Estatística. Rio, 1924.

―――. Salários rurais: Inquerito organizado pelo Serviço de Inspecção e Fomento agrícolas sobre as oscillações dos salários ruraes em todo o paiz, durante o quinquennio de 1922–1926. Directoria Geral de Estatística. Rio, 1927.

―――. VII recenseamento geral do Brasil. Série regional. v. 3, tomo III: Censo industrial de 1960; Paraíba, Pernambuco, Alagoas. Instituto Brasileiro de Geografia e Estatística. Rio, 1963.

―――. 78 anos de receita federal (1890–1927). Ministério da Fazenda. Rio, 1968.

―――. Sexo, raça e estado civil, nacionalidade, filiação, culto e analphabetismo da população recenseada em 31 de dezembro de 1890. Directoria Geral de Estatística. Rio, 1898.

―――. VI recenseamento geral do Brasil, 1950: Estado de Pernambuco. Instituto Brasileiro de Geografia e Estatística. Rio, 1955.

―――. Synopse do recenseamento realizado em 1 de setembro de 1920: População do Brasil. Directoria Geral de Estatística. Rio, 1922.

Bruneau, Thomas C. The Political Transformation of the Brazilian Catholic Church. London, 1974.

Buber-Neumann, Margarete. Kriegsschauplatze der Weltrevolution: Ein Bericht aus der Praxis der Komentern, 1919–1943. Stuttgart, 1967.

Buley, E. C. North Brazil. New York, 1914.

Byars, Robert S., and Joseph L. Love. Quantitative Social Science Research on Latin America. Urbana, Ill., 1973.

Caldas, Joaquim Moreira. Porque João Dantas assassinou João Pessôa. Rio, n.d.

Callado, Antônio. As indústrias de sêca e os "galileus" de Pernambuco. Rio, 1960.

Callado, Pedro Eloy Pereira. A revolução de 29 de outubro de 1931 em Pernambuco. Rio, 1944.

Calogeras, João Pandia. Res Nostra. São Paulo, 1930.

Cámara, Clementino. Décadas. Recife, 1936.

Camargo, José Francisco. Exodo rural no Brasil. Rio, 1960.

Campello, Netto. História parlamentar de Pernambuco. Recife, 1923.

Cardim, Padre. Tratados da terra e gente do Brasil. Rio, 1939.

Carvalho, Alfredo de. "Cartografia e demographia de Pernambuco," *Annaes do 4°
Congresso Brasileiro de Geografia*, v. 2. Recife, 1916.

———. "Jornaes pernambucanas de 1821–1898," *Revista do Instituto de Arqueologia, História e Geografia de Pernambuco*, no. 52 (1889). (Republished as
a monograph; Recife, 1899.)

Castro, Josué de. A cidade do Recife: Ensaio de geografia urbana. Rio, [?] 1955.

———. Death in the Northeast. 2d ed. New York, 1969.

———. Documentário do nordeste. São Paulo, 1957.

Cavalcanti, Clovis de Vasconcelos. "A renda familiar e por habitante na cidade do
Recife," *Pesquisa e Planejamento Econômico*, 2, no. 1 (June 1972): 81–104.

Cavalcanti, Paulo. Os equívocos de Caio Prado Júnior. São Paulo, 1967.

———. A verdade sobre o "Pernambuco Tramways." Recife, 1954.

Cavalcanti de Albuquerque Mello, Félix. Memórias de um Cavalcanti; trechos do
livro de assentos de Félix de Albuquerque Mello (1821/1901), escolhidos e an-
notados pelo seu bisneto Diogo de Mello Menezes. São Paulo, 1940.

Chacon, Vamireh. A Capibaribe e o Recife (história social e sentimental de um
rio). Recife, 1959.

———. Da Escola do Recife ao código civil. Rio, 1969.

Chaves, Nelson. Problema alimentar do nordeste brasileiro. Recife, 1946.

Chevalier, Louis. Laboring Classes and Dangerous Classes in Paris During the
First Half of the Nineteenth Century. New York, 1973.

Cintra, Assis. Os escandalos da 1ª República. São Paulo, 1936.

Coimbra, Estácio. Politica de Pernambuco: A opinião do meu estado e do paiz.
Recife, 1927.

Congrès internationaux de 1900 à 1919, Les. Paris, 1920.

Correia de Andrade, Manoel. "População e movimentos migratórios no nordeste,"
Estudos Políticos e Sociais (Recife), 1, no. 1 (Jan.–June 1968): 135–48.

———. A terra e o homem no nordeste. 2d ed. São Paulo, 1964.

Costa Pôrto, José. Os tempos de Barbosa Lima. Recife, 1966.

———. Os tempos de Dantas Barreto. Recife, 1973.

———. Os tempos de Rosa e Silva. Recife, 1970.

Cowell, Bainbridge. "Cityward Migration in the Nineteenth Century: The Case
of Recife, Brazil," *Journal of Interamerican Studies and World Affairs*, 17, no.
1 (Feb. 1975): 43–63.

Cunha, Euclides da. Rebellion in the Backlands. Samuel Putnam, trans. Chicago,
1944.

Cunha, Mário. "O ensino primário em Pernambuco," in Diário da Manhã e Diário
da Tarde, comp., Anuário de Pernambuco para 1934. Recife, 1933.

Cuniff, Roger L. "The Birth of the Drought Industry: Imperial and Provincial
Response to the Great Drought in Northeast Brazil, 1877–1880," Paper delivered at American Historical Association meeting, New Orleans, Dec. 1972.

———. "The Great Drought: Northeast Brazil, 1877–1880," Ph.D. dissertation,
University of Texas. Austin 1970.

Dantas, O. R. Directório commercial brasileiro, edição de 1922 (Estado de Pernambuco). Recife, 1922.

Dantas Barreto, E. Commentários. Rio, 1922.

———. Conspirações, Rio, 1917.

Dé Carli, Gileno. A açúcar na formação económica do Brasil. Rio, [?] 1937.
———. Aspectos açucareiros de Pernambuco. Rio, 1940.
———. Aspectos de economía açucareira. Rio, 1942.
———. Geografia económica e social de canna de açúcar no Brasil. Rio, 1938.
———. História contemporánea de açúcar. Rio, 1942.
———. O processo histórico da usina em Pernambuco. Rio, 1942.
Degler, Carl N. Neither Black nor White: Slavery and Race Relations in Brazil and the United States. New York, 1971.
Della Cava, Ralph. "Catholicism and Society in Twentieth-Century Brazil," *Latin American Research Review*, 11, no. 2 (1976): 7–50.
———. Miracle at Joaseiro. New York, 1970.
Denslow, David, "Sugar Production in Northeastern Brazil and Cuba, 1858–1908," Ph.D. dissertation, Yale University. New Haven, Conn., 1974.
Diário de Pernambuco; Livro do Nordeste; commemorativo do primeiro centenário do Diário de Pernambuco: 1825–1925. Recife, 1925.
Dias, Público. Condições higiénicas e sociais do trabalhador dos engenhos de Pernambuco. Recife, 1937.
Diaz, Arthur. The Brazil of To-Day. Nivilles, Belgium, [?] 1906.
Diegues Júnior, Manuel. "Caracteristicos das populações nordestinas," *Boletim Geográfio*, 6, no. 70, (Jan. 1949): 1205–1207.
———. Regiões culturais do Brasil. Rio, 1960.
DiTella, Torcuato S. "The Dangerous Classes in Early Nineteenth-Century Mexico," *Journal of Latin American Studies*, 5, part 1 (May 1973): 79–105.
Dombre, L. F. Viagens do Engenheiro Dombre ao interior da Província de Pernambuco em 1874 e 1875. Recife, 1893.
Dutra, Francis A. "Centralization vs. Donatorial Privilege: Pernambuco, 1602–1630," in Dauril Alden, ed., Colonial Roots of Modern Brazil. Berkeley, Calif., 1973.
———. "Duarte Coelho Pereira," *The Americas*, 29, no. 4 (April 1973): 415–41.
Eisenberg, Peter L. "From Slave to Free Labor in Sugar Plantations: The Process in Pernambuco." Paper delivered to American Historical Association meeting, Boston, 1970.
———. The Sugar Industry in Pernambuco: Modernization Without Change, 1840–1910. Berkeley, Calif., 1973.
Elliott, J. H. The Revolt of the Catalans: A Study of the Decline of Spain (1598–1640). Cambridge, Eng., 1969.
Escobar, José Ribeiro. Educação nova. Recife, 1930.
———. O ensino de didática. Recife, 1929.
Establecimentos de ensino superior. Campanha Nacional de Aperfeiçoamento de Pessoal de Nivel Superior. Serie informação, 7. Rio, 1960.
Estudos afro-brasileiros (trabalhos apresentados ao 1º Congresso Afro-Brasileira reunida no Recife em 1934. v. 1. Rio, 1935.
Estudos de desenvolvimento regional: Pernambuco. Campanha Nacional de Aperfeiçoamento de Pessoal de Nivel Superior. Rio, 1959.
Estudos pernambucanos dedicados a Ulysses Pernambucano. Recife, 1937.
Facó, Rui. Cangaceiros e fanáticos. 2d ed. Rio, 1965.
Fafe, Egas [M. Paes de Figueiredo Moraes]. O governador de Pernambuco e a morte de José Maria. Recife, 1895.

Falcão, Annibal. Fórmula da civilização brasileira. Rio, n.d.

Fausto, Boris, ed. História geral da civilização brasileira. v. 3: O Brasil republicano. São Paulo, 1975.

Fernandes, Anibal. Um senhor de engenho pernambucano. Rio, 1959.

Fernandes, Antônio P. C. Jacques Maritain, as sobras de sua obra. Recife, 1941.

Fernandes, Gonçalves. Mobilidade, caráter e região. Recife, 1959.

Fernandes, Gonçalves, et al. Problemas do abastecimento alimentar no Recife. Recife, 1962.

Ferraz, Alvaro, and Andrade Lima Júnior. A morfologia do homem do nordeste. Rio, 1939.

————. Perfil morfofisiológico do nordestino. Recife, 1967.

Ferraz de Sá, M. Auxiliadora. Dos velhos aos novos coronéis. Recife, 1974.

Fleischer, David Verge. "Political Recruitment in the State of Minas Gerais, Brazil (1890–1970)," Ph.D. dissertation, University of Florida. Gainesville, 1972.

Frank, André Gunder. Capitalism and Underdevelopment in Latin America: Historical Studies of Chile and Brazil. New York, 1969.

Freire, Anibal. Rosa e Silva, centenário do seu nascimento, 1857–1957. Rio, 1957.

Freise, Friedrich W. "The Drought Region of Northeastern Brazil," Geographical Review, 28 (July 1938): 363–78.

Freitas, Octávio de. Medicina e costumes do Recife antigo. Recife, 1943.

————. Os trabalhos de hygiene em Pernambuco. Recife, 1919.

Freyre, Gilberto. Um engenheiro francês no Brasil, 2d ed., 2 v. Rio, 1960.

————. "O Estado de Pernambuco e sua expressao no poder nacional: Aspectos de um assunto complexo." Lecture given to Associação dos Diplomados da Escola Superior de Guerra, Recife, 1964.

————. Guia prático, histórico e sentimental da cidade do Recife. 3d ed. Rio, 1961.

————. "Manifesto regionalista de 1926," Boletim do Instituto Joaquim Nabuco (Recife), 5, no. 1, (1952): 21–43.

————. The Mansions and the Shanties: The Making of Modern Brazil. New York, 1963.

————. The Masters and the Slaves: A Study in the Development of Brazilian Civilization. Samuel Putnam, trans. New York, 1964.

————. Nordeste: Aspectos da influência da cana sobre a vida e a paisagem do nordeste do Brasil. 3d ed. Rio, 1961.

————. Oliveira Lima: Don Quixote gordo. Recife, 1968.

————. Ordem e progresso. v. 1. Rio, 1959.

————. Perfil de Euclides e outros perfis. Rio, 1944.

————. Região e tradição. Rio, 1941.

Freyre, Gilberto, et al. Novos estudos afro-brasileiros. v. 2: Trabalhos apresentados ao 1º Congresso Afro-Brasileiro do Recife. Rio, 1937.

Furtado, Celso. The Economic Growth of Brazil. Berkeley, Calif., 1963.

————. A operação nordeste. Rio, 1959.

Galloway, J. H. "The Last Years of Slavery on the Sugar Plantations of Northeastern Brazil," Hispanic American Historical Review, 51, no. 4 (Nov. 1971): 586–605.

————. "The Sugar Industry of Pernambuco During the Nineteenth Century,"

Annals of the Association of American Geographers, 58, no. 2 (June 1968): 285–302.

Galvão, Sebastião de Vasconcellos. "Município do Recife: Estudo histórico e topográphico," in Diccionário Chorográphico, Histórico e Estatística de Pernambuco. v. 3. 2d ed. Rio, 1921.

Gayoso, Armando. A verdadeira verdade. Recife, 1925.

Geiger, Pedro Pinchas. Evolução da rede urbana brasileira. Rio, 1963.

————. "Migrações inter-regionais no Brazil," in Migrações, v. 2, cited below.

Genovese, Eugene D. The World the Slaveholders Made: Two Essays in Interpretation. New York, 1971.

Gerson, Brasil. O sistema político do Império. Bahia, 1970.

Gonçalves, Antônio Carolino. As migrações para o Recife, v. 2: *Aspectos do crescimento urbano*. Recife, 1961.

Gonçalves Fernandes, Albino. Região, crença e atitude. Recife, 1963.

Gondim, Umberto. Pôrto do Recife: Sua história . . . . 2d ed. Recife, 1968.

Gorringe, H. H. The Coast of Brazil. v. 1, no. 43. Washington, D.C., 1873.

Gorton, William W. "The Northeast of Brazil: Economic Information on a Problem Area," unpublished manuscript, United States Development Mission. Rio, 1959.

Graham, Douglas H., and Sérgio Buarque de Hollanda Filho. "Interregional and Urban Migration and Economic Growth in Brazil," in *Migrações*, v. 2, cited below.

Graham, Richard. "Brazilian Slavery Re-examined," *Journal of Social History* (Summer 1970): 431–53.

————. Britain and the Onset of Modernization in Brazil: 1850–1914. Cambridge, Eng., 1968.

Great Western of Brazil Railway Company Limited. Reports of the Directors, 1900–1922. London.

Griz, Jayme. Palmares, seu povo, suas tradições. Recife, 1953.

Guerra, Flávio. Lucena: Um estadista de Pernambuco. Recife, 1958.

Guerra, Otto. "Pequenos aspectos da política social e económica do nordeste," *Fronteiras* (Recife), 6, no. 25 (June 1937).

Haas, Ernst. The Uniting of Europe: Political, Social, and Economic Forces, 1950–1957. Stanford, Calif., 1968.

Harris, Marvin. Town and Country in Brazil. New York, 1956.

Havighurst, Robert J., and J. Roberto Moreira. Society and Education in Brazil. Pittsburgh, 1965.

Hirschman, Albert O. Journeys Toward Progress. New York, 1963.

Hobsbawm, E. J. Bandits. London, 1969.

————. Primitive Rebels: Studies in Archaic Forms of Social Movements in the 19th and 20th Centuries. New York, 1959.

Ianni, Octávio. Estado e planejamento econômico no Brasil (1930–1970). Rio, 1971.

"Immigrantes entrados nos pôrtos do Brasil, 1820–1926," *Boletim do Ministério da Agricultura e Commércio*, 16, v. 2, no. 3 (Sept. 1927): 328–29.

Jobim, José. Brazil in the Making. New York, 1943.

Johnson, Allen W. Sharecroppers of the Sertão: Economics and Dependence on a Brazilian Plantation. Stanford, Calif., 1971.

Klein, Herbert S. "The Internal Slave Trade in Nineteenth Century Brazil," *Hispanic American Historical Review*, 51, no. 4 (Nov. 1971).

Lacaz, Carlos da Silva. Vultos da medicina brasileira. São Paulo, 1963.

Lafetá, João Luiz. "Estética e ideologia; o modernismo em 1930," *Argumento* (São Paulo), 1, no. 2 (Nov. 1973).

Lamartine, Juvenal. Velhos costumes do meu sertão. Natal, 1965.

Laslett, Peter. The World We Have Lost: England Before the Industrial Age. New York, 1965.

Leal, Victor Nunes. Coronelismo, enxada e voto. Rio, 1948.

Leão, A. Carneiro. A sociedade rural: Seus problemas e sua educação. Rio, [?] 1937.

Leff, Nathaniel. "Economic Development and Regional Inequality: Origins of the Brazilian Case," *Quarterly Journal of Economics*, 86 (May 1972): 243–63.

———. "Long-Term Viability of Slavery in a Backward Closed Society," *Journal of Interdisciplinary History*, 1 (Summer 1974).

Lemos Filho. Clã de açúcar. Rio, 1960.

Levine, Robert M. "The First Afro-Brazilian Congress," *Race*, 15, no. 2 (Oct. 1973): 183–94.

———. "Some Views on Race and Immigration During the Old Republic," *The Americas*, 27, no. 4 (April 1971): 373–80.

———. The Vargas Regime: The Critical Years, 1934–38. New York, 1970.

Lima, Manoel de Oliveira. Pernambuco: Seu desenvolvimento histórico. Leipzig, 1895.

Lima Castro, Eduardo de. Memórias de um político pernambucano. Rio, 1955.

Lima Cavalcanti, Carlos de. Manifesto ao povo pernambucano. Recife, 1935.

———. Pernambuco saqueado (reminiscências de um desgoverno). Rio, 1927.

Linhares, Hermínio. "As greves operárias no Brasil," *Estudos Sociais*, 1, no. 2 (July-Aug. 1958): 215–28.

Lins de Albuquerque, Ulisses. Um sertanejo e o sertão: Memórias. Rio, 1957.

Lloyd, Reginald, et al. Twentieth Century Impressions of Brazil: Its History, People, Commerce, Industry, and Resources. London, 1913.

Lôbo, Eulália Maria Lahmeyer, et al. "Evolução dos prêços e do padrão de vida no Rio de Janeiro, 1820–1930, resultados preliminares," *Revista Brasileira de Economia*, 25, no. 4 (1971): 235–65.

Love, Joseph L. "Political Participation in Brazil, 1889–1969," *Luso-Brazilian Review*, 7, no. 2 (Dec. 1970): 3–24.

———. Rio Grande do Sul and Brazilian Regionalism, 1882–1930. Stanford, Calif., 1971.

———. São Paulo in the Brazilian Federation, 1889–1937. Stanford, Calif., forthcoming.

Lubambo, Manoel. Capitães e grandeza nacional. São Paulo, 1940.

———. Contra Nassau. Recife, 1944.

Lyra, João. Cifras e notas: Economia e finanças do Brasil. Rio, 1925.

McCann, Frank D. "The Nation in Arms: Obligatory Military Service in Brazil During the Old Republic," unpublished manuscript, 1975.

Macedo, Nertan. Capitão Virgolino Ferreira da Silva: Lampião. 2d ed. Rio, 1968.

Machado, Cristina Matta. As táticas de guerra dos cangaceiros. Rio, 1969.

Magalhães, Agamenon. O nordeste brasileiro. Rio, 1936.

————. "Relatório apresentado ao exmo. sr. Presidente da República, 1938–39," unpublished manuscript, Arquivo Público Estadual de Pernambuco. Recife, 1940.

Maia, J. Gonçalves. Horas de prisão (notas históricas). Recife, 1923.

————. A política do assassinato: Uma página de história pernambucana. Recife, 1895.

————. Questões de limites: Relatório apresentado ao sr. dr. José Bezerra, Governador de Pernambuco. Recife, 1920.

Maia, Newton da Silva. Apontamentos para a história da Escola de Engenharia de Pernambuco. Recife, 1967.

Maranhão, Jarbas. Municipalismo e ruralismo. Rio, 1960.

Marc, Alfred. Le Brésil, excursion à travers ses 20 provinces. v. 1. Paris, 1890.

Martins, Henrique. Lista geral dos bachareis e doutores que tem obtido o respectivo grau na Faculdade de Direito do Recife desde sua fundação em Olinda, no anno de 1828, ate o anno de 1931. 2d ed. Recife, 1931.

Maurício, Ivan, and Daura Lúcia. "Na terra dos usineiros," Opinião, July 16–23, 1973.

Mello, Diogo Cabral de. Lista geral dos bachareis e doutores na Faculdade de Direito do Recife (em continuação de junho de 1931 a dezembro de 1941), appendix to Revista Académica, 49 (1941).

Mello Barreto, Joaquim Tavares. "A crise da lavoura," Revista Académica (Recife), 15 (1907): 112.

Mello Neto, José Antônio Gonsalves de. "Por uma história do Império vista do nordeste," Estudos Universitários, 6 (1) (Jan.-March 1966): 51–59

————. Tres roteiros de penetração de território pernambucano (1738 a 1802). Recife, 1966.

Melo, Mário. "Chorographia de Pernambuco," Revista do Instituto de Arqueologia, História e Geografia de Pernambuco, 24, no. 115–18 (1922): 5–148.

————. "A evolução da capital de Pernambuco," Revista do Instituto de Arquelogia, História e Geografia de Pernambuco, 31, no. 147–50 (1931): 75–85.

————. "Genealogia municipal de Pernambuco," Revista do Instituto de Arqueologia, História e Geografia de Pernambuco, 32, no. 151–54 (1932): 23–25.

————. A imprensa pernambucana em 1918. Recife, 1918.

————. Pau d'Alho: Geographia physica e política. Recife, 1918.

————. "Sinopse cronológica de Pernambuco," Revista do Instituto de Arqueologia, História et Geografia de Pernambuco, 38 (1943): 9–146.

————. Toponymia pernambucana. Recife, 1931.

Melo, Mário Lacerda de. As migrações para o Recife. v. 1: Estudo geográfico. Recife, 1961.

————. Paisagens do nordeste em Pernambuco e Paraíba. Rio, 1958.

————. Pernambuco: Traços de sua geografia humana. Recife, 1940.

————. Tipos de localização de cidades em Pernambuco. Recife, 1958.

Melo, Oscar. Recife sangrento. 3d ed. Recife, 1953.

Memorial que ao exm. sr. Dr. Affonso Penna, Presidente eleito da República apresenta a Associação dos Empregados no Commércio de Pernambuco sobre as necessidades do commércio neste Estado. Recife, 1906.

Menezes, Djacir. O outro nordeste. Rio, 1937.

Menezes, João Barreto de. Libello contra um tyrannia. Recife, 1922.

Migrações internas e desenvolvimento regional. Centro de Desenvolvimento e Planejamento Regional da Universidade Federal de Minas Gerais. 2 v. Belo Horizonte, 1973.

Milet, Henrique Augusto. Os Quebra-Kilos e a crise da Lavoura. Recife, 1876.

Montenegro, Olívio. Memórias do Ginásio Pernambucano. Recife, 1943.

Moraes, Manuel H. A. de. "O nordeste: O meio e o homem," Síntese Política Economica e Social, 5, no. 17 (Jan.-March 1963): 7–17.

Moraes, Octávio, and Eurydice Amorim de Moraes. Roteiro do Barão Rodrigues Mendes. Recife, 1967.

Morse, Richard. From Community to Metropolis: São Paulo, Brazil. Gainesville, Fla., 1958.

Mota, Leonardo. No tempo de Lampião. 2d ed. Fortaleza, 1967.

Mota, Mauro. Paisagem das secas. Recife, 1958.

———. Votos e ex-votos: Aspectos da vida social do nordeste. Recife, 1958.

Nabuco, Joaquim. Minha formação. 2d ed. São Paulo, 1934.

Nascimento, Luiz do. História da imprensa de Pernambuco (1821–1954). v. 1–5, Recife, 1966–67.

Nery, M. F. J. de Santa-Anna. Le Brésil en 1889 avec une carte de l'empire en chromolithographie . . . . Paris, 1889.

Paachans, Gustavo L. "O bolshevismo e o afro-brasilismo," Diário do Nordeste (Recife), Nov. 1, 1937, p. 9.

Paes Barreto, Carlos Xavier. Os primitivos colonizadores nordestinos e seus descendentes. Rio, 1960.

Paes Barretto. A abolição e a federação no Brasil. Paris, 1906.

Paim, Antônio. A filosofia da Escola de Recife. Rio, 1966.

Pang, Eul-Soo. "The Changing Role of Priests in the Politics of Northeast Brazil, 1889–1964," The Americas, 30, no. 4 (Jan. 1974): 341–72.

———. "The Politics of Coronelismo in Brazil: The Case of Bahia, 1889–1930," Ph.D. dissertation, University of California. Berkeley, 1970.

Parahym, Orlando. O problema alimentar no sertão. Recife, 1940.

Passos Guimarães, Alberto. Quatro séculos de latifúndia. São Paulo, 1963.

Patrick, George F. Desenvolvimento agrícola do nordeste. Rio, 1972.

Pearse, Arno S. Cotton in North Brazil. London, 1923.

Peçanha, Carlos. Nilo Peçanha e a revolução brasileira. Rio, 1969.

Peixoto, Alzira Vargas do Amaral. Getúlio Vargas, meu pai. 2d ed. Pôrto Alegre, 1960.

Pereira, Nilo. Agamenon Magalhães: Uma evolução pessoal. Recife, 1973.

———. "A expulsão dos jesuitas de Pernambuco," Estudos Universitários, 9, no. 1 (Jan.-March 1969): 53–72.

Pereira, Nilo, and Vamireh Chacon. Trajano Chacon, escritor. Recife, 1970.

Pereira da Costa, F. A. Comarcas da Província de Pernambuco. Recife, 1884.

———. "Notícia sôbre as instituções de crédito bancário em Pernambuco," in Relatório da Direcção da Associação Comercial Beneficiente de Pernambuco. Recife, 1898.

———. Em prol da integridade do território de Pernambuco. Recife, n.d.

Peres, Apollónio, A indústria pastoril em Pernambuco. Recife, 1917.

———. Pernambuco na primeira grande feira annual de Distrito Federal. Recife, 1898.

Peres, Apollónio, and Manoel Machado Cavalcanti. Indústrias de Pernambuco. Recife, 1935.

Peres, Gaspar. "Accidentes de trabalho," *Boletim Agrícola*, 8, no. 2 (Feb. 1914).

Pernambuco. Annaes, 1896–1926. Câmara dos Deputados. Recife.

——. Annuario Estatistico de Pernambuco, 1927–42. Recife.

——. Constituição do Estado de Pernambuco de 10 julho de 1935. Recife, 1935.

——. Demografia. Conselho de Desenvolvimento. Recife, 1966.

——. Estado de Pernambuco: Obra de propaganda geral. Rio, 1922.

——. Exposição apresentada ao chefe do govêrno provisório da República . . . pelo Interventor Federal Carlos de Lima Cavalcanti. Recife, 1933.

——. Mensagem do exm. sr. Dr. José Rufino Bezerra Cavalcanti, Governador do Estado. Recife, 1922.

——. Mensagems apresentados ao Congresso Legislativo do Estado em 1893, 1895 e 1896 pelo Dr. Alexandre José Barbosa Lima quando governador de Pernambuco. Recife, 1931.

——. Observações estatísticas sôbre os mocambos do Recife. Recife, 1939.

——. Recenseamento do Recife: 1923. Recife, 1924.

Pernambuco, José Antônio de Almeida. Esgôtos da cidade do Recife. Recife, [?]1905.

Perruci, Gadiel. Favelas do Rio e mucambos do Recife. Recife, 1962.

——. "Le Pernambouc (1889–1930): Contribution à l'histoire quantitative du Brésil," Thèse de Troisième Cycle, Université de Paris. Paris, 1972.

Pessoa, Laurita Raja Gabáglia. Epitácio Pessôa (1865–1942). 2 v. São Paulo, 1951.

Pimenta, Joaquim. Retalhos do passado. Rio, 1949.

Pinto, Estévão. A Associação Comercial de Pernambuco: Livro comemorativo do seu primeiro centenário (1839/1939). Recife, 1940.

——. História de uma estrada-de-ferro do nordeste. Rio, 1949.

Pinto, Eudes de Souza Leão. "Considerações agronômicas objectivando e aproveitamento do potencial económico de Pernambuco," Mimeographed document. Recife, 1963.

Pinto, Ferreira. Pernambuco e seu destino histórico. Recife, 1950.

Pinto, Octávio. Velhas histórias de Goiana. Rio, 1968.

Rabello, Dácio de Lyra. O nordeste: Pernambuco centro e origem de toda civilização nordestina. Recife, 1932.

Raffalovich, Isaiah. Zionism and Bitterness. Tel Aviv, n.d.

Ramos, Graciliano. Infância. Rio, 1956.

Recife, Município de. Recenseamento realizado em 12 de outubro de 1913. Recife, 1913.

"O Recife de outr'ora," *Jornal Pequeno* (March 1929), in *Revista do Instituto de Arqueologia, História e Geografia de Pernambuco*, 29, no. 5 (1928–29): 84–142.

Reina, Ruben E. Paraná. Austin, Tex., 1972.

Reis, Jaime. "Abolition and the Economics of Slaveholding in North East Brazil," Occasional papers, no. 11, Institute of Latin American Studies, University of Glasgow, 1974. Published in *Boletin de Estudos Latino-Americanos y del Caribe*, no. 17 (Dec. 1974): 3–20.

——. "From Bangüe to Usina: Social Aspects of Growth and Modernisation in the Sugar Industry of Pernambuco (1850–1920)," manuscript supplied to me by the author. Glasgow, 1973.

————. "The Realm of the Hoe: Plantation Agriculture in Pernambuco Before and After the Abolition of Slavery," manuscript supplied to me by the author. Glasgow, 1974.

Reis, Naura de Farias. "Alguns aspetos da comunidade judaica do Recife (século XX)," unpublished manuscript in the possession of its author, Recife, Nov. 1970.

Rey Alvarez, Julian. O transporte ferroviário no nordeste do Brasil. Recife, 1962.

————. Transporte marítima e portos do nordeste. Recife, 1961.

Ridings, Eugene W. "Elite Conflict and Cooperation in the Brazilian Empire: The Case of Bahia's Businessmen and Planters," Luso-Brazilian Review, 12, no. 1 (Summer 1975): 80–99.

Ringawa, Marcel. "An Exploratory Study of the Elites of Pernambuco, 1879–1889," M.A. thesis, New York University. New York, Jan. 1971.

Rocha, Tadeu. Roteiros de Recife (Olinda e Guararapes). 3d ed. Recife, 1967.

————. "Sindicalismo revolucionário," Fronteiras, 6, no. 20 (June 1937): 8–9.

Robock. Stefan. Brazil's Developing Northeast: A Study of Regional Planning and Foreign Aid. Washington, D.C., 1963.

Rodrigues, Mário. Meu Pernambuco. Recife, 1931.

Roett, Riordan Joseph Allenby III. "Economic Assistance and Political Change in the Brazilian Northeast," Ph.D. dissertation, Columbia University. New York, 1968.

Saffioti, Heleieth I.B. A mulher na sociedade de classes: Mito e realidade. São Paulo, 1969.

Schmitter, Philippe C. Interest Conflict and Political Change in Brazil. Stanford, Calif., 1971.

Sette, Hilton, and Mário Correia de Andrade. Pontos de geografia e história de Pernambuco (para o curso de formação de professores). 2d ed. Recife, 1954.

Silva, Moacir M. F. "Tentativa de classificação das cidades brasileiras," Revista Brasileira de Geografia, 8, no. 3 (1946).

Silva, R. Fernandes e. Notas econômicas sôbre a indústria pastoril de Pernambuco. Recife, 1927.

Silva Bruno, Ernani. História do Brasil: Geral e regional. v. 2: Nordeste. São Paulo, 1967.

Singer, H. W. "Economic Development of North-Eastern Brazil," unpublished manuscript, United Nations Technical Assistance Program. New York, Aug. 15, 1956.

————. "Estimate of Capital Requirements for the Economic Development of the North-East," unpublished manuscript in Superintendência Para o Desenvolvimento do Nordeste library. Recife, 1952.

Singer, Paul. Desenvolvimento econômico e evolução urbana. São Paulo, 1968.

Singlemann, Peter. "Political Structure and Social Banditry in Northeast Brazil," Journal of Latin American Studies, 7, part 1 (May 1975): 59–83.

Skidmore, Thomas E. Black into White: Race and Nationality in Brazilian Thought. New York, 1974.

Slater, Charles, Harold Riley, et al. Market Processes in the Recife Area of Northeast Brazil, Research Report #2, Latin American Studies Center, Michigan State University. East Lansing, 1968.

Soares, Gláucio Ary Dillon. "Brasil: A política do desenvolvimento desigual," Revista Brasileira de Estudos Políticos, 22 (Jan. 1967): 19–70.

Sociedade de Amigos de Alberto Torres, Sociedade de Amigos de Alberto Torres; 1932–1939, no sétimo aniversário de sua fundação. Rio, 1939.

Sodré, Nelson Werneck. Memórias de um soldado. Rio, 1967.

Souto Maior, Pedro. Fastos pernambucanos. Rio, 1913.

Souza, Washington Albino de. "O planejamento regional no federalismo brasileiro," Revista Brasileira de Estudos Políticos, 28 (Jan. 1970): 113–224.

———. Souza Barros. A década 20 em Pernambuco (uma interpretação). Rio, 1972.

———. Velhos e novos problemas vinculados a economia de Pernambuco. Recife, 1956.

Stein, Stanley J. The Brazilian Cotton Manufacture: Textile Enterprise in an Underdeveloped Area, 1850–1950. Cambridge, Mass., 1957.

Stein, Stanley J., and Barbara H. Stein, The Colonial Heritage of Latin America: Essays on Economic Dependence in Perspective. New York, 1970.

Stone, Lawrence. The Crisis of the Aristocracy, 1558–1641. London, 1967.

Sund, Michael Dean. "Land Tenure and Economic Performance of Agricultural Establishments in Northeastern Brazil," Ph.D. dissertation, University of Wisconsin. Madison, 1965.

Tarrow, Sidney, Peasant Communism in Southern Italy. New Haven, Conn., 1967.

Taylor, Kit Sims. "Brazil's Northeast: Sugar and Surplus Value," Monthly Review, March 1969, pp. 20–29.

Teixeira de Mello, Alcino. Nordestinos na Amazônia. Rio, 1956.

Tejo, Limeira. Brejos e carrascaes do nordeste: Documentário. São Paulo, 1937.

———. Enéias: Memórias de uma geração ressentida. Rio, 1956.

Theophilo, Rodolpho. A secca de 1919. Rio, 1922.

Torres, Mário. Primeiro Congresso Econômico Sertanejo. Recife, 1935.

Trabalhos do Congresso Agrícola do Recife em outubro de 1878. Recife, 1878.

"O transporte ferroviario no Brasil e seus problemas," Estudos Diversos (Rio), 1954, pp. 11–149.

Tricart, Jean. As zonas morfoclimáticas do nordeste brasileiro. Salvador, 1959.

Valente, Waldemar. Serrinha. Recife, [?] 1968.

Vasconcelos Sobrinho, João de. As regiões naturais de Pernambuco: O meio e a civilização. Rio, 1949.

Vaz da Costa, Rubens. "As disparidades intra-regionais de crescimento econômico no nordeste," Revista de Finanças Públicas, 277 (Nov. 1968): 23–31.

Venâncio Filho, Alberto. A intervenção do estado no domínio econômico. Rio, 1968.

Vergolino, Honorato. Denúncia apresentada ao Tribunal de Segurança Nacional. Processo no. 204, Estado de Pernambuco. Rio, 1937.

Vianna, Barbosa, see Barbosa Vianna.

Vidal, Ademar. Importância do açúcar. Rio, 1945.

Vilaça, Marcos Vinícius. Presença na Faculdade. Recife, 1962.

———. Em torno da sociologia do caminhão. Recife, 1961.

Vilaça, Marcos Vinícius, and Roberto Cavalcanti Albuquerque. Coronel, coronéis. Rio, 1965.

Villela, Annibal Villanova, and Wilson Suzigan. Política do govêrno e crescimento da economia brasileira, 1889–1945. Monograph no. 10, Instituto de Planejamento Econômico e Social, Instituto de Pesquisas. Rio, 1973.

Viotti da Costa, Emília. De senzala a colônia. São Paulo, 1966.

"Vocabulário pernambucano," Revista do Instituto de Arqueologia, História e Geografia de Pernambuco, 24, no. 159–62 (1936).

Walle, Paul. Au Brésil, Etat de Pernambuco. Paris, 1912.

Walter, E. V. Terror and Resistance: A Study of Political Violence. New York, 1969.

Wanderley, Eustórgio. Tipos populares do Recife antigo. Recife, 1953.

Waterton, Charles. Wanderings in South America. London, 1903.

Webb, Kempton E. The Changing Face of Northeast Brazil. New York, 1974.

Wileman, J. P. The Brazilian Year Book, 1909. London, 1909.

"Yearly Floods in the Northeast," Reflector, United States Consulate, Recife, April 14, 1970.

Wirth, John D. Minas Gerais in the Brazilian Federation, 1889–1937. Stanford, Calif., 1977.

Wright, Marie Robinson. The New Brazil, Its Resources and Its Attractions. Philadelphia, [?] 1902.

Zeldin, Theodore, France: 1848–1945. v. 1: Ambition, Love and Politics. Oxford, 1973.

Index